One Hundred Years of THE SUSSEX REGISTER

AND
County of Sussex
— New Jersey —

Record of Historical, Biographical, Industrial, and Statistical Events During a Century

1813-1913

Edited by
Whitfield Gibbs

HERITAGE BOOKS
2007

HERITAGE BOOKS
AN IMPRINT OF HERITAGE BOOKS, INC.

Books, CDs, and more—Worldwide

For our listing of thousands of titles see our website
at
www.HeritageBooks.com

A Facsimile Reprint
Published 2007 by
HERITAGE BOOKS, INC.
Publishing Division
65 East Main Street
Westminster, Maryland 21157-5026

Copyright © 1992 Heritage Books, Inc.

Published in cooperation with the Genealogy Society of Sussex County, New Jersey

Originally published by
The Sussex Register
Whitfield Gibbs, Editor
Newton, New Jersey
1913

— Publisher's Notice —
In reprints such as this, it is often not possible to remove blemishes from the original. We feel the contents of this book warrant its reissue despite these blemishes and hope you will agree and read it with pleasure.

International Standard Book Number: 978-1-55613-557-6

NEWSPAPER HISTORY OF SUSSEX COUNTY 1813 TO 1913 — THE MEN WHO HAVE MADE IT

THE SUSSEX REGISTER was founded by John H. Hall, who was a graduate of the Bucks County Intelligencer, published at Doylestown, Pa. The first number was issued on the 6th of July, 1813, in a small building in the rear of the Court House. In size it was 18x22 inches, printed on coarse paper in what is known to printers as small pica and English type and without column rules. The working force consisted of the proprietor and one assistant, and the proprietor's work also included the delivery of the papers to subscribers. The day of publication was Monday.

In 1818 the office was removed to a building which then stood on the present site of the M. E. Church. Column rules were procured and first appeared in the issue of July 13, 1818. In January 8, 1821, a change was made in the make-up, smaller type being used and the quality of the paper improved. On October 20, 1821, the publication day was changed to Tuesday. In 1882 the size of the type was still further reduced.

In May, 1827, Mr. Hall formed a copartnership with William H. Johnson and a store was started at Lewisburg, about one mile south of Deckertown, and at least a part of the profits of that venture were required to keep the paper going. In 1830 the store was moved to Newton and located in the building now owned and occupied by Dr. H. J. Mc-Cloughan, on Main street, in which building The Register was printed for six years.

In 1836 the office was removed to a building on the corner of Main and Division streets, where it remained for a period of 31 years. In February, 1867, it was again removed to the upper floor of the store building No. 27 High street, then occupied by the Merchants National Bank and the post office. The office remained there for a number of years, after which it in turn occupied quarters over Huston & VanBlarcom's store, in the building now occupied by Earl's Hotel; on the second floor of the building in which the office is now located, and then moved to the Rosenkrans building, where it remained until July, 1911, when it was removed to its present location in the Roof building, corner of Spring and Moran streets.

The first number of the paper on file in the office is No. 10, dated Sept. 7, 1813. There is also a break in the files from 1828 to 1830. During the latter period the paper was enlarged to 22x38 inches. In 1843 it was enlarged to 23x38 inches. On June 29, 1846, the size was again changed, this time to 20x40, and again in 1868 to 28x42 inches. Still another change was made March 8, 1906, when the size was changed from 4 to 8 pages and 35x44 inches. The last change was made in 1913 when two inches were added to the length of the column, making them 22 inches instead of 20.

From April 7, 1834, to March 26, 1836, the paper was published by John H. Hall and Nelson P. Moore. This partnership expired by limitation, and from that time until February 5, 1855, Judge Hall conducted it alone. On the latter date Benjamin B. Edsall, who had been connected with the paper as an editorial writer and printer from 1833, acquired a half interest in the business and continued to be the guiding spirit until his death, which occurred on March 28, 1868.

While others had been connected in a business way with The Register during Judge Hall's ownership Mr. Edsall was the only one who participated in the editorial management of the paper. On the 13th of January, 1864, Judge Hall sold his interest to his son-in-law, Richard B. Westbrook, and the business was conducted under the firm name of B. B. Edsall & Company until November 10th, 1866. Mr. Westbrook sold his interest to Joseph Coult, and upon the death of Mr. Edsall in 1868 the editorial management devolved upon that gentleman. July 11, 1868, Aaron C. Goodman, of New York, purchased the interest of the Edsall estate in The Register, and for a little more than a year the business was conducted under the firm name of Coult & Goodman.

On the first of October, 1869, Richard F. Goodman purchased the interest of his uncle and also that of Mr. Coult and became sole owner and editor of The Register, which relation he held for nearly forty-two years, or until June 1, 1911.

On the first of January, 1893, Robert E. Foster, who had commenced in 1858 to learn the printer's trade in the office and had been connected with the paper almost continuously from that time on, became assistant editor and held the position until his death on the 6th of July, 1912.

From the time it was established in 1813 until 1824, when the county of Warren was set off and the Belvidere Apollo was started, The Register was the only paper published in all that territory and the papers were delivered by carrier from Reiglesville to Tri-States.

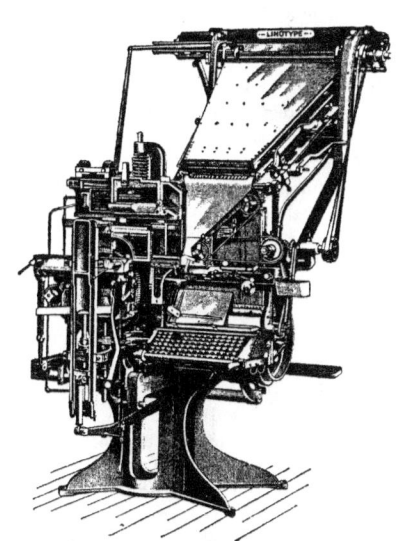

One hundred years ago The Register was set up by hand. To-day it is set on this machine.

JOHN H. HALL.

The death of Judge Hall occurred on Tuesday, December 4, 1865, and the following obituary, from the pen of his long-time associate, Benjamin B. Edsall, is taken from the files of The Register:

John H. Hall, Esq., the founder of this journal, and for nearly fifty-one years its proprietor, in whole or in part, departed this life at 7 o'clock on Monday evening, December 4, 1865. He was born in Kingwood township, Hunterdon county, April 25, 1791, and was at the time of his death 74 years, 7 months and 9 days old.

The son of a farmer of somewhat limited means, who was burdened with the care of a large family, his education was such only as could be acquired in the common schools of a primitive period in the history of this country. The greater part of his youth was devoted to agricultural pursuits, and when he arrived at the age of 17 years, he left the paternal home to learn the art of printing. He was apprenticed to Asher Miner, Esq., the founder of the Bucks county (Pa.) "Intelligencer," and derived from the example and counsels of that excellent man, those lessons of integrity, of system, economy and good order, which he adhered to and practiced throughout a long and useful life.

At the age of 22 years he came into Sussex county, and with the aid of a small capital acquired by his own labor, he established "The Register," issuing the first number on the 6th of July, 1813, and continuing its publication without the interregnum of a single week until the 22d of January, 1864, when he sold out his interest to his son-in-law, Richard B. Westbrook.

During this long period, it is safe to say Judge Hall continually gained a wider and deeper hold upon the affections and esteem of the people with whom his lot had been cast. Though never agreeing in political sentiment with the majority of the voters of this county, his sterling honesty and indisputable capacity for the correct and intelligent discharge of public business, early led to his employment in official position. He was deputy sheriff for nine years, a part of the time doing nearly all the duties of his principal. For thirteen years he was clerk of the board of freeholders, being annually re-elected although the members of the board almost unanimously differed from him in political sentiment. For fifteen years he was Judge of the Court of Common Pleas; in 1836 he was chosen one of the Presidential electors for New Jersey, and voted for Gen. Wm. H. Harrison; and in 1841 he was appointed Clerk of the county, serving in that capacity until 1846. In all these positions he acquitted himself with the greatest credit. He was painstaking, systematic, and scrupulously honest. As a judge no man could be more conscientious; he was cautious, considerate and impartial, and when once his judgment was formed, he was immovably firm; nor fear, nor favor, nor hope of reward, could swerve him a hair's breadth from what he believed to be right and just. The correctness with which Judge Hall discharged his public duties is proverbial in this county; and the one distinguishing trait in his character which those best acquainted with him most frequently speak of with admiration, was that no matter what business he transacted, whether small or great, it was thoroughly and completely done. He was as careful to keep a full and minute record of what he did as the trustee of a school district as of his doings as Clerk of the county. In all the relations of life, as a husband, a father, a neighbor and a citizen, he approached as near perfection as it is permitted for a human being to attain.

To those who knew but little of the man whose venerable form is now clad in the habiliments of the grave, this language may seem somewhat extravagant. But the writer of these lines, who is himself no longer young, and who has seen enough of the gloss and tinsel which in this world passes too often for pure gold, to make him somewhat cynical, is the last one to indulge at such a time in insincere compliments or in unmerited eulogiums. For over thirty years the closest personal and business intimacy subsisted between the deceased and the writer, and when we say that above and beyond all men that we ever knew, he was a model of manly probity, we are unconscious of uttering aught but the simple truth. There have existed many men of more capacious intellect—many of a brighter fancy, and better calculated to dazzle the multitude with sparkling rhetoric and radiant wit; but for the solid courtesy of a true gentleman, the jocund good humor of an every day companion, the ever ready sympathy and kindness of a warm friend, and the sound common sense, the sterling worth and the invincible integrity that may be relied upon either for wise counsel or safe example, there are few persons that ever lived who furnished a better model than Judge Hall. Ripe in years, in usefulness, in the love of kindred and friends, and in the esteem of the public, he sinks at last to his final rest. He leaves his family a fair amount of wealth honestly earned, as well as the richer legacy of a good name and social virtues which all admire and few emulate.

Judge Hall at the time of his death was the oldest newspaper publisher in New Jersey. All his original contemporaries disappeared some time since from the stage of action. Sherman and Wilson, of Trenton, Tuttle and Crowell, of Newark, Mann, of Morristown, Kollock, of Elizabeth, and Randolph, of New Brunswick, all worthy and faithful laborers in the editorial field, all men of large influence in moulding the character of the people of this State, have departed one by one, and now the last link which connected the press of to-day with the press of fifty years ago is severed.

Newspapers have improved greatly during the last half century; they have multiplied in number and their contents are far more comprehensive; but the personal character of the men who now officiate as editors has not improved. The pioneers of New Jersey journalism maintained to a man the dignity of their calling; and the lessons of honesty, economy and virtue which they set before their readers, they very generally practiced themselves. We fear that in the present day, the profession is not equally consistent. Let us all then heed the lesson. The small and dingy sheet that circulated as a newspaper fifty years ago may appear to some of us puerile and insignificant; but it effectually served the purpose of its day and generation; if it was unpretending, it was honest; if it was plain and practical, it accorded with the character of a people who had not at that period smothered to any considerable extent the noble simplicity of true manhood, by snobbish affectation and pompous assumption. Above all let us remember that the men who stood behind those little sheets, were earnest patriots, sincere lovers of truth, and practical exponents in their own walk and conversation of the virtues which they inculcated. Judge Hall was such a man; and all who were fortunate enough to come into close association with him were the better for such contact. Sincere, unaffected and humane; upright and exact in all his dealings; forbearing to the erring; kind to all, exhibiting the same courtesy and consideration towards the poor and dependent that he did to the rich and influential, "he was a man, take him for all in all, we ne'er shall look upon his like again."

Judge Hall was married in 1815, and was the father of ten children, four of whom survive him. His wife died in May, 1862. Of his six deceased children, only one left issue, viz: the wife of Maj. Gen. John B. Sanborn, of Minnesota. Judge Hall died from the effects of a carbuncle, which formed in the back of his head at the base of the brain, some twenty days prior to his dissolution. Though skillfully and carefully treated, it was exceedingly painful and malignant, and literally wore out the suffering patient by the intense agony which it caused.

BENJAMIN BAILEY EDSALL.

Benjamin B. Edsall, during the long years he occupied the editorial chair of The Register was undoubtedly the most noted editor in New Jersey, and no man who has since occupied an editorial position in the State has ever attained the prominence in the profession that Mr. Edsall enjoyed. The following obituary, presumably prepared by the late Robert E. Foster, appeared in The Register of April 2, 1868:

Benjamin Bailey Edsall, the editor and one of the proprietors of this paper, departed this life on Friday of last week, after a brief illness, at the age of 57 years, 2 months and 2 days. In his death The Sussex Register has suffered a bereavement which none know so well, or feel so painfully, as those connected with its management, and under the shadow of this great affliction we pause to pay a deserved tribute to his memory.

Mr. Edsall was born in Maspeth, L. I., on Jan. 25, 1811. His parents were poor and even unable to afford him a common school education. At the death of his father, when he was but little over ten years of age, he commenced an apprenticeship in the printing establishment of Harper & Brothers in New York, and continued with them until his term of service expired. In the fall of 1833 he came to this county and entered The Register office as a journeyman under the late John H. Hall. He soon began to take a leading part in the editorial management of the paper and, in 1855 became part owner of the establishment. Under the control of Hall & Edsall The Register increased in circulation, in influence and power, and soon attained a front rank among the weekly journals of the State. In politics, he was a Whig of the Henry Clay school, and followed the fortunes and earnestly advocated the measures of that organization until it sank beneath the heavy load which its pro-slavery adherents sought to place upon it, and the Republican party rose out of its ruins. He was among the first in the State to join in this new movement, and by his pen and voice added in no inconsiderable degree to its success. Firm in his adherence to principle, bold in his advocacy of measures which met his approval, fearless in his denunciation of corrupt and venal men, he was nevertheless fair and honorable with political opponents.

It may be truly said of him that he was "self-made." Without any of the aids now within the reach of the humblest, he stored his mind with a vast fund of information from which a most wonderful memory enabled him to draw at will, as from an inexhaustible fountain. His style of writing giving praise wherever due, so that among his warmest political friends are numbered many with whom he combatted most strenuously. Among the members of his own party he held the love and respect of all. He was so far above the tricks of the mere politician that no one ever accused him of duplicity or unfairness.

In private life, no man was more esteemed, carefully avoiding all personal controversies and neighborhood strifes, he attended faithfully and constantly to his own business. He was exceedingly industrious, preparing all or nearly all the editorial matter of The Register, and selecting with great care the miscellaneous reading which made its columns so attractive. He still found time to do a large share of the severe physical labor of the office, and many of our readers will remember him toiling at the large hand press upon which, until recently, the paper was printed. His style of writing was terse and forcible, and so peculiar to himself, that the habitual reader could easily detect the occasional articles from other pens which appeared in editorial garb.

Although not a member of any religious organization, he had for a long time prior to his death been a generous supporter of the M. E. Church, in the secular affairs of which he took a deep and active interest.

As a citizen he was liberal and public spirited, contributing to every laudable object and every worthy enterprise, even beyond the measure of his ability.

We are not alone in our grief, outside the domestic circle which has been broken, and from which a kind and affectionate husband has been taken, friends not few in number or hollow in profession, who had been drawn to him by his noble qualities through a long and useful life, will sincerely mourn his departure.

The funeral of Mr. Edsall was held in the M. E. Church

on Monday, March 29, and was attended by all the leading men of the county and by many from outside. The services were in charge of Rev. J. N. FitzGerald, pastor of the church. The following ministers also took part in the services: Rev. C. S. Coit, Rev. S. W. Hilliard, Rev. G. S. Mott and Rev. Myron Barrett.

No mention is made in the above account of the life and death of Mr. Edsall of the fact that in 1860 he was nominated by the Republican party as its candidate for Congress. The district then comprised the counties of Bergen, Morris, Passaic and Sussex, and his opponent was Hon. George T. Cobb, of Morris, who was elected by a majority of 1,078.

Leonard & Coult, and they commenced making a specialty of municipal law. Mr. Coult was especially active in this direction, serving as Prosecutor of Pleas for one year and as counsel for the city of Newark. In the latter capacity it was due in a great measure to his individual efforts that the present water supply for Newark was put into operation and it was under his personal leadership that the "Martin Act" was passed. He made the original draft for this act and was indefatigable in his endeavor to have it passed in the legislature and by its passage a number of cities now escape a heavy burden of taxation.

As an earnest Republican he has taken an active and beneficial interest in the party, and has served as delegate to numerous conventions, among them being those which renominated Lincoln for a second term, and Grant and Hayes. His ability as a counsellor has been widely and frequently recognized, and in many important cases he is consulted by his legal confreres. His fraternal affiliations include membership in the Union, the North End and the New York Republican clubs.

Mr. Coult married at Branchville, New Jersey, May 25, 1859, Frances A., daughter of Joseph A. and Margaret Osborne, of Sussex county, and they have had four children: Margaret, Eliza, Lillian and Joseph Jr.

JOSEPH COULT.

Mr. Coult was the son of Joseph and Hannah (Coursen) Coult, and was born in Papakating, Sussex county, New Jersey, May 25, 1834. He attended the Rankin School at Deckertown, where he acquired a thorough classical education, but he was obliged to abandon the hope he had entertained of being permitted to go to college, as his parents wished him to follow a mercantile life. Determined, however, to engage in the legal profession, he commenced the study of law under Thomas N. McCarter, and subsequently became a student in the Law School at Albany, New York, from which he was graduated with the degree of Bachelor of Laws. Admitted to the bar in the State of New York in 1858, he commenced active practice in the city of New York, returning after a short time to New Jersey, where he was admitted as an attorney-at-law in February, 1861.

For several years he was successfully associated in a partnership with Thomas Anderson in Newton, and was made a full attorney and counsellor-at-law under the laws of the State of New Jersey in 1864. In 1871 he formed a partnership with Lewis VanBlarcom, withdrawing from the firm two years later and removing to Newark, where he became the junior partner in the firm of Leonard & Coult. When Chancellor Theodore Runyon withdrew from the practice of law in 1893, upon his appointment as United States Minister to Germany, his extensive law practice fell into the hands of

RICHARD F. GOODMAN.

Richard F. Goodman was born in Hartford, on the 12th day of April, 1841, was graduated at the Harris Military Academy in 1858, and a year later entered Trinity College, at which institution he was graduated with honor in 1863. After a short vacation he was appointed, early in the following February, to the position of acting assistant paymaster in the United States Navy and stationed at the Brooklyn navy yard. Later he was ordered to the United States steamer Nightingale, which then lay in the gulf of Mexico, but after a short cruise of two months returned north. The department complimented him upon the fact that in this, his first report, his accounts were found to be complete and without error. In August he was transferred to a more important position, being ordered to join the Miami, at Hampton Roads, Virginia. This was the first vessel of the navy to ascend the James river, and Paymaster Goodman was sent there to take charge of the storeship of the large fleet which followed, performing that important duty until they returned in May, 1865. The cruise being ended, he declined a place among the regular assistants with the promise of speedy promotion, and resigned at the end of the leave granted for making up his accounts. A further leave of two months was accorded him, at the end of which time he was excused from active duty and given leave without date. He received his honorable discharge in 1868.

Entering the Albany Law University, Mr. Goodman won the degree of Bachelor of Arts, was afterward admitted to the bar in Connecticut, and entered into partnership with his father, Edward Goodman, with whom he remained until he purchased The Sussex Register and removed to Newton on the 1st of October, 1869.

Mr. Goodman is a most able and entertaining writer, and has made The Register one of the most progressive and creditable papers in New Jersey. He has attained marked success in this field of endeavor, and his worth to the community in advancing all measures for the general good cannot be overestimated.

He has been a member of the Board of Directors of the H. W. Merriam Shoe Company Building & Loan Association since its organization in 1890. Since its organization, in March, 1888, he has been a member of Company G, Seventh New Jersey Regiment of National Guards, of Newton, and soon was selected captain, while in February, 1897, he was promoted to the rank of Major. He was a member of Newton Steamer Company during the first nine years after its organization and during the two last years was foreman of the company. Socially he is connected with Harmony Lodge, No. 8, F. & A. M.; Baldwin Chapter, No. 17, R. A. M., of which he was secretary for 35 years; DeMolay Commandery, K. T., and is a noble of Salaam Temple, A. A. O. N. M. S. He is also a member of Captain Walker Post, G. A. R. and of the Military order of the Loyal Legion of the United States. He is one of the directors of the Newton Library Association and a charter member of the Newton Club. And in military, political, social and professional circles occupies a position of due relative distinction, his strong mentality and ability making him a leader, while his genial, cordial manner renders him a favorite with all.

Mr. Goodman is President of the Newton Board of Trade, having been elected in 1912. He is also President of the Sussex County Branch Society for the Prevention of Cruelty to Animals, succeeding the late Rev. James E. Hall in December, 1912. He is greatly interested in the work of both organizations and much of their usefulness is due to his untiring efforts.

He was appointed Postmaster of Newton by President McKinley in October, 1897, and was reappointed twice by President Roosevelt, serving until 1910, when he was succeeded by James E. Baldwin. His administration of the office made it one of the best in the country. To him is due the credit of the establishment of the carrier service in Newton, his recommendation being favorably acted upon by the Postmaster General in 1901, the service beginning on October 1 of that year.

During his term of office the receipts increased fifty per cent. Two additional New York mails were put on and an early morning mail from New York was secured. Three rural routes were established, taking in a big section of the county about Newton.

In 1890 Mr. Goodman was the Republican candidate for Congress. This district comprised Hunterdon, Somerset, Sussex and Warren counties. The Republican candidate ran ahead of his ticket, but was not elected to Congress.

WHITFIELD GIBBS.

Whitfield Gibbs, the present editor of The Register, was born at Hope, Warren county, January 28, 1851. After obtaining a common school education he spent three years in a store at Hope and one year at Hackettstown.

In 1871 he entered the office of The Sussex Register for the purpose of learning the printing business, and after gaining a general knowledge of the art during the next three years, spent about four years as a journeyman printer in Newark and New York.

On the first of October, 1878, he entered into partnership with John J. Stanton and they purchased the Sussex Independent, at Deckertown, of the late Jacob L. Swayze. As the story of the stirring times of his connection with that paper is fully covered in the history of the Independent printed on another page it will not be recapitulated here.

In 1882 he retired from the Independent and spent three years in the lumber business, operating a steam saw mill in this and Orange counties. In 1885 he conducted the Passaic Daily Times for about six months, or until it was sold, for the late Thomas M. Moore, who had been compelled to take it for debt.

Upon the sale of the Times Mr. Gibbs became city editor of the Jersey City Daily Argus, and remained there until the work of building the Pennsylvania, Poughkeepsie and Boston Railroad was resumed in 1888, when he became connected with that road and was later made purchasing agent, which position he held until the line was absorbed by the Philadelphia & Reading road.

In 1897 he purchased the Citizen at Walden, N. Y. Before taking possession the plant was entirely destroyed by fire. He then purchased the subscription list, put in a new plant, and after running it for two years, during which time its circulation increased from 600 to 1,500, sold out, as there didn't seem to be much prospect of profit in a dollar newspaper.

Mr. Gibbs then became connected with the American Milling Company and was located at West Point, Va., for two years superintending the construction of a large mill. He represented the company at different points through the country, and in 1908 went to Superior, Wis., where he superintended the construction of another large mill. He remained there two years and then returned East and in May, 1911, purchased The Sussex Register of Richard F. Goodman and took possession on the first of June.

ROBERT E. FOSTER.

For thirty-five years the local editorship of The Sussex Register was under the direction of the late Robert E. Foster. Through all the changes in editorship and ownership he continued at his post and gave to the reading world the best that was in him. Born in Newton in 1843, the son of David Lunn Foster and Sarah Knapp, he attended the district school until thirteen years old. He then entered the store of Stoll & Dunn, but his ambition turning toward the printing trade, he was apprenticed when fourteen years old to John H. Hall, the founder of The Register, becoming an inmate of Mr. Hall's home. Every department of the business was mastered by him. He was devil, typesetter, pressman, foreman, reporter and associate editor. In 1870 Mr. Foster left The Register and went to Newark where he was employed on the old Newark Advertiser, now The Star. In 1872 he returned to Newton and again became associated with The Register, remaining until the time of his death on July 6, 1912.

Pre-eminently a journalist, under conditions now changed by modern methods, he gave to the readers of the paper the results of ceaseless vigilance and hard labor. He won a reputation throughout the State as a news editor and perhaps none of the writings of his contemporaries were copied as much as his. Long years of experience, aided by a journalistic instinct, a knowledge of what was "news" and what would interest the people, coupled with a love for truth, made him one of the foremost of his profession. Throughout his long career as a newspaper man, he used with great tact the ability given him. His saving sense of humor was exercised throughout his life and sustained his spirit until the close of his career.

In his later years he continued his work under conditions which would have discouraged a majority of men. Failure of eyesight and a loss of the faculty of hearing did not drive him from his post and it was not until weakened by the onslaught of a mortal disease that he dropped his weary pen from hands which almost refused to push themselves across the page and tottered to his home to linger but a few days and then pass into the presence of the great Editor of the Universe.

SUSSEX COUNTY HOME JOURNAL.

The first paper published in the Borough of Sussex, then Deckertown, was the "Sussex County Home Journal," which made its initial appearance on June 2, 1850. The founder and publisher was J. L. Barlow, who was born in Neversink, N. Y., on October 27, 1819. Prior to his advent in Sussex county he had published the "Western New Yorker" in his home town. The "Home Journal" survived but two years, but it was an exceptionally good paper for those times. After discontinuing the paper Barlow moved to Port Jervis where he, together with John Dow, published the "Mirror of Temperance." Barlow was afterwards ordained as a Baptist preacher and became pastor of a church at Seymour, Conn. He died at Hagadorn's Mills, N. Y., October 24, 1906.

ERNEST ARTHUR SHAY.

Ernest Arthur Shay became associated with The Register in October, 1911, as a reporter. Following the death of Robert E. Foster in July, 1912, he became associate editor and shortly afterward business manager. He was born near Branchville, February 5, 1882, his parents being James and Susan (Compton) Shay. When he was a little over a year old they removed to Wantage township. He attended the Union public school, graduating in 1898. He then attended Seeley's Select School, Sussex, for two terms. After being in the mercantile business for a short time, Mr. Shay entered the Newton Business College. Finishing the business course he entered the law office of Judge Henry C. Hunt, of Sussex, but believing the city offered better opportunities, obtained a position with J. S. Bailey & Company, wholesale and retail meat dealers, Christopher and Hudson streets, New York. A few months later he resigned to take a position as secretary to the manager of the New York office of the Vacuum Oil Company, of Rochester, N. Y. When his chief was promoted to the managership of the Foreign Shipping Department of the company, with offices at 29 Broadway, Mr. Shay accompanied him and was later made traffic manager of the company.

In 1907 a nervous breakdown compelled him to resign his position and return to Sussex county, locating at Branchville. He was appointed carrier on rural route No. 1, which included the territory around Culver's Lake. In 1909 he was appointed county representative of the Newark Morning and Evening Star, leaving that paper to become associated with The Register. For a number of years he has been a special writer on the staff of the Newark Sunday Call, and following the removal of I. L. Hallock to Newark in October, 1913, was made the Sussex county representative of that paper. He is also the county representative of the New York Herald and New York World.

While a resident of New York city he served in Company K, Twenty-second Regiment Enigneers. An injury received in an accident in New York caused him to resign from the regiment after his removal from New York to Newark.

He is a member of the Newton Board of Trade, the Newton Club, Kittatinny Hose Company, Newton Lodge No. 654, Loyal Order of Moose, Newton Council No. 1313, Royal Arcanum; Culver Lodge No. 133, Independent Order of Odd Fellows, of Branchville, which he organized; Halsey Council, No. 92, Jr. O. U. A. M., of Newark; Frankford Grange, P. of H., of Branchville; Sussex County Pomona Grange, No. 2; is a Past President of Washington Camp, No. 82, P. O. S. of A.; first vice-president of the Sussex County Branch Society for the Prevention of Cruelty to Animals; secretary of the Branchville Water & Improvement Company; an honorary member of Protection Hook & Ladder Company, of Sussex; one of the charter members of the Branchville Fire Department and was the first secretary of the North Jersey Poultry Association. He is also Secretary and a member of the executive committee of the Sussex County Automobile Club.

THE NEW JERSEY HERALD.

The New Jersey Herald, published at Newton, was established in 1829 by Col. Grant Fitch, of Norwalk, Conn., on the site of what is now the W. W. Woodward Hardware Company building on Main street. Col. Fitch retired from the ownership in 1842, being succeeded by his son, Charles W. Fitch, of Washington, D. C. In November, 1843, the paper was purchased by Gilbert J. Beebe, of Orange county, who sold it to Victor M. Drake, of Goshen, in 1845. In 1853 the paper was purchased by Judge Thomas Anderson, who was succeeded in August, 1855, by Col. Morris R. Hamilton, of Oxford, Warren county. He was followed in August, 1858, by James J. McNally, of Orange county. In August, 1861, Henry C. Kelsey purchased the paper. In 1862 Mr. Kelsey purchased the Sussex Democrat, published by George R. Mc-Carter, and consolidated the two papers under the name of the Herald. The Sussex True Democrat, published by George D. Wallace, was also purchased by Mr. Kelsey and consolidated with the Herald. At the time of the purchase of the Sussex Democrat, John W. Gillam, its foreman and assistant editor, became a partner of Mr. Kelsey. On June 28, 1866, Mr. Kelsey sold his interest to William H. Bell, of Branchville. In March, 1867, Thomas G. Bunnell became local editor, succeeding George R. McCarter, who had gone with the Herald at the time of the purchase of his paper in 1862. In August, 1867, the paper was purchased by a stock company of Democrats, of which Thomas G. Bunnell was the principal stockholder and he became editor and publisher, with Edwin Owen as foreman. Owen was succeeded in August, 1868, by Henry C. Bonnell who, in 1873, succeeded John S. Gibson as local editor. In August, 1886, Thomas Kays succeeded Thomas G. Bunnell as editor and publisher, the paper being purchased by Mr. Bunnell and Jacob L. Bunnell in February, 1887. Jacob L. Bunnell later became sole owner and in July, 1902, formed a partnership with Martin J. Cox, who had been connected with the paper some time, under the name of Bunnell & Cox. The paper is still published by them. During its career it has changed locations a number of times, being established at its present location in 1873.

JOHN J. STANTON.

John J. Stanton, one of the well known editors of the county, began his newspaper career in the town of his birth, Newton, where he was born November 27, 1857. After attending several of the private schools in the town, he finished his course in the Newton High School in the class of 1873. Like the present editor of The Register, he served his apprenticeship in this office. In partnership with Whitfield Gibbs they became joint owners of the Sussex Independent October 1, 1878, purchasing the property of the late Jacob L. Swayze, of Newton. The town was then known as Deckertown.

Mr. Gibbs retired from the paper in 1882, since which time the paper has almost entirely been under the ownership and management of Mr. Stanton. It is needless to say that it has always been among the foremost local papers of the State and district, and its editor a leading factor in every public enterprise and betterment movement for his town and county, always taking an active interest in all public matters, political, social and commercial.

The paper has a fine plant in its own town, and in addition to the Independent Mr. Stanton is the owner and publisher of the Milk Reporter, the organ of the fluid milk trade of the country.

Aside from the printing and publishing business, the subject of our sketch is extensively interested in real estate, the handling of real estate; is manager of several large estates, and is president and general manager of the Woodbourne Electric Light, Heat and Power Company, of Sussex, the company being organized largely through his efforts.

It was through him that the late United States Senator John F. Dryden and his son-in-law, Colonel A. R. Kuser, and many other wealthy and prominent men purchased handsome estates in the county of Sussex. Although largely interested in a variety of enterprises for thirty-five years he has never missed a week in supplying copy and supervising the publication of the Independent. Mr. Stanton is widely known in the county, adjoining counties and State. He has a comfortable home on Newton avenue, while his offices are located on Fountain Square, in the Borough of Sussex.

THE SUSSEX INDEPENDENT.

The Sussex Independent, printed at Sussex borough, formerly Deckertown, was established May 4, 1870, by Stephen H. Sayer, then of Montgomery, Orange county, where for a time he was engaged in the publication of Sayer's Dollar Weekly.

The paper was printed in the second story of a building now occupied by Irwin Smith, as a blacksmith shop, and across the street from the upper hotel in the then small village.

About a year later William H. Noble, of Waverly, N. Y., who removed to Sussex county with his family and the family of his father, became a partner in the business with Mr. Sayer, under the firm name of Sayer & Noble. This was soon after the building of the Midland Railroad to Deckertown, when the town was enjoying the greatest boom in its history, and new families were coming to the place almost every week. Mr. Noble was a most excellent job printer. Soon after these men joined hands they purchased much new material and machinery and installed the first new steam driven press in the county.

In 1873 came the famous panic when everything went back and made very hard work for the two men then running a paper in a town like Deckertown, and the concern became somewhat embarrassed. They managed to struggle along for a time, but finally organized the plant into a stock company, known as The Independent Printing Company, stock being taken by many of the merchants and leading business men of the town and township. At this time business was still slow.

In 1878 the late Jacob L. Swayze, President of the Merchants National Bank of Newton, purchased a controlling interest in the paper, installing Henry A. Van Fredenburg, the present editor of the New York Farmer, as editor of the Independent. October 1st Mr. Swayze sold the paper to Whitfield Gibbs, of Newark, and John J. Stanton, of Newton, both graduates of The Register office, under the mechanical management of the late Robert E. Foster, with Richard F. Goodman as editor. Mr. Van Fredenburg remained with the new management until the spring of the following year.

Being practical and experienced the new management began a lively hustle for business, going actively after the then existing Democratic ring in county politics. The struggle from that time on for two or three years was a most memorable one, and the paper gained much prominence in the county and State, and had among its contributors and supporters such men as Jacob L. Swayze, William A. Stiles, General Judson Kilpatrick, John Loomis, A. F. Fellows, H. A. Van Fredenburg and a number of others prominent in county affairs. It was the first time in the county history that the then dominant party received a setback. At this time the county expenses were $109,000 per year. In 1879 an anti-ring Board of Freeholders was elected. The ring in Warren county had also been attacked and a fight started by a young prosecutor named Henry S. Harris, afterwards Congressman, which resulted in twelve or fifteen men prominent in county affairs being sentenced to the State prison.

Politics reached a very high pitch and in 1878, in a three-cornered fight for Sheriff, J. B. Hendershot, Republican; James L. Decker, of Sparta, Democrat, and George B. Cole, Greenback, were the candidates. The plurality for Decker was only 56 on the count over Cole. It was charged at the time that this was secured in Sparta by alleged irregularities. The Independent favored fusion and endeavored to have Hendershot withdraw. Failing in this it advocated the election of Cole, with results as stated above.

Politics continued high. In the general elections of 1880, the Independent supported Republican policies and candidates and favored the election of Garfield as against Hancock. As a result the county gave greatly reduced majorities for the entire Democratic ticket, Hancock only carrying the county by about 800, while in 1879 Lewis J. Martin for Assembly had only carried the county by a majority of 126.

During the year of 1880 there was much personal journalism in Sussex county. James L. Decker, who was then Sheriff of Sussex county, packed a grand jury hostile to Jacob L. Swayze, Whitfield Gibbs and John J. Stanton, against whom indictments were jointly procured at the December term of the Court of Oyer and Terminer, 1880, for libel.

To the indictments pleas in abatement were interposed, which were overruled by the court.

On June 7, 1881, Mr. Swayze died and the case was continued against Gibbs and Stanton, editors of the Sussex Independent. In October 1881, an arrangement between the counsel for the State and the defendants was made, that if the defendants should plead guilty to the technical charges, that only a nominal fine would be imposed. The counsel of the State betrayed the counsel of the defendants. The defendants were sentenced for a term of six and ten months to State prison, which however, they were never compelled to serve.

Then appeared plainly the treachery of the men they were dealing with as opponents. The people of the county were up in arms. While held temporarily in Newton they were given keys to the jail and received their friends in the parlors of the court house. The first night caused a riot in the court yard and the court was burned in effigy on the public square. The first Sunday was a regular ovation to the editors and over 500 people from all parts of the county visited them in the court house. Then came on the election.

It was one of the most desperate and hard fought battles ever known in the history of the county. The result was the election of Jacob E. Hornbeck, of Deckertown, the father-in-law of Editor Gibbs.

After this came a great legal battle. Former Governor Joseph D. Bedle, a great Democratic leader of Jersey City, and Martin Rosenkrans, Esq., were employed. The editors were released on the day after election on a writ of error to the Supreme Court and from thence to the Court of Errors and Appeals. The fight continued for several years and was finally won out by the editors in July, 1884. This was the second plea of the kind ever made in the United States, the first being that of Aaron Burr, challenging the entire array of Grand and Petit Jurors on the grounds of personal prejudice. The final result was forever an end of that kind of politics in Sussex county. It resulted for many years in a saving of more than $50,000 a year to the taxpayers of Sussex county, and at the next session of the Legislature in a complete revision of the libel laws of the State. John J. Stanton went to Trenton, but he went there as Journal Clerk of the House of Assembly, which position he occupied for two or three years.

One by one the members of that Grand Jury passed away and every actor in the drama of those days, who were in the fray as prosecutors of the young editors, passed out of county politics and all but one are now with the great majority.

Through the wide publicity given by the metropolitan papers this became a celebrated case and was discussed by the leading papers throughout the country, and among them all the New Jersey Herald was the only one that did not condemn the action of the Sheriff and the perfidy of the Prosecutor.

THE MILK REPORTER.

The Milk Reporter, the organ of the fluid milk trade, is published monthly at the office of the Sussex Independent, Sussex, N. J. The editor and manager is John J. Stanton.

The paper was originated by Amzi Howell in 1885, then Secretary of the New York Milk Exchange, and was then a small four page pamphlet devoted mostly to milk statistics and the milk carrying trade of the railroads.

At the death of Mr. Howell the paper passed into the hands of Mr. John B. Kimber, a pioneer in the milk business, a milk salesman and collector.

In 1893 the paper was purchased by John J. Stanton, who removed the paper to Sussex, then Deckertown, a great milk shipping centre, Orange and Sussex counties at that time being the most extensive milk producing counties in the New York milk district.

In the hands of Mr. Stanton the paper has been continuously enlarged until it is now a sixteen page standard size paper, nicely printed on book paper, and has a wide scope, covering a large and successful advertising patronage. It is a standard authority on the milk business and is so recognized by the national government in the year book and the different State experiment stations. In the courts its statements are accepted as an authority on all sides. Nearly all the experts in the milk business in all parts of the country are contributors to its columns. Mr. Kimber is still connected with the paper as a regular contributor, and Mr. Irvin D. Shorter is assistant manager.

CHARLES E. STICKNEY.

Charles E. Stickney, the editor and owner of The Wantage Recorder, published at Sussex Borough, was born in the town of Wawayanda, Orange county, New York, January 1, 1841, being the son of the late Hon. Erastus Stickney. He received only a common school education, but being a reader, and a close observer became one of the best informed men in his native town. His perseverance and determination to win, coupled with his natural ability, made him a successful teacher, adviser and business man. A collector of historical data, he has written a number of interesting books on the early history of both New York and New Jersey, the most widely known perhaps, being "A History of the Minisink Region," published in several editions and which is recognized as the official history of that section.

For a number of years Mr. Stickney was engaged in the mercantile business in Slate Hill. In 1883 he sold his business at that place and removed to Sussex (then Deckertown) when he purchased a general store near the Susquehanna railroad depot. On January 1, 1894, he established the Wantage Recorder, a Democratic weekly, published on Friday of each week. The paper has steadily grown under his management.

In 1905 he was elected Mayor of Sussex, serving two terms. In 1912 he was appointed Mayor by the Common Council to fill the unexpired term of Edward C. Feakes, resigned. During the last year of its existence he was Clerk of the sixteen member Board of Freeholders.

As Mayor, he has given the people of Sussex a fair, just, economical and honest administration. Both in the mercantile and newspaper business he has obtained an enviable reputation for honesty and straightforwardness and while many differ with him as to his political convictions, none question his integrity.

GEORGE T. KEECH.

George T. Keech, editor and owner of the Stanhope Eagle, was born at Lower Merion, Montgomery county, Pa., January 28, 1852. He attended the public school until seventeen years of age, then attended Freemont Seminary, a private school at Norristown, Pa., for one and a third years. He then taught school for one year at Clarksboro, Gloucester county, New Jersey. In September, 1871, he entered the Bridgewater (Mass.) State Normal School, graduating in July, 1873. He taught one year in Massachusetts, returning to New Jersey in 1874, teaching successively at Richwood, Mantua and Harrisonville, all in Gloucester county. In 1880 he took the principalship of the Kennet Square Public School, resigning in 1881 to enter the ice business in Philadelphia. Leaving that business in 1882, he again took up teaching at Broadway, Warren county. Nights and mornings he conducted a small printing business, doing mostly a mail order business.

In 1884 he retired from teaching and on February 1, 1885, removed his printing establishment to Netcong, then called South Stanhope. On June 30, 1885, he issued the first edition of the Stanhope Eagle, which because of the absence of a post office at what is now Netcong, was entered as second class matter at the Stanhope post office. On the establishment of the post office at Netcong, the paper was mailed from that place but the name of the publication was not changed.

Mr. Keech has been active in the affairs of Netcong and has twice been elected Justice of the Peace, first serving from 1886 to 1891. He was again elected to that office in 1911, his term running to 1916. From 1907 to 1910 he was Borough Clerk and as such official had the entire charge of drawing up the papers for the election and bonding of the Borough for its municipal water plant. He has also served a number of terms as Borough Recorder.

SUSSEX COUNTY

A Few Brief Facts About Its History From the Time of Early Settlement to the Present Time

To properly write the history of Sussex county would necessitate the filling of more pages than can be allotted in this anniversary number. It would necessitate the telling of the deeds of heroism performed not only by the men of the county but also by the women, the wives, mothers and daughters of the early settlers; not only of the deeds of valor performed by the men who stood against the British in the early days of the country and against the assaults of their Southern brothers at the Bloody Angle, at Spottsylvania, at Gettysburg and the Wilderness, but by those who, in the early days, left their homes with their rifles in their hands to till the fields far from their homes in the little clearing, knowing not whether they would find their homes in ashes and their wives and daughters captives in the hands of cruel and treacherous Indian foes, where death would be a welcome release from the torture and indignity practiced. It would mean the writing of the history of the men who have risen from the ranks to be leaders in the State and Nation, and they are many, for Sussex county's contribution to the business and professional life of the country is perhaps larger than that of any other county of its size of any State. It would also mean the writing of the records of the men and women who have stayed in the old county and added to its fair name. All of this cannot be done and we shall devote ourselves to the main facts of the story of its early settlement and the events which lead up to the present time.

Sussex as a separate county began its existence under an act of the Legislature on June 18, 1753, being the thirteenth county in order of erection in the State of New Jersey. The name was derived from the family seat of the Duke of Newcastle, located in the County of Sussex, England, and was bestowed on the new division by Jonathan Belcher, Esq., then governor of New Jersey. At that time it included the lands now known as Warren county, the partition of the two having been made in 1824. Prior to 1738 the northern part of the State was included in the county of Hunterdon, and the public business of this section was done at Trenton. On March 15 of that year, Morris county was taken from Hunterdon and the seat of public business was transferred to Morristown, where it remained until 1753.

In order to give a detailed account of the history of the county we are proud to call our home, it becomes necessary to go back still farther than the erection of the various counties. Imagination must be drawn on to a certain extent as to the exact time the first white man set foot on the land now included in the county. When the English invaded the country prior to 1664, abandoned lead mines and excellent roads were found, presumably worked and made by those who had wandered down the Minisink Valley from eastern New York, perhaps around the year 1650. Evidently these men were Hollanders from Ulster county, New York. After locating the lead mines, they saw the necessity of building a suitable road over which to transport the mineral, and the old Mine Road, running from Pahaquarry, in Warren county, to Esopus, N. Y., a distance of about one hundred miles, was built.

This is thought to be the first road of any considerable length built on the western continent. In those days the expense was born by the builders. There was no 40 per cent. of State aid or any 10 per cent. from the districts through which the road passed. The territory was a howling wilderness. The construction was doubtless attended with considerable danger, both from the wild natives and the still wilder animals. The fact that it remains to-day is a monument to the skill of the men who spent their time, their money and possibly their lives in its construction. The sole excuse for building the road doubtless lay in the fact that a few men saw a chance for personal gain and attainment. These parties, however, were driven from this section of the country in 1664 when the British captured New Nethernlands and ended the Dutch rule in America. With the capture of the British came the return to their homes of the majority of the Dutch settlers. A few of the heartiest, however, remained and from them sprang the men who were the ancestors of our old Dutch friends in Sussex county.

Through the length and breadth of northern Jersey, from the Hudson to the Delaware, roamed the Leni Lenape Indians or Delawares. For a period of time, the length of which no man knows, the Turkey and Wolf branches of this tribe occupied what is now the counties of Sussex and Warren. Their emblem, the "tortoise" is claimed to be 2,000 years old. Before the whites, came the fierce and warlike tribe of Iroquois who practically made slaves of the Leni Lenapes, and in 1742 the latter tribe was forced to cross the Delaware into Pennsylvania. The last rights of the Indian lands of New Jersey were purchased by the State in 1832 under an act of the Legislature at the memorial of Shawuskukhking, whose English name was Bartholomew S. Calvin, born in 1756 and was educated at Princeton. The sum of $2,000 was paid by the State for these rights.

This section of the county evidently had no particular, dominant nationality. The Hugenots, the Hollanders, the Swedes, the Irish, the Welsh and the Scotch all figured in its make-up, more or less. As early as 1614 settlements were being made in parts of the State, especially along the upper part of the Delaware Valley. The settlers came from Esopus, New Paltz and Kingston on the Hudson, gradually spreading down the upper Delaware to Port Jervis and thence down along the river through the western townships of the county, meeting a similar stream of Protestants and Dissenters of Continental Europe coming north along that stream. Even in 1609, some of the Hollanders who came to Amsterdam with Hendrick Hudson, wandered into what is now Monmouth county and settled there.

The advent of the English into the New World caused a change in the upper portion of New Jersey. On June 23 or 24, 1664, the Duke of York executed a lease and release to Lord John Berkeley, Baron of Stratton, and Sir George Carteret, of Saltrun in Devon, granting to them and their heirs all the land west of Long Island and Manhitas, or Manhattan, the Hudson River and the main sea to the Delaware Bay and river, extending southwest to the main sea as far as Cape May and northeast to the northermost branch of the Delaware River to the forty-first degree of latitude, to be called New Caesarea or New Jersey. A constitution for the new division was signed on February 10, 1664, and Philip Carteret, a brother of Sir George Carteret, one of the grantees, received his commission as governor of the section. From that time on until 1709, the history of the county is told in the story of efforts to colonize the various sections, the area embraced by the county as at present laid out containing less than 500 people. Even in 1738, not more than 600 people resided among the hills and valleys of the northern county of the State, while the population of the entire State was only 47,369.

All the territory comprised in the old county belonged to West Jersey. By the act of 1709, the land in the northern part of the State was defined as Burlington county. When Hunterdon was erected in 1713, we were shifted to that and still another change of name was made in 1738 when Morris county was erected. Between 1738 and 1753 a number of townships were erected, being composed of Walpack, New Town, later Newton, Hardwick and Greenwich, the latter being erected by Royal Patent. The two former townships comprised practically all the present county of Sussex, with the exception of what is now Stillwater, Fredon and Green townships, these being included with what is now Warren county in the townships of Greenwich and Hardwick.

From 1753 to 1793 the population of the county as then formed largely increased, German immigrants adding considerably to the population.

In 1750 the residents of the county became dissatisfied with the necessity of having to go to Morristown to attend to public business and a petition was made to the Provincial Assembly to divide the county and allow the building of a Court House and jail in the northern section. On June 8, 1753, the Assembly granted the petition and designated the upper part of Morris county as Sussex county. At the time of granting the petition, the Assembly gave the right to the legally qualified citizens to appear at Trenton or elsewhere in the County of Hunterdon and there vote in conjunction with the citizens of Morris and Hunterdon counties for two members of Assembly. Because of the distance and lack of roads Sussex was practically deprived of direct representation at Trenton until 1768 when on May 10 of that year an act was passed authorizing the county to elect two representatives. This was confirmed by the King on Dec. 9, 1770. The confirmation was proclaimed in New Jersey in 1771 and the first election for representatives was held on Aug. 17, 1772, when Thomas Van Horne and Nathaniel Pettit were elected. The first court ever held in Sussex county was opened on May 20, 1753, in the residence of Jonathan Pettit in Hardwick township. A proclamation issued by Governor Belcher called for the holding of the court of general sessions of the peace, an inferior court of common pleas, on the third Tuesday in November, the third Tuesday in February, the fourth Tuesday in May and the fourth Tuesday in August of each year, each term not to exceed four days. Nothing was done at the first term except to grant tavern licenses. It was then that Sussex county actually began its existence as a separate county. The first meeting of the Board of Freeholders, by which the county was then to be governed, was held on Nov. 21, 1753, in what is now Johnsonburg, the residence of Samuel Green being used as the meeting place. The principal business at that meeting was the ordering of an election to be held on April 16, 17 and 18, 1755, for the purpose of selecting a place for the jail and Court House. At the election it was decided to build the jail upon land owned by Samuel Green, and the log jail so well known in the county history was the result. On May 8, 1755, Thomas Wolverton was elected as the county collector and on the 18th of June of that year the citizens of the county were assessed one hundred pounds to be raised by taxation. At the May term of court, 1754, a commission appointed by the court formed three new divisions in the county, Wantage, Oxford and Mansfield Wood-House. On May 12, 1756, the Board of Justices and Freeholders began holding meetings at the house of Thomas Wolverton, near Huntsville, and this house was used as a meeting place until 1762.

The township of New Town soon became the most important township. By 1761 the residents of the township had made themselves felt in county progress and on Dec. 12 of that year an act was passed by the Assembly authorizing the erection of a Court House and jail on a spot to be fixed by a majority of the Justices and Freeholders. The requirement, however, was made that the buildings were to be erected either on the plantation owned by Henry Hairlocker or within a half mile of his dwelling house, which stood where the Horton mansion now stands. From various sources it would appear that Hairlocker was not the actual owner of the land but that the real owner was Jonathan Hampton, an Essex county resident. By stretching the surveyors' tape the site of the Court House was fixed part way up the steep hill to the south of the Hairlocker home. The sum of 500 pounds was voted toward building the Court House and jail. Twelve hundred pounds were afterward appropriated and a stone building was erected, which stood until 1847. At the time of the building of the Court House the county did not own the land and the deed was not passed until August 31, 1764. Two and eight-tenths acres were conveyed for the purpose of a site for the building of a Court House, yard and county park, the land to revert to the heirs of Jonathan Hampton or their assignees at any time court may cease to be held there. The ground at present occupied by Spring street, High street and Park Place have all been taken from the land given for county purposes, thereby narrowing it down considerably.

In 1764 Knowlton township was set off from Oxford, in 1782 Independence from Hardwick; 1792, Vernon from Hardyston; 1797, Frankford from Newton; 1798, Byram from Newton. No other townships were set off until the county of Warren was taken from the land embraced by Sussex in 1824.

In addition to the townships already mentioned others were erected as follows: Andover in March, 1864; Andover Borough, March 25, 1904; Branchville Borough, March 9, 1898; Fredon, 1904; Hampton, March, 1864; Brooklyn Borough, (now Hopatcong) April 7, 1898; Franklin Borough, 1913; Green, 1824; Lafayette, 1845; Montague, 1759. The Borough of Deckertown was incorporated in October, 1891, the name being changed to Sussex in April, 1901.

In 1801 the County Clerk's office was built on the green in front of the Court House, to which a Surrogate's office was added in 1825. In 1844 the Court House was remodeled at a cost of about $5,000. This building, however, was totally destroyed by fire on Jan. 28, 1847. In February of that year the county appropriated $8,500 and the citizens appropriated $6,500 more for the building, in all a total of $15,000 to rebuild on the site of the burned building. At this time an effort was made to have the county seat moved to either Branchville or Augusta, but the proposition was defeated in the Board of Freeholders by a vote of 14 to 12. The building of the new Court House was at once started and speedily completed. On Dec. 29, 1911, fire damaged the Court House so that it necessitated the complete rebuilding of the interior of the second floor. A new clerk's office was built in 1859 and a jail was erected in the rear of the Court House in 1868. This was replaced by the present jail in 1896. The County Clerk's building was remodeled in 1907.

In the earliest wars and Indian struggles which have occurred since the founding of the county, Sussex county always bore a prominent part. Between 1720 and 1740 there was continual strife between the people living in the northern part of the county and those living in the southern part of Orange county over what should be the border line of New York and New Jersey. From 1753 to 1764 the county was a scene of many Indian outrages. Sussex county was upon the frontier, as to the west stretched the wilderness whose farthest borders touched on the French settlement along the Ohio river. The English defeat at Pittsburg afforded the Indians a chance to even up scores made by the unscrupulous English surveyors and the people in the eastern part of Pennsylvania were the first to feel the Indian ravages. At the command of Governor Belcher seven hundred Jerseymen, including one hundred men from Sussex county, went to the assistance of the Pennsylvanians. In 1756 the Indian trouble began to sweep Sussex county itself and before the treaty of peace was made in 1759 scores of its citizens were massacred or carried away by the Indians and sold into slavery. It was early during this troublesome period that 10,000 pounds was authorized by the Legislature for the defense of the frontier along the Delaware River in Sussex county. Seven block houses were erected. The first fort reading "12 miles above Easton"; the second, "18 miles further north"; the third, "Fort Walpack, 6 miles further"; the fourth, "Headquarters of the officers commanding these forts, 6 miles from Fort Walpack"; the fifth, "Fort Nomanock"; the sixth, "Fort Shipeconk"; the seventh, "Fort Cole, 12 miles from Nomanock." These forts have crumpled into ruins but will be marked by suitable tablets given to the county by Freeholder John J. Van Sickle. From the close of these Indian struggles, during 1774 the inhabitants of the county continued in their work of subduing the wilderness. Early in 1774, however, the storm of the Revolution began to break in Sussex county and on July 16 a meeting was held at the Court House, presided over by Hugh Hughes, at which resolutions drawn by John Cleves Symmes asserting the right to be taxed only by their consent and denouncing the act of Parliament in imposing taxes and closing the port of Boston as oppressive, unconstitutional and injurious to American freedom were read. During the war Newton was the scene of many meetings of those interested in the independence of the colonies in the struggle for liberty. One thousand of Sussex citizens were enrolled in the Continental army and militia and at the close of the combat the Continental Congress passed resolutions thanking the county for her response to the call for men and supplies. In the year 1781 the amount raised by Sussex county for the purpose of carrying on the struggle for Independence was about $40,000, while the following year nearly $30,000 was raised. Following the war Sussex county became the dwelling place of many of the residents of New York and Philadelphia who owned land in the county.

The war of 1812 made very little impression on Sussex county and it was necessary to resort to a draft in order to secure the quota required of it. The Civil War, however, was quite a different matter. Mere boys vied with the grown men in the rush to enlist for the preservation of the Union.

From the county went the pick and flower of her manhood; some to return racked with fever and disease; some to return maimed and wounded and some to never return, for many gave their lives on Southern battlefields and in Southern prisons that the Union might be preserved. From the county went the dashing Kilpatrick, whose deeds as a calveryman made him the best known man in that branch of the service and whose valor brought him the title of Brigadier General; Lieut. George V. Griggs, who gave his life on the field of battle; Colonel Henry Ogden Ryerson; Quartermaster Sergeant Oliver W. Cooke, Colonel Samuel Fowler, Chaplain Alanson A. Haines, Colonel Edgar A. Hamilton, Captain James Walker, Captain James S. McDanolds, Captain Lewis VanBlarcom, Virgil Broderick and the scores of others who faced the bullets of their Southern brothers on many a battlefield. Sussex county has no reason to be ashamed of her citizen soldiers. The Fifteenth New Jersey Infantry, composed in a large part of sons of Sussex, left more than half its number on the field at Spottsylvania Court House; the First New Jersey Cavalry had no equal in the service, participating in nearly a hundred battles; the men scattered in the various New Jersey and New York Regiments from the old county all gave splendid accounts of themselves.

Since the end of the Civil War the history of the county has been one of quiet agricultural and industrial development. Newton, Sussex, Hamburg, Franklin and Stanhope have large industrial establishments employing many men.

Diversified farming has been succeeded to a large extent by the production of milk alone and the county is one of the principal sources of the milk supplies of New York and Newark. Through the efforts of the Sussex County Farm Bureau during the past year, efforts are again being made to induce the farmer to do more general farm work, especially along the line of growing live stock, grains and vegetables.

POPULATION.

According to the census reports of 1910, the total population of Sussex county was 26,781 as against 24,134 in 1900, an increase of 11 per cent. Of this number 14,802 were males and 11,979 were females. Of the total number 168 were negroes. The legal voters number 9,767. Of the population 20,238 were of native parentage, while 2,224 were of mixed native and foreign parentage. Of the foreign born, Hungary leads with 1,465 people in the county born on her soil. Italy is second with 997 and Austria third with 366. The balance of the foreign born population is scattered between 19 other countries. There are 6,059 separate and distinct families in the county, residing in 5,592 houses.

With a land area of 529 square miles, the population per square mile in 1910 was 50.6, while the rural population per square mile was 42.2.

LAKES.

Situated the farthest north of any county in the State, with its area of 529 square miles seamed from end to end with parallel ranges of mountains, the northern termination of one of which is High Point, the highest spot in New Jersey, 1,819 feet above sea level, Sussex county boasts of more natural lakes than any other county in the State. There are within its borders over 50 natural lakes, whose elevations range from 486 to 1,570 feet, varying in size from a few acres to over 500 acres in extent. There is also Lake Hopatcong, containing 2,445 acres, on the southeastern border lying partly within the county. In addition to these lakes are the scores of artificial ponds, used for commercial purposes and for gathering the family supply of ice during the winter. No matter how small the pond, however, there are only a few which do not contain fish. Practically all the larger lakes and many of the private ponds have been stocked with game fish by the State and also have in their waters the ordinary varieties, furnishing a more varied sport to the disciple of Isaak Walton than even the far-famed Adirondacks or the lakes of the Pennsylvania mountains.

Following are the principal ones, together with their area in acres and elevation in feet above sea level: Culver's Lake, 486 acres, 848 feet; Lake Owassa, 299 acres, 861 feet; Lake Musconetcong, 339 acres, 859 feet; Swartswood Lake, 505 acres, 480 feet; Wawayanda Lake, 240 acres, 1,152 feet; Cranberry Lake, 154 acres, 771 feet; Little Swartswood, 100 acres, 486 feet; Morris Lake, 136 acres, 929 feet; Lake Grinnell, 40 acres, 564 feet; Panther Lake, 41 acres, 766 feet; Lake Marcia, 23 acres, 1,570 feet; Lake Mashipacong, 46 acres, 1,124 feet; Lake Rutherford, 75 acres, 1,302 feet; Long Pond (Andover township) 117 acres, 576 feet; Lake Pochung, 76 acres, 806 feet; Losee Pond, 137 acres, 1,020; Sucker Pond, 95 acres, 913 feet; White Lake, 17 acres, 575 feet; Lake Kiamesia, 43 acres, 943 feet.

These lakes have caused the county to become famous as a summer resort and around nearly every one of them cottages have been erected. Culver's Lake has perhaps the largest summer colony, there now being about 125 cottages around its shores. On the shore of Lake Kiamesia is the summer camp of the Newark Y. M. C. A. Swartswood Lake has been kept from being a popular summer resort because of the closing of the lake to fishermen by the Albright estate. There are hopes, however, that an appropriation may be secured from the State for the purchase of the lake and that it will be thrown open to the public. Morris Lake belongs to the town of Newton. Lake Marcia is on the High Point estate of the Dryden family and is a private lake. Lake Rutherford is the source of the Sussex Borough water supply. Lake Pochung is owned by a club composed of Sussex Borough residents.

ELEVATIONS.

The most northern county, Sussex has the highest point in New Jersey, the top of the mountain to the east of the summer home of the Dryden estate at High Point, being 1,819 feet above sea level. From the highlands of Sussex many beautiful views may be obtained. This is particularly true of the Kittatinny Mountains stretching across the western end of the county with an almost unbroken crest the whole distance, rising sheer up in many places, hundreds of feet, seldom dropping below the elevation of 1,200 feet. In Wantage township it reaches its highest points. The crest of the mountain at Beemerville is 1,650 feet, at Lake Rutherford 1,642 feet, culminating at High Point, 1,819 feet. From one point twenty towns and villages may be seen from the top of the mountain.

Elevations at various points are as follows:

Sussex, summit of Newton turnpike at VanSickle residence, 520 feet, summit of hill east of railroad station, 516 feet, hill northeast of village (Space's), 740 feet; Branchville, a cross on southeast corner of Cook building, 579.69 feet; Carpenter's Point, top of Tri-States monument, 414.99 feet; Colesville, lower hotel, level of flagstone under porch, 791.95; Culver's Gap, summit of road, 915.35 feet, observatory in Gap (now decayed) 1,382 feet; Franklin Furnace, stone water table near depot, 560.13; Hainesville, rock 40 yards north of school house, 639.20 feet; Montague, a cross on water table of Brick House hotel, near barroom door, 520.82 feet; Newton, Clerk's and Surrogate's office, 649.63 feet, a cross on east end of stone door sill, corner of jamb at central entrance to Presbyterian Church, 678.46; Stanhope, cross cut on northwest corner of cap stone of turret supporting cable at southeast corner of the bridge over the Morris canal, outlet of reservoir, 871.13 feet; Waterloo, a cross cut on southwest corner of the north abutment of Sussex R. R. bridge Musconetcong river at head of Waterloo pond, 655.44 feet; High Point, 1,819 feet; Bevans, stone sill entrance to hotel, 499 feet; Beemerville, cross on foundation of old wheelwright shop, 755.02 feet; Glenwood, on maple near school building, 724.04 feet; Vernon, bolt in guard stone corner of fence east of Wallace's store, 561.06 feet; McAfee, west rail at railroad crossing, 434.02 feet; Hamburg, east rail at railroad station, 421.02 feet; Libertyville, cross on stone, northeast corner of cross roads, 742.05 feet; Mt. Salem, State line monument at road north of, 872 feet; Ogdensburg, rail at station, 664.02 feet; Plumsock, pyramid shaped stone in fence south of store, 660.04 feet; Quarryville, east side of station, 556.09 feet; Sparta, top of stone in sub-foundation at southeast corner of Presbyterian church, 713.07 feet; Stockholm, guard stone northeast corner of J. M. Lewis's store, 982.05 feet; summit of Port Jervis turnpike, 1,391 feet; the Inn at High Point, 1,657 feet; Lafayette, an arrow on limestone boulder at the east corner of the main crossroad in the village, 546.94 feet; Wallpack Center, arrow on conglomerate rock, west side of crossroads, 452.08 feet.

RAILROADS.

On January 7, 1836, a public meeting was held at Sussex, then Deckertown, to advocate the building of a railroad across the county between the Hudson and Delaware. This resulted in a survey being made through Culver's Gap, but nothing came of the project. On April 17, 1847, a meeting was held at Newton to consider the building of a road to connect with the Erie Railroad at Port Jervis, but nothing came of that. In 1848 the Sussex Mine Railroad was incorporated to connect the mines, being operated near Andover by Messrs. Cooper and Hewitt, with the Morris canal at Waterloo. This was the first railroad to be built within the bounds of Sussex county. Between that date and 1852 the building of a road from Newburg across the county to the coal mines of Pennsylvania, a line to run from Dover to the Water Gap and one to follow the Musconetcong Valley and connect with the Central Railroad of New Jersey were discussed. On August 28th of that year, however, a meeting was held in Newton to plan for the extension of the Sussex Mine Railroad to that place and a loan of $100,000 secured by the first mortgage bonds was finally secured.

On January 3, 1853, subscription books were opened at Newton. On February 26 The Sussex Register announced that $90,000 of the bonds had been taken and the construction of the road begun. The whole amount asked was subscribed on March 19, ninety-two persons taking the bonds. The work on the road was pushed and on November 27, 1854, the first train pulled into the Newton station. The road was formally opened on December 11 of that year.

In 1864 an attempt was again made to revive the road across the county through the Water Gap but the attempt to secure money was unsuccessful.

Through the enterprise of William H. Bell, of Branchville, rights of way from Drake's Pond had been secured and in 1866 work was begun on an extension of the Sussex road from Drake's Pond to Branchville. The first train reached Lafayette January 1, 1869. The road opened through to Branchville on July 3 of that year. In 1870 Franklin Furnace became the next objective point of the Sussex Railroad.

In 1870 it was decided to extend the Sussex Railroad to Franklin Furnace and as an inducement to the company to build the road across the meadows instead of using the Bell road from Drake's Pond, the citizens of Newton voted to issue $25,000 in bonds, which were accepted by the company and the line built as desired.

Under the charter secured in 1832 the building of a railroad was begun near Sussex on February 16, 1870, known as the New Jersey Midland, connecting with the Sussex Railroad at Franklin Furnace and on June 19, 1871, a train was run through from Newton to Deckertown over the two roads. On the 4th of July of that year the Midland was formally opened between Franklin and Unionville. Work on the Midland was continued eastward and on January 22, 1872, a train was run into Newfoundland. And soon after the road was built to West End Jersey City where it connected with the Pennsylvania to Tidewater. An effort made in 1873 to extend the Midland Railroad by way of Newton, Johnsonburg and Hope to Belvidere was abandoned. In 1882 an extension was built from Ogdensburg through Sussex and Warren counties to Stroudsburg and later to the Pennsylvania coal fields. The Midland Railroad became known as the "New York, Susquehanna & Western."

About the same time the Lehigh & Hudson River Railroad was built through the counties of Warren and Sussex, connecting Belvidere with the Erie at Greycourt. Later the Boston and South Mountain Railroad Company started the construction of a road from the coal fields of Pennsylvania through Sussex county but the project was not carried on. This corporation, however, under the name of the Pennsylvania, Poughkeepsie and Boston Railroad Company constructed a road leading from Slatington, Pa. to Campbell Hall, N. Y., where it connects with the Central New England Railroad for Boston and the East. Later the road became known as the Lehigh & New England R. R.

The present railroad mileage in Sussex county is 108.7 with a total valuation of $313,200.

BANKS.

The development of the county at the close of the Revolutionary War necessitated the establishment of some banking institution and in 1818 the Sussex Bank was opened. The first president was Daniel Stewart, his successors having been: Ephriam Green, David Ryerson, David Thompson, David R. Hull, Theodore Morford and Theodore Simonson. Samuel D. Morford was the first cashier, being succeeded by his son, Theodore Morford, who on becoming the president of the bank was in turn succeeded by his son, Lewis M. Morford.

The Farmers Bank in Wantage was established in 1850, the charter having been obtained in 1849. The first president was James C. Havens, his successors being Jonathan Whitaker, John A. Whitaker, Theodore F. Margarum and Ford W. Margarum.

Both these institutions became National Banks in July, 1865.

The Merchants National Bank of Newton was established in 1865. Robert Hamilton was the first president, his successors being: Jacob L. Swayze, Samuel H. Hunt, John C. Howell, John L. Swayze and Dr. Ephriam Morrison.

The Newton Trust Company was organized in 1902, with Frank M. Hough as the first president. Mr. Hough resigned the presidency in 1910 and he was succeeded by Hon. Levi H. Morris.

The First National Bank of Branchville was organized in 1904 with A. J. Canfield as president, and he still occupies that position.

The Hardyston Bank was organized in 1906, with Horace E. Rude as the first president. Since his death that office has been filled by Thomas D. Edsall. The total deposits of the banks in the county at the present time are $4,953,720.25. This does not in any way cover the financial business of Sussex county as thousands of dollars are on deposit in various banking institutions outside of its boundaries.

COUNTY GOVERNMENT

The Men Who Hold the Offices and Conduct the Affairs of the County Locally and in the Law Making Body of the State

HON. ALLEN R. SHAY,
County Judge

was born in Sandyston township August 10, 1850, his parents being Timothy E. and Catherine Shay. He was educated in the district schools, being prepared for college at the Newton Collegiate Institute. He graduated from Wesleyan University, Middletown, Conn., in 1872, with the degree of Bachelor of Arts, receiving his M. A. from the same institution in 1875. From 1872 to 1875 he was principal of the Hamburg school. Studying law under Thomas Kays and Charles J. Roe, he was admitted to the bar as an attorney in 1877 and as a counsellor in 1880. For the past thirty years he has practiced in Newton, being considered one of the most active and successful practitioners of Northern New Jersey. He ranks among the foremost members of the Bar and is noted for his interest in all civic affairs. From 1881 to 1883 he served as County Counsel. From 1883 to 1885 he was a member and director of the Board of Freeholders. He served as a member of the County Board of Taxation until May 26, 1913, when Governor Wilson honored him with the appointment as County Judge, which position he is eminently qualified to fill.

For a number of years he occupied part of the suite of offices of Hon. Levi H. Morris, but following his appointment as Judge he took the office formerly occupied by the late Lewis J. Martin, on High street.

In his dealings with first time offenders, Judge Shay has followed closely in the footsteps of Judge Ben B. Lindsey, of Denver, believing that if there is a possibility of bringing out the good qualities of the boy or man brought before him, he should be given an opportunity.

His first wife was Miss Amanda J. Hill, who died in 1889. Three children blessed this union. On December 26, 1893, he married Miss Cora Shiner, a well known teacher in the Newton schools.

Lewis J. Martin was born at Deckertown, February 22, 1844, his parents being James J. and Eleanor McCoy Martin. After graduating from the Newton Collegiate Institute in 1862, he assisted his father, who had been elected as County Clerk. On the death of his father in March, 1869, he was appointed to fill the vacancy. While assisting in the Clerk's office he had studied law and was admitted to the bar in 1867. He commenced the practice of law in Deckertown in 1870, and became counsel and a director of the Farmers National Bank. He remained there until 1892, when he removed to Newton.

He was elected to the Assembly in 1878 and was twice re-elected. In 1881 he was appointed Law Judge of the county and filled that office very acceptably for fifteen years. In 1897 he was elected State Senator and served two terms. In 1911 he was again appointed Law Judge and was holding that position at the time of his death on May 5th, 1913. At the November election 1912 Judge Martin was elected a Member of Congress from the Sixth District and was attending a special session of that body at the time of his death.

He was the leader of his party in the county for twenty years, and was minority leader while in the Senate.

In 1868 he married Miss Frances M., daughter of the late George C. Shaw, who together with four sons, survive: George S., of Branchville, Sayre and Scott, at home, and Lewis, at Factoryville, Pa.

Judge Martin was a member of Harmony Lodge, No. 8, F. & A. M.; Baldwin Chapter No. 17, R. A. M., of Newton; DeMolay Commandery, Knights Templar, of Washington, N. J., and Salaam Temple, Order of the Mystic Shrine; the Newton Board of Trade, the Newton Club, the Woodlawn Driving Park Association, the Newton Fire Patrol, and various other organizations.

OUR CONGRESSMAN

HON. A. C. HART

Archibald C. Hart, of Hackensack, N. J., is the present Representative in Congress of the Sixth New Jersey District. He was born February 27, 1873. He received his education in the public schools of Brooklyn, N. Y. and Hackensack until his fourteenth birthday, when he worked upon his father's farm for two years. He then became Secretary of Walter G. Berg, Engineers Dept. L. V. R. R., where he remained for three years; then entered the office of Governor Bedle, of Jersey City, where he studied law, being admitted to the bar in 1896. He was admitted to the United States Supreme Court in 1910, and at present has the most extensive law offices in Bergen county, specializing in real estate law.

He is a veteran of the 23rd Regiment, N. Y. Vol. Inf., and of the Spanish American War, having volunteered in the 2nd N. J. Vol. Inf. During his term he served as Secretary in Gen. Fitzhugh Lee's Headquarters, 7th Army Corps, and then at General Arnold's Headquarters, 2nd Division.

Mr. Hart is President of the First National Bank of Lodi, N. J., and is otherwise interested in banking institutions; is director of three Bergen county Building & Loan Associations, and President of several real estate companies, being individually largely interested in Bergen county realty.

Mr. Hart is a member of Pioneer Lodge, F. & A. M. Past Exalted Ruler of Hackensack Lodge, B. P. O. E.; Past Noble Grand, Bergen County Lodge I. O. O. F., a Forester of America, and until lately was a member of the National Union and Royal Arcanum. He is a member of all the important clubs of Bergen county, and the President of the Hackensack Club.

He was a delegate to the Democratic National Convention in Denver in 1908, and in 1907 was Bergen county candidate for Senator, being defeated by Hon. Edmund W. Wakelee by only 678 votes.

He served in the 62nd Congress as the successor of Hon. Wm. Hughes, now U. S. Senator, at which time he so distinguished himself as to receive the unsolicited written endorsements of President Wilson, Speaker Champ Clark, and Hon. Oscar W. Underwood, of the House of Representatives, when he was again elected in 1913 to succeed Hon. Lewis J. Martin, deceased, in the 63rd Congress, receiving about 63 per cent. of all the votes cast.

In 1901 he was married to Miss Lily L. Fenwick, of East Orange. They have four children, all of whom are boys.

State Senator

HON. SAMUEL T. MUNSON

was born on the Munson homestead, near Franklin Furnace, and has lived there ever since. He graduated from the New York Military Academy in 1895, immediately beginning his mercantile career. He was collector of taxes in Hardyston township seven years; member of Democratic County Committee ten years; was Journal Clerk in the House in 1907 and elected to the Senate in 1912, defeating Huston, Republican, by about 800 votes. The Senator stands high in the councils of his party, is one of the county's most public spirited citizens and has the confidence of all who know him.

Member of Assembly.

HON. HENRY T. KAYS.

Resident of Newton, and prominent member of the Bar. He was born in Newton, September 29, 1878. Graduated from Princeton University in 1903, and for two years held the chair of Sciences in the English and Classical School at Newton. He read law with his father, Thomas M. Kays, and was admitted to the Bar in 1910. He served as Freeholder in 1910 and 1911 and was made County Counsel in 1911. Is at present attorney for the Town of Newton. Was elected to the Assembly in 1912 on the Democratic ticket, defeating his Republican opponent by about 1,500. Mr. Kays takes a keen interest in civic and political matters and is regarded as an able lawyer, and in the Legislature stood faithful to his constituents.

Member and Director of the Board of Freeholders.

JOHN J VAN SICKLE

Born in Sandyston township in 1851. Educated in the public schools. Taught four years. Engaged in the mercantile business in Bevans. Was an extensive hay and grain buyer in Bucyrus, Ohio, for 11 years. An active Democrat and public spirited. First elected a Freeholder thirty years ago, and has been a member under all the different laws and terms of office. Elected again in 1912, and re-elected in 1913.

Married Miss Alice V. Losey in 1880. She died in 1908, and in 1910 married Miss Abbie Montross. Resides in Bevans and is very popular everywhere.

Member of the Board of Freeholders.

WILLIAM ILIFF.

Born in Hope township, Warren county, in 1861. Came to Andover, Sussex county, N. J., in 1876, and engaged in farming, which occupation he still follows. Served fifteen years as Assessor. A prominent Democrat, and of sterling character, he was chosen a member of the Board of Freeholders in 1912. Married Miss Anna Cox in 1882. One daughter blesses the union. Is an Odd Fellow, Red Man, Granger and an R. A. One of our most popular citizens.

FRANK J. COE.

Member of the Board of Freeholders.

Born and reared in the county, near Sussex. Educated at the district schools and Sussex Academy. Has a fine 104 acre farm; active in public affairs, and a staunch Democrat. For 12 years Township Committeeman, 9 years on the school board. Elected Freeholder in 1912. Is making a splendid record. Married Miss Carrie Nyce in 1888, and one daughter blesses the union. Is prominent in the P. O. S. of A., and very popular in the county.

Sheriff.

EDWARD C. MAINES.

Was born in Lafayette township in 1855. He attended the Lafayette and Hampton township public schools.

1867 he was made assistant superintendent at the Sussex County Almshouse under James Smalley, Steward. At the death of the latter Mr. Maines was appointed Steward to fill the unexpired term. The following year he was re-appointed, holding the position for fourteen years.

After leaving the Almshouse Mr. Maines conducted the Albert O. Smith farm in Hampton township. He was elected Freeholder from Hampton township, serving two terms. In 1910 he was elected Sheriff of Sussex county, defeating his opponent, Leon C. McKim, by a large majority. He was a successful cattle dealer and auctioneer, crying some of the largest sales held in Northern New Jersey.

County Clerk

HARVEY S. HOPKINS

Was born December 1, 1878, on a farm near the village of Lafayette. Graduated from Lafayette Public Schools and later took a course at the Newton Collegiate Institute. Had considerable earlier experience in newspaper work and was, for a time, associated with his father in the feed and grain business at Lafayette under the firm name of B. K. Hopkins & Son. Was appointed a copyist in the County Clerk's office in March, 1900, by former County Clerk Ora C. Simpson, who made him his Deputy in the following June. Continued in that position until the end of Simpson's term in 1907, when he succeeded him as County Clerk. Was unanimously re-elected to that position in 1912, without opposition either at the primaries or general election. Is a Past Master of Harmony Lodge, No. 8, F. & A. M.; the present High Priest of Baldwin Chapter, No. 17, R. A. M.; a Past Grand of Ivy Lodge, No. 221, I. O. O. F.; and a member of the Newton Board of Trade and Board of Education. Was married on October 15, 1903, to Miss Alice R. Wilson, of Blairstown, N. J., and has four children.

Surrogate

EMMET H. BELL

Was born on a farm in Walpack township in 1862, being the son of Robert and Sarah Berk Bell. He was educated in the district schools and Hackettstown Seminary. He followed farming as a vocation, and was active politically. A staunch, hard working Democrat, his party and the people have honored him with places of trust. He served eight years on the Board of Freeholders, four of which he was Director. Served as Postmaster at Walpack four years, also as Tax Collector and Town Committeeman. He is a trustee of the M. E. Church and prominent in fraternal orders, being a Mason, Knight of Pythias, Red Man and Elk, a member of the Newton Club and identified with every civic plan for improvement. He was elected Surrogate in 1908, and re-elected in 1913. He has made a most efficient, accommodating official, and stands high in the community.

Prosecutor of the Pleas

WILLIAM A. DOLAN

Was born in Ogdensburg, Sussex county, March 31, 1883, being a son of Patrick J. Dolan. He studied law with John L. Swayze, at Newton, and was admitted as an attorney in 1904, and as Counsellor in 1907. He was an assistant in Attorney General's office in Trenton, and in the legal department of the American Telegraph and Telephone Co. of New York, locating in Newton in 1908, becoming a partner of Judge Joseph Coult, Jr. In March, 1912, he was appointed Prosecutor by Governor (now President) Wilson and is making a conscientious and vigorous official. Mr. Dolan is the president and counsel of the Newton Slate Co. and president of the Newton Club.

Deputy County Clerk.

H. CLARENCE COLE.

Was born at Colesville June 20, 1876, being the son of Mr. and Mrs. Jackson Cole. He attended the Newton grammar and High Schools, graduating from the latter with the class of 1894. He attended the Newton Collegiate Institute for one term, leaving the school to enter the drug business. He later attended the Eastman Business College, Poughkeepsie, graduating from that College in December, 1898. After engaging in office work for some time he entered the grocery business with his father at the corner of Spring and Adams streets, Newton, remaining there four years. After leaving the grocery business he was an instructor in the Success Shorthand School, New York, leaving that position to accept the Deputy County Clerkship which had been offered him by County Clerk Harvey S. Hopkins. He was first sworn into office in 1907 and was reappointed in 1912. He is thoroughly versed in the work of the office and has made a most capable and efficient official.

Under Sheriff.

ALBERT T. LYONS.

Was born in Wiretown, Warren county, on November 22, 1878. In 1881 he came to Newton. He attended the parochial school, leaving there to go with M. P. Tully in the clothing business, where he remained six years. He then was made manager of the clothing department of the Park Block, holding the position eight years. In 1908 he was appointed Under Sheriff by Sheriff George N. Harris, being reappointed in 1911 by Sheriff Edward C. Maines. He is a fearless official and has an enviable reputation for bravery and discretion.

Deputy Surrogate.

SAYRE S. MARTIN.

Was born in Sussex on October 31, 1878, being the son of the late Lewis J. Martin. He graduated from the Newton High School in 1896, and from the Newton Business College in 1897. He was employed for four years in the law office of James M. Trimble, of Newark. He then spent five and one half years in the West with headquarters at Pueblo, Cal. In 1908 he was appointed Deputy Surrogate, being reappointed in 1913. He is Secretary of the Woodlawn Driving Park Association. Mr. Martin is an enthusiast in all outdoor sports and is prominently identified with local athletics. He is unmarried, residing with his mother at 29 Trinity street.

Assistant County Clerk.

HARRY E. DEMAREST.

Was born in Lafayette on October 27, 1881, being the son of Mr. and Mrs. J. M. Demarest. He attended the Lafayette public school, the Newton High School and the Newton Business College. He served as Deputy Surrogate from 1903 to 1908. In 1909 he was appointed assistant in the Sussex county clerk's office by County Clerk Harvey S. Hopkins. He is married, his wife being a daughter of William F. Howell, residing on Academy street.

County Superintendent of Schools.

RALPH DECKER.

Was born February 23, 1873, at Flatbrookville, and is a son of Sarah E. Rosenkrans and Martin Decker. He was educated in the Flatbrookville public school, Newton Collegiate Institute, Blair Presbyterial Academy and the State Normal School at Trenton, graduating from the latter in the class of 1896. Before entering the State Normal he taught school at Harmony and Walpack Center. After graduating from the Normal School, he was principal for one year of the school at Stockton, N. J., and for five years was principal of the Sussex Borough High School. On October 7, 1902, he was appointed County Superintendent of Schools to succeed Luther Hill, of Andover, and has made a splendid record for hard work and devotion to duty. He is regarded as one of the leading educators of the State.

He is a resident of Sussex Borough, at which place he has a pleasant home on Unionville avenue. He is an elder of the Sussex Presbyterian Church; secretary of the Sussex Board of Trade; president of the Sussex Literary Society; a member of Samaritan Lodge, No. 98, F. & A. M.; a member of Gen. Kilpatrick Council, No. 1631, Royal Arcanum.

On June 28, 1899, he was married to Miss Amelia Stickney, daughter of Charles E. Stickney, editor of the Wantage Recorder. They have three children, Martin, Alice R. and Helen A.

County Engineer.

HARVEY SNOOK.

Was born on a farm in Hampton township in 1883, being the son of Hiram Snook. He was educated in the Branchville school, Blair Hall and Lafayette College, graduating from the latter with the class of 1907, with the degree of C. E. Served in the engineering corps of the N. Y. C. R. R. Located in Newton 1908. Appointed County Engineer in 1912. He is regarded very highly by the members of his profession, and is making a splendid record. He is a member of the Newton Water Commission, a Mason and an Odd Fellow. In 1908 he was married to Miss Lu Ella Roy.

HON. LEVI H. MORRIS.
County Counsel.

A prominent and successful member of the Sussex County Bar, son of Abraham S. and Susan (Howell) Morris, born in Hampton township, near Newton, December 23, 1870. Educated in the District Schools, Newton Collegiate, State Model School, Trenton, and Eastman's Business College, Poughkeepsie, N. Y. Studied law under Theodore Simonson and was admitted to the Bar in 1899, as attorney, and later as Counsellor.

Began practice in Newton where his ability and eloquence as an advocate soon brought him a large and influential clientele. Served as attorney for the Town of Newton several terms.

He has represented many of the townships in the county, besides being identified with some of the most important litigation in this section. Is President of the Newton Trust Company, Vice President of the H. W. Merriam Building & Loan Association and Treasurer of the Lafayette Slate Company.

During 1906-7-8 he served as a member of the Legislature, and for two terms was attorney for the Board of Freeholders, and is now County Counsel. Is active in civic and fraternal matters, being a member of Harmony Lodge No. 8, F. & A. M., Baldwin Chapter, No. 17, DeMolay Commandery Knights Templar, Salaam Temple Ancient Arabic Order Nobles of the Mystic Shrine of Newark, and member of Ivy Lodge, I. O. O. F., trustee and member of the First Presbyterian church, and is one of the county's most public spirited and progressive citizens. His business interests are vast as well as varied, among them a 380 acre model dairy farm, near Newton, one of the most up-to-date places in the county.

Mr. Morris was united in marriage on October 7th, 1903, to Miss Laura B. Snyder, of Lafayette, daughter of Raymond Snyder.

MEMBERS OF TAX BOARD

S. FRANK QUINCE.

S. Frank Quince, president of the Sussex County Tax Board, was born at Peters Valley, October 10th, 1864. He is a Democrat and was appointed to the Tax Board in 1911 by Governor Wilson. He is a resident of Sussex Borough, where he holds the office of superintendent of the town water supply system. He is active in public affairs and is a member of the Democratic County Committee. His term will expire in 1914.

ROBERT T. JOHNSON.

Robert T. Johnson was appointed a member of the Sussex County Tax Board in July, 1913, to fill the vacancy caused by the resignation of Allen R. Shay. He was born June 2, 1845, at Marksboro, Warren county, being a son of John Johnson. He attended Blair Academy and later Wyoming Seminary. He was admitted to the Bar of New York both as an attorney and counsellor in 1868. He was admitted as an attorney and Master in Chancery in New Jersey in 1870. He was a member of the Board of Freeholders in 1887-1888, and has represented the Town of Newton on the Town Committee.

MARTIN W. BOWMAN.

Martin W. Bowman, the Republican member of the Sussex County Tax Board, was born in Frankford township, but for more than thirty years has resided in Wantage township. For many years he has been a member of the Republican County Committee and has taken an active part in politics in Wantage township. He is a farmer and is considered one of the most progressive in his township. He is a close student of current and public events, and is the only representative the agricultural interests of the county have had on the board in many years.

OBADIAH E. ARMSTRONG.

O. E. Armstrong, secretary of the Sussex County Tax Board, was born in Lafayette on March 16th, 1861. His father was the late Bradford C. P. Armstrong. He attended the Lafayette school, after leaving which he entered the feed business with his uncle at Lafayette. In 1892 he received an appointment in the New York Custom House and remained there for five years. He was connected with the Hopkins & Williams Company for two years and then formed a copartnership with Gilliam Demarest, under the firm name of Armstrong & Demarest, and has since conducted the flour, feed and grain business at Lafayette. He was appointed secretary of the Tax Board in 1906 and has been reappointed by each successive board.

BOARD OF ELECTIONS

DAVID W. McCARTHY.

David W. McCarthy, one of the Republican members of the Sussex County Board of Elections, was born at Franklin June 2d, 1875. He was a member of the Board of Freeholders for six years, and filled the position of Postmaster for twelve years. He has been a member of the Republican County Committee for sixteen years and was chairman one year. For a number of years past he has conducted the Washington Hotel at Franklin Borough. He was appointed to the Board of Elections by Governor Wilson in 1912, his term expiring in 1915.

ROBERT T. SMITH.

Robert Thompson Smith, secretary of the Sussex County Board of Elections, was born at Marksboro, Warren county, May 7, 1836, being the same age as Uncle Joe Cannon. During the years 1862-63-64-68-69 he served as township clerk of Frelinghuysen township. He has been Mayor of Andover Borough since its incorporation in 1904. In 1870 he was elected Justice of the Peace and holds nine State commissions as such. Has been notary public, holding four commissions, the first one extending sixteen years without renewal. He has been appointed a member of the Board of Elections for six successive terms and is a Commissioner of Deeds. He is considered one of the leading citizens of the county and has taken an active part in Democratic politics for many years.

SAMUEL E. INGERSOLL.

Samuel E. Ingersoll, one of the Democratic members of the County Board of Elections, was born in Lafayette in 1851 and has resided there since. He was appointed postmaster at Lafayette by President Cleveland and served under both administrations. He was a member of the Board of Freeholders from 1903 to 1909. He was Justice of the Peace from 1887 to 1902 and is a Notary Public.

RAYMOND CASE.

Raymond Case, one of the Republican members of the County Board of Elections, was born near Hamburg, November 16, 1868. He is at present a resident of Ogdensburg, being the proprietor of one of the well known hotels of that thriving town. He was appointed to office in February, 1913. He is at present a member of the Board of Education of Sparta township and prominent in township affairs.

Manager Sussex County Farm Bureau.

H. W. GILBERTSON.

Born and reared in the country, he has devoted most of his efforts in the study of science and agriculture and has performed every kind of farm work. In 1905 he graduated from the Minnesota State Normal School at Mankato. For two years he was principal of a four room school in Minnesota. He entered the College of Agriculture of the University of Minnesota in 1907, and completed the four year course in 1910, with the degree of B. S. in agriculture. Attended the Graduate School of Ames, Iowa, and then took a post graduate course in Cornell University, specializing in Farm Management. Received degree of M. S. in agriculture in 1911 from the New York State College of Agriculture. In 1908 he was employed by the Northern Pacific Railroad Co. in the soil survey of Montana lands, and in 1909 was employed in the soils department of the Minnesota State College of Agriculture. He entered the office of Farm Management of the U. S. Department of Agriculture, and was assigned the district comprising Montana and the western half of the Dakotas. On March 16, 1912, he took up the Farm Bureau work in Sussex county, and is tireless in his labors in behalf of the agricultural interests of this section.

LEWIS S. ILIFF.

Lewis S. Iliff, County Collector and former assemblyman, was born in Andover township, being the son of the late James and Anna (Ayers) Iliff. His early education was obtained in the public schools of Andover township and of Hope, Warren county, where his parents removed when Mr. Iliff was in his youth. When twenty years old he returned to Sussex county and shortly after married Miss Lucy Cox, daughter of Charles C. Cox, of Andover township. He farmed in Sparta township until 1889 when he entered into partnership with Nathan H. Hart and purchased the coal and lumber business of I. L. Hallock, near the Lackawanna depot, Newton. The following year the firm purchased the coal and lumber business of Peter S. Decker, consolidating the two plants. Mr. Iliff is prominent in public affairs in Newton, having taken an active part in the establishment of the various industries of the town. He is a member of the Newton Board of Trade, the Newton Club and various fraternal and social organizations. He is also active in the affairs of the Newton M. E. church. In politics he is a Democrat, and during the years 1902, '03 and '04 represented Sussex county in the New Jersey Legislature as a member of the Assembly. He was appointed County Collector in 1912 to succeed the late Wm. E. Ross, being reappointed in 1913 and 1914.

Steward and Stewardess of the Sussex County Almshouse.

MR. AND MRS. FLOYD DICKISON.

Mr. and Mrs. Dickison were appointed in April, 1913, and are making a splendid record for the care of the inmates and the thoroughness of their management.

JOHN A. McCARRICK.

To be a successful newspaper reporter requires natural ability, persistence, unfailing courage and a strong sense of honor and responsibility. There must be ability to distinguish news from chaff, the persistence to secure all the details in order that the story may be as correct as it is possible to make it; unfailing courage to do the duty required and to use all, rich or poor, high or low, alike, regardless of the persuasion that may be brought to bear from different sources; a sense of honor that all may have justice and a responsibility to do your duty as it may appear to you, regardless of what may be your personal desires.

There is perhaps no representative on any paper in the country who has the territory to cover as has John A. McCarrick, the well known representative of the Newark Evening News in Sussex county. Although nearly 600 square miles in extent, without the instant trolley and train service which distinguishes most counties, but few matters of importance escape his trained newspaper mind. He is always on the job and no storm is too severe or no day's work too long to prevent him from covering a story. That his services are appreciated by his superiors is seen in their utmost confidence in him and the high esteem in which he is held at the main office of the paper.

John A. McCarrick was born at Branchville on June 23, 1880. He attended the Branchville Public School and the Newton High School, graduating from the latter with the class of '97. In June, 1898, he became connected with the Branchville Times. When that paper was consolidated with the Newton Record, Mr. McCarrick went into the Newton office of that paper. He served in all capacities, from devil to editor. Previous to the discontinuance of the Record, he became connected with The Register. In June, 1908, he severed his connection with that paper to take the managership of the Sussex county branch of the Newark Evening News, succeeding Harvey L. Hallock, who went to the main office of the News. He then, as now, maintained an office in the office of The Register.

He is a resident of Branchville, where he is vice-president of the Board of Education, Borough Recorder, registrar of vital statistics, secretary and inspector of the Board of Health, foreman of Hose Company No. 1, Overseer of the Poor. He is a Past Master of Kittatinny Lodge, No. 164, F. & A. M., and Past Worthy Patron of Owassa Chapter, No. 43, Order of the Eastern Star. He is a member of Culver Lodge No. 133, I. O. O. F. of Branchville, Baldwin Chapter No. 17, R. A. M. of Newton, DeMolay Commandery, Knights Templar of Washington, and Salaam Temple Ancient Arabic Order Nobles of the Mystic Shrine, Newark.

HENRY S. LOSEE.

Henry S. Losee, the Sussex county representative of the Standard News Association, the New Jersey member of the American Press Association, was born in New York city March 10, 1885. When seven years old he came to Newton where he has since made his home. He attended the Newton High School, the Newton Collegiate Institute and the Newton Business College. In 1904 he entered the newspaper business, reporting for the New York Sun, being appointed the representative of the Standard News Company the following year. He is a special representative of The Sussex Register and does considerable special work for the Sun and the New York American.

Beside his newspaper work he is largely interested in real estate in Newton and vicinity, and in other business enterprises. He is conscientious, a tireless worker and enjoys the friendship of a large number of people.

WILLIAM D. WILSON.

William D. Wilson, sealer of weights and measures, was born in Wantage township, April 7, 1867. Until a few years ago he resided on a farm in the Clove valley, from which he removed to Sussex borough. He was appointed sealer of weights and measures Feb. 21, 1912. Since removing to Sussex he has served on the Board of Education of that place. In both positions he has made an excellent record. He is married.

DAVID COUSE.

David Couse was born in Newton township, but in what is now Hampton, on the 10th of December, 1828. In 1850 he, in partnership with the late Richard V. Northrup, operated the Moden wool carding mill, on the road running from the J. L. Lawrence farm to the Dr. Smith farm. In 1851 they leased the woolen mills at Branchville and commenced the manufacture of cloth.

Mr. Couse moved into Newton in 1856 and was appointed deputy Sheriff in 1861 by the late Sheriff Arvis, and was elected constable for thirty years in succession. In 1880 he was appointed Court Crier and has never missed a court term during the thirty-four years he has served. In fact he has attended every term of court during the past fifty-eight years.

Mr. Couse was a son of Henry and Mary Northrup Couse, and was married in 1859 to Miss Mary Kays, daughter of Henry Kays, of Lafayette. They have two children, H. D. Couse, the jeweler, and Mrs. Minnie Hawkins.

ANDOVER BOROUGH.
By Robert T. Smith.

Mayor Robert T. Smith.

In rounding up a century of existence in the one locality, the county seat of Sussex county as has The Sussex Register, in commemorating that event it seems meet that each locality or municipality of the county at least, should take interest in the event and supply as far as possible a history of the conditions existing at that time, and following as far as possible the changes that have come to that locality during the regime of The Sussex Register. One hundred years since its first issue.

How are we to cover it? For the first sixty years backward we have living evidence for history, but for the forty years beyond, tradition. Our Historical Society is so young in years as to afford little assistance, but thanks be to B. B. Edsall, (whose name seems to form an integral part of The Sussex Register) in his Sussex County Centennial address—furnished much toward building history.

Andover, the first and foremost town in the County of Sussex (alphabetically) was founded in the year 1492. There is no historic evidence to verify this date, and in the absence of such evidence we have placed this date, believing that the town was in at the beginning.

At any rate when Newton consisted of one residence, that being the farm house and tavern of Henry Hairlocker, and when the Court House a half mile distant from this house was built, the second in the town, Andover was busy mining iron ore from its hills, and smelting it in substantially built stone buildings still in good condition and in daily use, although in different lines of business. The principal building, the furnace, was changed by Joseph Northrup to a grist mill in 1816, Northrup having purchased in 1810, 700 acres which included these buildings

Some have suggested that the mill, furnace and the other stone buildings were built by the Moravians coming from Bath, Pa., the famous builders of the town of Hope in Warren county, but these buildings were here long before the Moravians were known to this section of the country, they coming to Hope in 1769 and remained only some thirty or forty years. Our buildings show by their firmness to-day, that their builders were at least equal to the Moravians.

As to the origin of the name "Andover," we have never been able to trace satisfactorily, but that it was not imported we have full belief, as we have, after considerable research, failed to find the name, or even heard of it in any foreign country. Therefore we conclude it must have been here when the first settlers arrived. While all the other towns were named after famous persons or places, Andover alone seems to support the claim of originality. We have loaned the name to a few places, as Andover, Mass.; Andover, N. Y.; Andover, N. H. and Andover, Pa., etc., but although we have not had the name copyrighted, we have kept it quite seclusive.

In 1813 there were no railroads or canals in Sussex county, and the rest of the State were little better off. Stages for passengers and teams and wagons for freight traffic to the markets of the city of New York. This mode of travel necessitated many hotels, or places for rest and refreshment along the line, and Andover Borough as now formed, included two of these hotels, one at either extreme, the Borough being two miles in length. One was situated where former Freeholder A. P. Kinney now lives, the other two miles south where the old Spitzer residence stands at White Hall, both the houses now standing being we think, the reconstructed originals of a century ago.

Seventy years ago the first one was occupied by Elihu M. Freeman, the grandfather of our merchant, V. B. Freeman; the one at White Hall by John Cox. There was no hotel near the centre of the present borough until in 1856, when William M. Iliff having finished the building now occupied as a hotel by Joseph R. Rose, Peter VanNess took possession and during that year conducted a "temperance hotel."

At the April term of court of 1857, VanNess made application for and received a regular hotel license which ran for one year. During that year Alexander and John McKain put up the building directly opposite (the one lately burned) and secured a license from the court to keep a "temperance hotel." In the spring of 1858 VanNess again made application for license which, through a remonstrance headed by Wm. M. Iliff, the owner of the property, was denied. The scheme of a temperance hotel of the McKains proved unsuccessful and was soon abandoned, and a house was built on the lot now occupied by the Freeman-Thompson block by Lewis McKinney who obtained a license, conducted it for several years, after which it passed from one to another, the late J. Britt Slater with Elias Goodrich conducting it for a time, after which Wm. Vannatta, of Newton, for two or three years, when Charley Adams bought it, ran it for two years and in 1876 sold it to Oscar Simpson, when it burned the night before he was to take possession and before he had made a payment thereon. Oscar Simpson immediately bought the Iliff property, the old hotel opened, enlarged and conducted it until his death, which occurred May 6th, 1880. The place was retained and run by the family until 1888 when it was bought by William K. Caskey, who conducted it until his death on August 12th, 1900. In April, 1901, Joseph R. Rose bought the property of the Caskey estate and has conducted the place since.

No other hotel or saloon has ever been licensed within the borough limits, or in Andover township until the T. J. Cuff license two years ago.

Churches. Tradition has it that in the early years of 1800 numerous families in and around the present site of the borough were affiliated with the Newton Episcopal Church, and were wont to drive there each Sabbath for worship, until 1834, when a church was built on the present site of the M. E. Church. This was ostensibly for the Baptists, but was really used by all denominations for about twenty years, when it was taken by the Methodist Episcopal Church and rebuilt. This building stood until 1892, when the present structure was erected. The Presbyterian Church was erected in 1857.

Physicians. Previous to 1846 Andover had never required a resident physician. In 1846 Dr. John Miller located here, coming from Warren county. He continued practice here until his death in August, 1888. Studying under and associated with him for a short time, were Levi D. Miller and

Calvin K. Davison. After 1876 came at intervals and staying from a month or two to three or four years, Drs. Joe Struble, Hugh D. Struble, Fithian, Condit, Potter, Smith, Young, Straley, Rosenberg, Shumo, Meeker and Dr. Jeptha C. Clark, who came in 1885 and is still here, our only physician.

Schools. The first record we have of a school house in Andover was the stone building, still standing and to-day used as a dwelling on the eastern end of High street, adjoining the Sussex railroad. This was built in 1824, and used until 1856, when a lot was procured where the present school house stands, and a two-story building erected thereon. During the next year, 1857, the trustees of the school sold to the Presbyterian Church trustees the better part of the school grounds on which the Church was then built.

This school house was used until 1890 when a prolonged school controversy was finally ended by the building of the two room part of the present building, the third room of the present building being added in 1901.

Cemetery. The Andover cemetery was opened, and the first interment made in November, 1858. The body of Rhoda, wife of Dr. John Miller, being the first interment made. This cemetery was opened by William M. Iliff, who in 1878 sold it to the Cemetery Association formed at that time, and in 1888 from necessity, some two and a half acres were added thereto, which to-day is nearing its final apportionment.

Family representation. Of the earlier settlers of Andover and its immediate vicinity, representatives of families left are few. Of the Northrup family, none are left; of the Willsons, Youngs, Freemans, Lawrences, VanSyckles, Kinneys and perhaps a few others, a small number of each are left. Of the McDavitts, the McConnells, the McKains, and the McKinneys, all of whom were formerly numerous, the McDavitts alone hold their own in numbers, while the McKains have but a single scion left, the others without the name representation. Of the early land owners, the Stackhouses alone, we think, hold their original farm.

Of course we have the Hills; in fact the hills were here to help to locate and found Andover. The Iliffs are all gone, as are the Strubles and Slockbowers. The Drakes, who were no doubt at the beginning, have gone out and returned several times, and to-day the old stock are again represented in our Borough. We had it from the late William Drake, of Newton, that in 1824 he as a boy was living in Andover, and he pointed out the house, still standing and occupied by George Losey, in which he lived when Joseph Northrup set out the apple orchard above the railroad, many of the trees still standing, two being left on the lot of the writer.

Post Office. In 1811, two years before the birth of The Sussex Register, history says there were but 87 post offices in New Jersey, six of which were in Sussex county, (then including Warren county) and one of the six was at Andover, with Lemuel D. Camp as postmaster, the other five being at Belvidere, Hackettstown, Hamburg, Johnsonburg and Newton, where Charles Pemberton was the P. M. In 1837, thirteen years after Warren was set off, Sussex county alone had twenty-five post offices. The postmasters at Andover being beside the one named above Joseph Northrup, John Crate, Alex McDaniels, S. R. White, Jehiel T. Smith, W. R. Ayers, N. A. Stackhouse, V. B. Freeman and Wm. S. Slater, the present incumbent. Previous to three years ago, the post office was kept in one of the stores, when at that time the office was raised to third class, and Mr. Slater built the present office building in which it is now housed.

On the first day of April, 1850, while the mines were running full force, an occurrance took place which cast a gloom over the whole community. William Johnson, an uncle of Robert T. Johnson, of Newton, lived in the house now occupied by A. P. Kinney, then known as a "tavern," which accommodated many workmen, overseers and others of the mines as boarders. Mr. Johnson had two sons, about eight and ten years old who would carry dinners to the workmen, a half mile distant, in a basket. On the day above noted, the boys took the dinners to the men, and as usual awaited the return of the basket and plates. The men retired to their wonted places to eat, and were thus engaged, when the powder house, a stone building containing many tons of powder, blew up with a report heard and felt ten to fifteen miles away. The bodies of the two children were gathered up in shreds. No other person was injured, and only a surmise left as to the cause.

In 1868 an epidemic of cholera broke upon the place, which automatically quarantined the town for months, and added bodies to the cemetery as victims.

Borough—During the winter of 1904 the Borough of Andover was incorporated and in the spring the first borough officers were elected as follows: Mayor, Robert T. Smith; Councilmen, Luther Hill, Nathan A. Stackhouse, Virgil B. Freeman, Emery Bonker, Watson R. Ayers and John W. Thompson, with Frank N. VanSyckle, Clerk.

Numerous deaths have occurred, principally those who were virtually worn out, on the first part, and marriages of others who are destined to take their place on life's stage, to fill their part in the program of life's play.

The most notable change in the Borough, especially as to scenery, is the Lackawanna cut-off railroad which, towering a hundred feet above streets, is both unsightly and annoying through its heavy traffic overhead. The present officials of the Borough are: Mayor, R. T. Smith; Council, George O. Young, President; Joseph Ackerson, Henry Hinds, Andrew Dobbins, Charles A. Meyer, Watson R. Ayers, with Frank N. VanSyckle (who has filled the office from the beginning) as Clerk, and Ludlow S. Cornine as Marshall, who has also served from the first. Assessor William E. Willson; Collector, Harry Stackhouse.

While we have for a greater part of its life been a reader of The Sussex Register, commencing at a time when it was delivered at Marksboro and Johnsonburg by Jep Denee from his saddle-bags, and while not a prophet or the son of a prophet, yet we can offer sincere congratulations to Sussex Register and its successful managers, and with others hope for many centuries of continued usefulness, and leave prophesy to those better able to forsee.

J. W. THOMPSON.

Established the business at Andover, N. J. in 1888, which consists of a complete line of General Hardware, Stoves, Furnaces, International line of Farm Machinery, Gasoline Engines, Farm and Garden Seeds. Mr. Thompson also does Heating, Plumbing and Repairing. He also enjoys a good business and invites all to call.

F. N. VAN SYCKLE.

Is a native of Sussex county. Established the mercantile business at Andover, N. J. in 1885, the firm being known as Valentine & Van Syckle. In 1893 Mr. Van Syckle became the sole proprietor and has since conducted the business.

He has been Borough Clerk of Andover since its incorporation in 1904, and is President of the Sussex County Sunday School Association.

S. J. WILLSON.

Is the Wheelwright and Wagon Maker of Andover, where he began business in 1875. Born and lived in the county all of his life. Has a fine trade and is an expert in his lines. Served on the Board of Elections many years and is a prominent Odd Fellow. He is located near the center of the town in one of the oldest buildings in the town.

Charles A. Meyer was born in Hoboken, December 31, 1864, and is a civil engineer. At the outbreak of the Spanish-American War he went to the front, being mustered out as Captain on November 17th, 1898. In 1901 he removed from Hoboken to Andover, where he has since lived. He is a member of Harmony Lodge, No. 8, F. & A. M., and Baldwin Chapter, Royal Arch Masons, of Newton; DeMolay Commandery, of Washington, and Salaam Temple, of Newark. He is also a member of the K. of P. He is a member of the Army and Navy Club and various other social and fraternal organizations. Prior to his removal to Sussex county he was secretary of the Hudson County Democratic Committee, serving from 1894 to 1897. After his removal to Andover he was elected a member of the Borough Council of that place and for three years was president of that body. In 1908 he was elected to represent Sussex county in the New Jersey Assembly, being re-elected in 1909, 1910 and 1911. He was the father of the Delaware River Drive Bill. He also introduced what was known as the Milk Bill, an act in favor of the milk producers of the State. He was a member of many of the important committees of the Assembly and was decidedly popular with his associates. After the expiration of his last term as Assemblyman, he was appointed by Governor Wilson as a member of the State Water Supply Commission. He takes a keen interest in civic affairs and can always be depended upon to take a leading part in all matters which will be of benefit to the borough and county.

CHARLES ANTHONY MEYER.

S. S. WILLS

Merchant Miller
Custom Grinding

Proprietor of Andover Electric Plant

ANDOVER, N. J.

BEEMERVILLE.

Beemerville is situated in the southwestern portion of Wantage township, receiving its name about 1830 from Henry Beemer, who at that time conducted the hotel at that place. The village is divided in two parts, Beemerville proper, and what is familiarly known as Plumsock. At one time it was quite a prominent manufacturing center, two carriage manufactories, a saw mill, harness shop, tannery and other industries being located there. Here was also located one of the earliest churches built in the county, the "Old Log Meeting House," which was torn down about 1823. The nearest railroad station is Sussex Borough, which is also the express and banking town, five and one-half miles distant. The town now boasts of a creamery, woodworking plant, a general store and a blacksmith shop. "Belle-Ellen Stock Farm," owned by J. N. Jarvie, of Montclair, is located partly within the village.

WESTFALL BROS.

This is a well known firm of wood workers and stair builders, who began business in Beemerville in 1863. They have an up-to-date planing and wood turning mill, and their work is known all over Sussex and Orange counties. The members of the partnership are G. W. and Willis Westfall. Their standing in the community is very high, and the excellence of their stair work is unsurpassed. They have a large trade, and enjoy the esteem of all.

D. C. TRUEX.

D. C. Truex is Beemerville's well known and popular merchant. He is a native of the county, and established his Beemerville store 18 years ago. Appointed postmaster in 1904. Is Vice President of the Sussex Mutual Insurance Company. Served on the school Board, is trustee and secre-

tary of the Beemerville Presbyterian Church, and treasurer of the Cemetery Association. Carries a fine line of goods, dairymen's supplies, hardware and dry goods. Is an extensive buyer of country produce. Fraternally an Odd Fellow. One of the town's most public spirited citizens.

Holstein-Friesan Registered Cattle

OF PONTIAC, KORNDYKE, HENGERVELD, DE KOL and JOHANNA FAMILIES.

We Are Breeders, Not Dealers.

SUSIE PONTIAC HENGERVELD
Butter 7 Days 28.28 lbs.

Is one of our many good ones. Nearly all milking cows are in the A. R. O. and many with enviable records. **FOR SALE** just now two young males about a year old, and they are worth looking into. Also several 7 to 8 months of age, suitable to head good herds. Prices $100 and up. **COME AND SEE FOR YOURSELF** or write for pedigrees and prices of individuals that you would not be ashamed to show your neighbors.

KING COLANTHA KORNDYKE
Our Herd Head No. 84782.

Bred along high producing lines and in addition is in the direct blood lines of modern ring requirements. Our herd now numbers 56 and growing rapidly. We sell only the surplus of our production, and to those who appreciate honest representation and moderate prices. Health, vitality and stamina are regarded above short time high records and all other factors. The Profitable, Producing, Practical Farmer's Dairy Cow is found here. Visitors welcome.

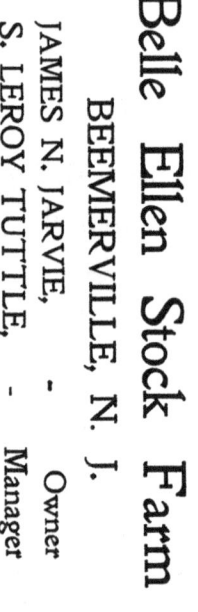

Belle Ellen Stock Farm
BEEMERVILLE, N. J.

JAMES N. JARVIE, - - Owner
S. LEROY TUTTLE, - - Manager

Aside from cattle we breed FANCY Single Comb White and Brown Leghorn and Barred Plymouth Rock Fowls. Stock and Eggs in Season.

Also in Season
PEACHES OF FINEST FLAVOR.

BEVANS.

Bevans, or it was commonly known a few years ago "Peters Valley," is situated in the southern part of Sandyston township, and was named about 1772 from Peter Vanness, who conducted the hotel at that place. From the hills surrounding the town a view of unexcelled beauty is obtained. A store, hotel, blacksmith shop and two churches, together with a number of dwellings comprise the town.

GEORGE V. JOHNSON.

A young but wide awake merchant of Bevans who established himself in the general merchandise business January 1st, 1913. Appointed postmaster August, 1913. Has an up-to-date store, and large variety of dry goods, groceries, farm implements, dairymens' supplies. Is a native of the county, an Odd Fellow fraternally. Is building up a fine trade and has the confidence of the community.

BRANCHVILLE.

Branchville was settled about the year 1700 by imigrants, principally from Connecticut. Ten years before that time, however, one lonely dwelling house might have been seen along the stream which flows through the town. Among the early settlers were the Coult, DeWitt, Beemer, Price and Gustin families. The land on which the town is now situated then belonged to James Haggerty, who later left it to his son, Uzal C. Haggerty, by whom it was sold to Judge John Bell, Joseph Stoll and Samuel Price. About 1820 the land was divided into building lots. The town was named Branchville by the school teacher of that district, Samuel Bishop. Prior to that time it had been known as Brantown.

Branchville is situated in one of the most beautiful sections of the county and as a healthful summer resort enjoys a deservedly high reputation. Situated at the western end of the Sussex branch of the Lackawanna, it is a freight, express and disembarking station for the townships of Frankford, Sandyston, Walpack and Montague. It is the station used by thousands of summer residents of Culver's Lake and vicinity.

Thousands of dollars worth of farm produce, fruit, dressed pork, calves and milk pass out through the railroad station at that place each year.

Branchville has an excellent graded school, two churches, Methodist and Presbyterian, and a number of fraternal organizations. The streets and many of the homes and stores are lighted by electricity furnished by a plant run by the waters of Culver's Lake and the town has an excellent water supply, originating from springs along the base of the Blue Mountains near Beemerville. Fire protection is provided for by a volunteer department.

The town is absolutely free from mosquitoes and malaria in any form.

C. H. CRISMAN.

Merchant Miller of Branchville and Proprietor of the Town's Electric Light Plant.

A busy and prominent citizen of the county is Mr. C. H. Crisman, of Branchville, who conducts a flour, feed and buckwheat mill and operates the town's electric light plant. Mr. Crisman is virtually the founder of the light plant, and established the business first over 20 years ago. Within two years the demand was so great that increased machinery was added, but this failed in a short time to afford service for all who applied. In 1898 new turbine wheels were required and a 1,000 light alternator Edison system was installed. Five years later a company was incorporated, with Mr. Crisman at its head. A new power house, with entire new dynamos and modern accessories was erected; a 160 horse power turbine wheel, and a capacity of 4,000 candle power now enables the plant to supply Branchville, Culver's Lake and the entire rural community within a radius of 3 miles with excellent electric light service. Mr. Crisman is a practical electrician, and has installed plants at Blairstown, Stanhope, Andover and Sussex, and is now the manager of the Blairstown plant. His knowledge of electricity is self acquired, and he is regarded as expert in all electrical matters. The Branchville plant is now modern in every detail.

OREN D. ELLETT.

Dealer in fine family groceries and provisions at Branchville, N. J. The business was established 17 years ago by Wm. P. Ellett, father of the present proprietor.

Mr. Ellett has an up-to-date store and enjoys a growing trade. He is one of Branchville's live wires, and public spirited on all occasions.

THE SUSSEX HOTEL.
Branchville, N. J.

A popular and long established hotel, conducted for the past 21 years by Mr. John Henry, one of the county's most substantial citizens, who is engaged in many vast and important enterprises. He is a manufacturer and shipper of lumber, operating three saw mills, an extensive buyer and shipper of all kinds of produce, owns and manages three large farms, gives employment to a large number of men, and seven or eight teams on the road all the time. Is prominent in civic affairs and very popular.

THE FIRST NATIONAL BANK
Branchville, N. J.
Established 1904.

A. J. Canfield, President.   N. H. Hopkins, Vice President.
M. L. Bond, Cashier.

Capital	$ 25,000.00
Surplus	44,000.00
Resources	350,000.00

Invites Your Business.

Security and courtesy assured.

Directors:

Alfred J. Canfield, Jacob C. Price, Noah H. Hopkins, Wm. P. Ellett, Marcus L. Bond, John H. Nelden, Frank Roe, Nicholas Tillman, John W. Crane, L. D. Wyker, George J. Bowman.

Commercial and Savings Departments.

Frank Roe.   Ernest Roe.

THE ROE COMPANY

Wholesale and Retail Dealers in

Feed, Grain, Salt, Flour, Baled Shavings, Fertilizer, Poultry Supplies, etc.

BRANCHVILLE, N. J.

Branch at Augusta, N. J.

General Merchandise, Flour, Feed and Coal.

You Always Get There with NEVERSLIP Red Tip CALKS

GARRIS BROS.

Horseshoeing and Blacksmithing

Wagon and Automobile Men.
BRANCHVILLE, N. J.

AMERICAN HOUSE
Branchville, N. J.
GEORGE S. MARTIN, Proprietor.

A modern Commercial Hotel, Steam Heat, Electric Lights, First Class Table.

HOPKINS, HOUGH & MERRILL CO.

Dealers in all kinds of Dairy Feeds, Grain, Coal, Lumber and Building Materials.
Branchville, - - N. J.

Park Place Hotel
BRANCHVILLE, N. J.
CHRIS ASHWORTH, - Prop.

EVERYTHING NEW AND UP-TO-DATE.

STABLES, LIVERY AND GARAGE.

WHEN HUNGRY, WEARY AND DRY,
DO NOT PASS US BY,
STOP TO FEED AND TO REST.
WE WILL DO OUR VERY BEST.

FRANK H. LOCKBURNER
Plumbing, Heating, Tinning.
Stoves and Parlor Heaters.
BRANCHVILLE, - N. J.

HOTEL BRANCHVILLE
Thomas Erb, Proprietor.   William R. Erb, Manager.
BRANCHVILLE, N. J.

Established in 1906.

One of the finest Hotels in Northern New Jersey. Modern in every detail. Enjoys the patronage of the high class tourists and travelers. Mr. Thomas Erb is 72 years of age, and most of his life has been devoted to the Hotel business. His son, William R., has had 15 years experience. They know the needs of guests and are sure to please you.

G. N. INGERSOLL
Dealer in Lumber, Coal and Builders Supplies.
BRANCHVILLE, N. J.
Established 1888.

CULVER'S LAKE HOTEL.

William H. Cooper, Proprietor.

This hostelry is situated at what is known as "The Inlet" at the southwestern end of Culver's Lake. It is an all-year-round house, capable of accommodating over one hundred guests. Its broad porches, excellent cuisine, nearness to the lake and the wild and mountainous scenery, make it an ideal spot in which to spend a vacation, either summer or winter. The proprietor, William H. Cooper, is an excellent hotel man and the visitor is sure of excellent treatment.

Street Scene in Colesville.

COLESVILLE.

Colesville is situated in one of the most picturesque parts of Sussex county, almost directly under the shadow of the highest point in New Jersey. It is in the midst of a fertile farming community, where dairying and fruit growing are the principal occupations. Sussex borough, six miles distant, is the nearest railroad station and banking town. The village has a public school and one church, Methodist, a well equipped general store, a blacksmith and wheelwright shop and a hotel.

COLESVILLE HOTEL
John Decker, Jr., Prop.
COLESVILLE, SUSSEX COUNTY, N. J.

Livery and automobile service. Tourists given special attention. The best to eat and drink.

The village store of Colesville is conducted by Mr. Raymond S. Coursen, who is a life-long resident of Sussex county. Born in Papakating and located in Colesville in 1877. Is farmer, fruit grower, merchant, dairyman and was appointed Postmaster 1905. Prominent as a Republican, and in fraternal orders, being an Odd Fellow and a Jr. O. U. A. M. Is an extensive buyer and shipper of produce. Full of civic pride and a substantial, popular citizen of the county.

W. MOTT.

Is the Blacksmith and Wheelwright at Colesville. He located there two years ago, and has a large trade. His work is regarded very highly in the community. He does wagon repairing, and general repairing in wood and iron. His shop is well equipped for all kinds of work in his line.

FRANKLIN BOROUGH.

Situated in the eastern part of the county, Franklin Borough, formerly known throughout the mining world as Franklin Furnace, lies in one of the most beautiful valleys of northern New Jersey. To the eastward rise the rocks and tree crowned summits of the Hamburg and Sparta mountains, while further to the west lie the foothills of the Blue Ridge. Underneath the surface of the ground on which the houses, factories and plants of the borough are built, is one of the richest deposits of mineral in the world. Here is located the richest and largest zinc mines of to-day, owned and operated

View From Crushing Plant.

by the New Jersey Zinc Company. The town has been primarily a mining town, and until recent years the foreign population has outnumbered the American or native born. Since its incorporation into a borough in 1913, new industries, the largest, a silk manufacturing plant, have been started and the growth of the place has been amazing. It is to the credit of the New Jersey Zinc Company, however, that Franklin Borough is the place it is to-day. Through the generosity of the Company, the town has gained an enviable reputation in educational, social, political and industrial circles. A community house, maintained at the expense of the company has recently been opened, being one of the most complete in the East.

Club House New Jersey Zinc Company.

Here the residents of the town, irrespective of religion, political affiliation or business connection, from the smallest to the largest, may go and spend an enjoyable evening. A public library and reading room, bowling alleys, pool and billiard tables are open to all. A dispensary and a nurse are at the disposal of the people. The company has also erected a hospital, primarily for the use of itself in the care and treatment of those injured in their plant, but which is open to any physicians of the county for operations, and to which may be brought patients for treatment at any time. This hospital is said to be the best equipped of any of its size in the country. The institution is in direct charge of Dr. Frederick P. Wilbur, a careful and experienced surgeon, and a corps of trained nurses. The hospital is situated on top of a hill overlooking the greater part of the town, and the valley and mountains to the east and south.

The Franklin Amusement Company, headed by State Senator Samuel T. Munson, have recently erected a theatre, said to be the largest and best equipped between New York and Pittsburg, having a seating capacity of 1,140 people and a stage on which the largest production now on the road may be accommodated.

At the present time the town has churches of the Catholic and Presbyterian denominations. A new Presbyterian church is being erected near the offices of the New Jersey Zinc Company. Connected with the Catholic church property is a lyceum and public hall, both the church edifice and lyceum being built of stone.

The Franklin school is different from the ordinary schools in New Jersey. Besides the regular work required by the State, much special work has been introduced. The school day has been lengthened to six hours; 9 to 12, and 1 to 4. This necessitates less home study and makes street and corner time less. The special features are as follows: First, a new

Zinc Company Tennis Courts.

kindergarten which is located in the Community House. The room, all the equipment, a kindergarten teacher, and a helper are donated by the New Jersey Zinc Company. The school supplies a regular kindergarten teacher also. There are about 75 children enrolled. A luncheon is served daily at 10.30. This consists of crackers and milk and fruit. Second, a teacher is in charge of the playground all day. There are no school recesses. One or more classes are on the playground all the time, have supervision, and receive instruction in marching, games, wand, indian club and dumb bell drills. The playground is equipped with a sand box, see-saws, volley ball, basketball, tether ball, small bowling alley, punching bag, quoits, horse lines, jumping ropes, and tug o' war ropes. Third, a special teacher has charge of the music. Besides the regular equipment, a victrola has been installed. Fourth, a special teacher has charge of cooking and sewing and elementary science. Fifth, the principal teaches manual training. Sixth, there is a special teacher for expression. This includes story telling and hand work, such as, raffia, reed, bent iron, weaving, knitting, paper folding, clay modelling and drawing.

Seventh, the kindergarten teacher devotes the afternoon to drawing in the intermediate and grammar grades. Eighth, school athletics, football, basketball and baseball are given special attention after school and Saturdays.

There are over 400 students enrolled. The teachers are: Stephen M. Case, Principal and Manual Training; Miss Matilda V. Driesbach, Household Arts and Elementary Science; Miss Grace Aungst, Music; Miss Mabel Van Reed, Expression; Miss Christie Crane, Playground; Miss Marguerite Krall, Kindergarten and Drawing; Miss Ellen Crawley, Mathematics and English; Miss Effie Fisher, Geography and History, and Elementary Science; Miss Lucy May, regular; Miss Lillian Treloar, regular, and Miss Irene Lasier, special kindergarten.

Principal of Franklin Borough Schools.

STEPHEN M. CASE.

Stephen M. Case is a native of Sussex county, born near Lafayette in 1884. His boyhood was spent on a farm. He attended district schools and the Newton High School from which he was graduated in 1901. Having decided to follow the profession of teacher, he entered the Trenton State Normal School and took the regular course and a special course in manual training. While at Trenton he was president of his class; a member of the Normal Dramatic Club, and also the Normal Debating Society; assistant business manager of The Signal, the school paper; athletic reporter for the Trenton Sunday Call; and a member of the baseball team.

He was graduated in 1904 and taught in the public schools of West Orange for five years. While there he had departmental work, manual training, and was director of high school athletics. He taught in the West Orange evening school; the Newark evening schools and summer schools, and was director of the Eighteenth avenue play ground in Newark. He has taken special work in New York University.

Mr. Case was elected principal of the Branchville public school in 1909 and remained there three years, when he resigned to accept the principalship at Franklin.

In June of his first year at Franklin he and a member of the Board of Education were sent to Gary, Indiana, to inspect the industrial and vocational schools there. Upon their report the Board of Education directed Mr. Case to start a similar school in September, 1913, making the system apply to local conditions.

JOSEPH HONIG.

An enterprising merchant of Franklin Borough, conducting one of the best clothing stores in the county. His store is on Main street, near the new theatre, where he has a fine line of Shoes, Hats, Caps, Clothing and Gents' Furnishings. See him and you will be pleased with his stock.

J. I. CRANE STORE.

J. I. Crane is one of the well-known and successful merchants of Franklin Borough. Came from Newfoundland to Franklin in 1879, and for two years was with the Franklin Iron Co. Nine years ago began business on his own account, and now has a large store, with a great and growing trade. Prominent in the town's affairs, serving on the School Board, Republican Town Committee, Borough Collector and Custodian of the School Funds, and Borough Treasurer.

S. KOHN, FRANKLIN BOROUGH.

A Miniature Department Store in Ladies' Cloaks, Suits, Dresses; also Infants', Children's and Misses' wear of every description. Ladies' and Gents' Furnishings. A store of quality and honest value.

JOSEPH HERZENBERG.

Mr. Joseph Herzenberg is the proprietor of the Franklin Borough Pharmacy. He has an up-to-date store and has conducted it five years. Is a graduate of the Brooklyn College of Pharmacy. Is keenly interested in the civic life of the new borough, a member of the Council and the School Board.

AN HISTORICAL SKETCH OF THE DEVELOPMENT OF THE ZINC MINES OF SUSSEX COUNTY, N. J.

The zinc and iron deposits now operated by The New Jersey Zinc Company, located at Sterling Hill (Ogdensburg) and Mine Hill (Franklin), in Sussex County, New Jersey, were known to exist in very early times. The records of the East Jersey Proprietary Co. describe a tract of land near Ogdensburg (which is known at the present time as the Sterling Hill Mine.) This tract was called the "Copper Mine Tract," and was returned to the heirs of Anthony Rutgers May 4, 1730.

The above fact would indicate that outcroppings of ore had been discovered prior to this date, and that the oxide of zinc was at that time considered to be a copper ore. This same tract was also known as the "Sterling" tract, from which it derived the present name of Sterling Hill and Sterling Mine.

No records of early mining are in evidence. The property with other lands came

Offices New Jersey Zinc Company.

into possession of the Ogden family in the latter part of the 18th century. One Elias Ogden, who died March 10, 1805, being a large land holder in this section, the present village of Ogdensburg takes its name from this Ogden family. Early in the 19th century Dr. Samuel Fowler acquired all the mineral lands at Sterling Hill. At his death his large land holdings were divided by will among his heirs. We find, however, that about the year 1848 his son, Col. Samuel Fowler, had acquired in his own name all the mineral lands of value. Soon after this date several mineral leases were taken from him by mining companies then organized to develop the mineral interests.

The court records would indicate these pioneer mining operations were not a commercial success. We find, however, that during the period between 1860 and 1870 considerable progress in mining had been made. From 1870 to 1896 the mines were successfully operated and produced considerable ore.

The history of the development of the mineral lands at Mine Hill, Franklin Furnace, N. J., is to a great degree coincident with that

General View of Works.

of Sterling Hill. A tract of land known as the "Mine Hill" tract was "returned to the heirs of Anthony Sharp," June 6th, 1750. This fact would indicate that mineral had been discovered at Franklin prior to 1750.

Dr. Samuel Fowler appears to have appreciated the mineral value of this section also since he acquired various tracts of mineral lands from Edward and Joseph Sharp during the period 1810-1814. James Scott and Dr. Samuel Fowler in 1821 owned practically all of what is the present Borough of Franklin, except the property of Asa Munson.

The first mine opening was on the southwest side of what is now known as the Open Cut (Taylor) Mine. The south end of Mine Hill was developed during the period between 1860 and 1870. The westerly outcrop of the vein was developed during the period between 1875 and 1890. The development of the north

Superintendent's Residence.

end of the deposit followed the sinking of the Parker shaft in 1894. In the early exploration of Mine Hill, Col. Samuel Fowler, son of Dr. Samuel Fowler, was a prominent figure, since he had acquired all the mining interests formerly held by his father.

The more extensive development of these Sterling Hill and Mine Hill low grade ores was facilitated by the invention

Where the Ore Comes Out.

and application of the Wetherill process of separation and the Rowand magnetic separators. The ore as mined is composed principally of the economic minerals Franklinite, Willemite, Zincite, and such other rock as may be attached to or com-

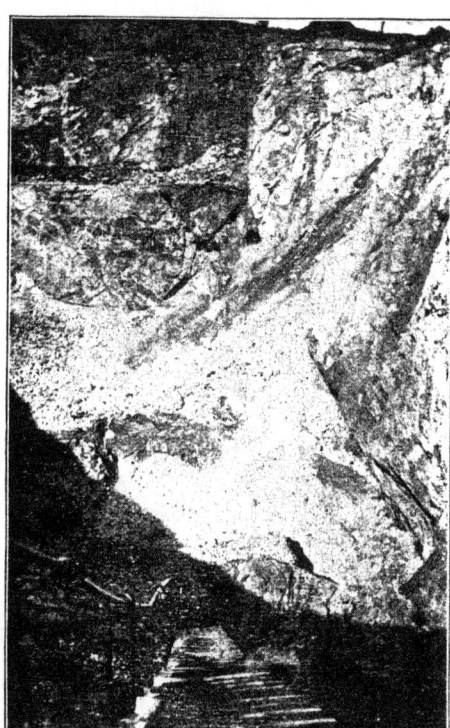

Mine Scene.

bined with it. In the metallurgical processes to recover the smelter products, it was desirable to have these minerals separated. This separation was accomplished by the perfecting of the magnetic separating process.

Two separating plants have been erected to handle the product of the mines. One crushing and separating mill (Mill No. 1) was built in 1896, and was operated until Mill No. 2, of larger capacity, was built in 1901 to replace it. This new mill, located along the Lehigh & Hudson River Railway, near Franklin Junction, is a part of the present Franklin plant and receives the ore direct from the Palmer shaft, which was completed in February, 1910.

The New Jersey Zinc Company in developing methods of operating their mines and plant have also undertaken exten-

Hospital, Franklin.

sive developments in the line of welfare work for the benefit of employes. A modern, well equipped hospital has been in operation for several years. All accident cases of employes are received here free of charge. The hospital is also open to countryside patients, who may, if preferred, be attended there by their own physician. A large change house, with individual lockers, shower baths, etc., is operated for the free use of employes. A community house and kindergarten, a domestic room, a reading room, a game room and bowling alleys, and is intended for the use of town people as well as the employes. An athletic field with grand stand, baseball, football, basketball and tennis grounds, affords an interesting part of the Zinc Company's sociological scheme. The accompanying views of the plant and the sociological features are of interest.

Time Office and Main Entrance to Plant.

REV. W. V. DUNN.

Church of Immaculate Conception, Franklin Borough.

The Church of the Immaculate Conception was erected at Franklin in 1902, being dedicated with appropriate ceremonies in 1903. The parish was established in 1864 by Rev. Father McCosker, at that time pastor of the Newton church. Mass was first said in Greer's Hotel by Father McMahon. The Church to-day is in a highly prosperous condition and services are held in a beautiful stone building located in the central part of Franklin. The churches at both Sussex borough and Ogdensburg are under the jurisdiction of the Franklin church. The pastors of the church since 1881 have been as follows: Rev. A. M. Kammer, 1881-1884; Rev. J. H. Boylan, 1894-1903; Rev. D. J. Brady, 1903-1906; Rev. M. F. McGuinness, 1906-1912; Rev. W. V. Dunn, 1912- . The trustees of the church at present are Myles O'Maley and Patrick Flynn.

St. Monica's Church, Sussex, (formerly Deckertown) was erected in 1880, through the untiring efforts and zeal of Rev. George W. Corrigan, at that time the parish priest at Newton. The efforts and personal contribution of the late General Judson Kilpatrick, the famous cavalry leader, whose old homestead is near the village, and whose wife was a Catholic, proved a very great aid to Father Corrigan.

General Kilpatrick's generosity, and that of the late Amos Munson, one of the town's most prominent and wealthy men, inspired the small band of loyal Catholics then living in the place, and which comprised only Daniel Rahaley and family, John Morrison and family, John Doran and family, and John J. and James E. Stanton, and the work of their friends, both Catholic and non-Catholic, furnished enterprise sufficient to secure the erection of the first edifice. Their efforts were coupled with the untiring efforts of their pastor. In 1888, during the great blizzard, the edifice was blown down. During the next year, and while the present Lehigh & New England Railroad was being built, the present edifice was built and since made free of debt. The little congregation was greatly aided by Mr. John R. Lee, the railroad builder, and family, of Paterson, who made their home in the borough during the construction of the road above mentioned.

St. Thomas a Quinas Church, Ogdensburg.

St. Monica's Church, Sussex.

COMMERCIAL MEN AND MOTOR PARTIES A SPECIALTY

— o —

FRANKLIN HOUSE

H. W. HARRISON   Proprietor

Franklin Borough, N. J.

— o —

CAFE WELL STOCKED   LIVERY ATTACHED

QUINN'S HOTEL
Franklin Borough, N. J.

Modern Colonial Hotel; very desirable for Transients. Special Service to Motor Parties. Many attractive rooms for permanent guests. Garage attached.

JOSEPH P. QUINN, Prop'r.

JOHN GLYNN,

one of the best known young men of Franklin, is engaged in the plumbing and heating business. He is agent for Thatcher Ranges and American Radiator Company boilers. All his work is guaranteed and he will be glad to submit estimates on heating, plumbing and bath room installation free of charge at any time. He has successfully handled many of the largest jobs in and around the borough.

Mr. Glynn is prominent in athletics. Is Director of the Sussex County League and plays first base. Is greatly interested in the welfare of the League and one of its most enthusiastic supporters.

The Washington Hotel
Franklin Borough

is a modern, first-class hostelry where everything of the best in the eating and drinking line awaits the guests. The proprietor, David W. McCarthy, is Mayor of Franklin. He is experienced in the hotel business and the traveller is always sure of prompt, courteous attention. He is also a member of the Sussex County Board of Elections.

D. W. McCARTHY,
Proprietor.

WASHINGTON HOTEL,
Franklin Borough.

D. W. McCARTHY.

JOSEPH HORVATH.

I. GREESPON

Is the enterprising and up-to-date Jeweler of Franklin Borough. He has a fine store and enjoys a large trade in Diamonds, Watches, Clocks and all kinds of Jewelry. Has been established five years and is located on the main street. He conducts an Optical and Repair Department.

WATSON LITTELL
Bottler of Beer, Ale, Porter and Soda Water
FRANKLIN BOROUGH, N. J.

Notary Public and Commissioner of Deeds, Fire, Life and Accident Insurance. All kinds of legal papers carefully drawn.

Mr. Horvath is the first and only Fire Insurance Agent in the Borough of Franklin. He represents all the leading companies in the Insurance line. If in need of Insurance, it will be to your interest to see him first.

HAMBURG.

Hamburg is situated in the northwestern end of Hardyston township, in one of the prettiest valleys of the county. Near the village flows the headwaters of the Wallkill River, which wends its way northward to the Hudson. Joseph Walling was the earliest pioneer, settling about the year 1750. His dwelling became the nucleus of a small settlement which was known as Sharpsboro. In 1792 a forge was established in the settlement, called Hamburg Forge. This name appealed to the residents of the place, and when the post office was established in 1759, the name Hamburg was adopted. Thomas Lawrence was the first postmaster.

Two railroads have stations in the town, the New York, Susquehanna & Western and the Lehigh & Hudson River. The express service is supplied by the Wells Fargo and the National. The banking interests are looked after by the Hardyston National Bank, one of the younger institutions of the county, but one which is on a solid foundation and growing stronger every year.

The town, which has a population of about 2,000, is progressive and highly prosperous. The principal industry is the Union Waxed and Parchment Paper Company, employing about 200 people. The East Jersey Lime Company, the New Jersey Lime Company and the Vanderhoof Lime Company all have kilns near the town. The soil of the surrounding country is particularly adapted to farming and pretty farmhouses and well equipped barns dot the hillsides for miles around.

Hamburg has three churches, Episcopal, Baptist and Presbyterian, an excellent public school, a well equipped volunteer fire department, and a number of fraternal organizations. The town is also represented by an excellent base ball team, which for two years in succession won the pennant in the Sussex County League. The houses of the town and the surroundings are well cared for, showing the thrift and town pride of the residents.

C. H. LINN.

Wholesale and Retail Druggist at Hamburg, N. J.

Sole manufacturer of the famous Ajax Remedies, which have long been favorites in so many households and are growing more popular year by year.

Mr. Linn also carries a full line of Drugs, Medicines, Toilet Articles, Ice Cream, Soda and Confectionery.

He enjoys a fine trade and is one of Hamburg's enterprising merchants.

C. L. KENT.

A native of Sussex county and a general merchant of Hamburg, N. J. Established the business in 1888. Has a large general store, well stocked with a fine line of goods, is agent for the famous Edison Phonograph and Records.

Mr. Kent is one of our enterprising citizens. Served 15 years on the school board and enjoys the confidence of all who know him.

C. E. THOMPSON.

Dealer in Paints, Oils, Varnishes, Dryers, Glass and Wall Paper, at Hamburg, N. J. Also Painting, Decorating and Paper Hanging. Estimates promptly given. Special attention given to picture framing.

Mr. Thompson established the business in 1902, and enjoys a large trade and the confidence of all who know him.

FRED VAN ORDEN.

deals in Confectionery, Ice Cream, Fruits, Nuts, Vegetables, Cigars and Tobacco, at Hamburg, N. J. Established the business eleven years ago and enjoys a good trade. Has a very attractive store.

HARDYSTON NATIONAL BANK

Hamburg, N. J. Established in 1906.

Capital stock, $50,000. Surplus, $30,000.
Average deposits, $27,600. Resources over $500,000.

Does a general Banking Business. Interest paid on savings. Deposit Boxes to rent.

Directors—President, Reeve Harden; vice presidents, J. Morehouse, W. S. Little; cashier, Thomas D. Edsall; teller, R. L. Martenis.

Directors—J. G. Coleman, A. S. Drew, Thomas D. Edsall, Reeve Harden, J. C. Kitchen, Wm. S. Little, S. C. Munson, John Morehouse, G. V. Schooley, J. K. Smith, Simon Wilson.

GEORGE PERLEE.

Established the grocery business at Hamburg, N. J. in 1907, in a small way and by preseverance and honest dealing has built up an extensive trade. Carries a fine stock of Staple Groceries, and makes a specialty of the famous brands of "Perlee" Teas and Coffee. Mr. Perlee extends his thanks to one and all for his success, and invites you to give him a call.

RUDOLPH RICKHORN.

Opened a cash grocery store at Hamburg, N. J., September, 1913, and is prepared to sell fine goods at the lowest prices and satisfaction guaranteed. Fine Teas, Coffees and sole agents for Rickhorn's XXXX Best Flour. You are invited to call and you will find a clean, up-to-date store, well stocked with staple groceries and the freshest that can be had.

```
* * * * * * * * * * * * * * * * * * * * * * * * * * * * * * * *
*                                                              *
*                    HAMBURG HOUSE                             *
*                    American Plan                             *
*                 HAMBURG,    -    N. J.                       *
*                 T. F. Booth, Proprietor.                     *
*       Up-to-date home of the commercial traveller,           *
*                       $2 per day.                            *
*                                                              *
* * * * * * * * * * * * * * * * * * * * * * * * * * * * * * * *
```

J. DYMOCK & SON

Designers, Contractors and Builders

HAMBURG, N. J. ESTABLISHED 1880.

DEALERS IN DIAMOND WALL PAPER, METAL, SHINGLES, PAINTS, OILS, BUILDING PAPER, LUMBER, LATH, ROOFING, SLATE, BRICK,

Residence of E. G. Sparks, Hamburg, N. J.

Designed and Built by J. Dymock & Son.

HOUSE FURNISHINGS, MACHINE OILS, and MANUFACTURERS OF WOODWORK OF ALL KINDS.

TELEPHONE 9-F 22.

ELLSWORTH ADAMS.

A well known furniture dealer and Undertaker of Hamburg, N. J. Is a native of the county and has lived therein all his life. Began business in Sussex in 1899, came to Hamburg in 1909. Has a fine store, and complete funeral accessories, morgue, and mortuary chapel. Is a graduate of the U. S. School of Embalming, New York, and licensed by the State of New Jersey. Mr. Adams' assistant is also a graduate of the same school. Mr. Adams stands high in the community. Is prominent in fraternal orders, being a Mason and Red Man.

A. B. CARD
Agent for Studebaker and Emerson Vehicles.

Livery, Sale and Exchange Stables.
HAMBURG, NEW JERSEY.

SYLVANUS SMITH.

Established the business at Hamburg, N. J. in 1907. Deals in Hardware, Tinware, Stoves and Housefurnishings, also does general repairing, steam heating and plumbing.

Enjoys a good trade and is one of Hamburg's enterprising citizens. Mr. Smith is a native of Sussex county, and takes a keen interest in the affairs of the community.

Hotel National
HAMBURG, N. J.

J. K. GUNN, Proprietor.

❧ ❧ ❧

First class accommodations, newly furnished, steam heat, gas light, livery. One of the county's up-to-date Hostelries. Designed and erected by J. Dymock & Son, Hamburg, and one of the handsomest buildings in this section.

HAINESVILLE STORE.

The proprietor of the Hainesville general store is Mr. James M. Stoll, who has conducted it for 41 years. He is a native of the county. Has a fine store and an extensive trade. Deals in Dry Goods, Boots, Shoes, Farm Implements, Machinery, Fertilizers and Dairymen's Supplies. Mr. Stoll is a heavy buyer and shipper of country produce. He served as postmaster 20 years. Is treasurer of the Cemetery Association and Commissioner of Deeds. James A. Stoll, his son, is now postmaster.

LESTER T. SMITH.

Enterprising merchant and postmaster at Layton. Is a native of the county, and has been in the general merchandise business for over 30 years. Has a fine store, and carries a large stock of Dry Goods, Boots, Shoes, Hardware, Crockery, and Farm Implements. Is a director of the Sussex Mutual Insurance Co. Served on the school board and member of Board of Elections. Mr. Smith has in his possession a copy of the "New England Journal," printed in Boston in 1728. It is a two page sheet, size 8x12, and is a curiosity as a newspaper.

THE HAINESVILLE HOUSE.

One of the county's oldest and most popular hotels. Erected and conducted for years by John Y. Clark and now managed by his son, Harry C. Clark, who has owned the place for about eight years. He is making an ideal host, giving special attention to summer guests, tourists and automobile parties. Mr. Clark takes a keen interest in fraternal affairs, and is prominent as a Mason and Odd Fellow.

THOMAS R. LANTZ.

Is the miller of Hainesville, and has an active business in the community grinding feed, and making a high grade Buckwheat Flour, which has a wide sale in the vicinity. He is a native of the county and has operated the mill about six years. The mill was built by his father 40 years ago. Mr. Lantz is a prominent Odd Fellow, and one of the town's enterprising citizens.

J. B. ROSENKRANS.

Is proprietor of the (haunted) mill, near Layton. The mill is haunted with a fine equipment of burrs and stones for grinding feed and buckwheat, and a press for cider making. Mr. Rosenkrans is a native of the county, and has operated the Layton mill for twenty-three years. Has a fine trade and is a jolly as well as a popular miller.

FRANK MAJOR.

Is the genial proprietor of the Hotel Layton, at Layton. He has conducted the place for the past three years, and keeps a first class, up-to-date Inn, where the best to eat and drink may always be had. Automobile parties, tourists and transients will find the Layton a most hospitable place of entertainment.

G. E. PHLEGAR.

Is the village smith at Layton. He is a native of Virginia, where he learned how to shoe a horse properly and repair a wagon quickly. Located in Layton March, 1912. Has a fine business. Repairs automobiles, and supplies accessories. Is a P. O. S. of A. and very popular with all.

SETH SHAY.

Is one of the enterprising merchants of Sussex county, who conducts a fine store at Layton. He has been in business there for about four years. Has built up a large trade, and is a buyer and shipper of country produce. Mr. Shay is an Odd Fellow fraternally, and a very popular merchant.

LAFAYETTE.

Lafayette was named in honor of the Marquis de la Fayette in 1824, the township in which it is situated taking its name from the same source. The first settlement was made by a German, Henry Bale, in the year 1750. Shortly after erecting his dwelling house he erected a log grist mill on what is now about the site of the mill of Armstrong & Demarest. This mill was the first in the township, and one of the first in the county. The original dam remained until 1858, when it was moved to reclaim a part of the flooded lands. The mill itself was in operation until about 1822, when it gave way to one of more modern equipment. Bale also erected a blacksmith shop which, with his sons he operated in connection with the mill.

The descendants of this family are numerous in Sussex county. Members of the family were the founders of Baleville. The town is situated on the Sussex branch of the Lackawanna, 65.7 miles from New York and 4.6 miles from Newton. Through the village runs the old Milford and New York turn pike, in the early days one of the great thoroughfares of the country.

The township of Lafayette was formerly embraced in the township of Newton and Frankford and was set apart by an act dated March 20, 1845.

Lafayette was for many years an active business center and was largely identified with the political history of the county. Between 1838 and 1842, Alexander Boyles conducted a foundry in the village, employing forty men. There were three stores, two flour and grist mills, a clover mill, a saw mill, a distillery, a blacksmith shop and various other smaller enterprises. In 1843 the slate deposits near the village were opened.

During the Revolutionary war, the American army passed through the village on its way from Morristown to Newburg.

At the present time but one mill is in operation, that of Armstrong & Demarest. Fire destroyed the plant of the Wolfe Brothers, formerly the Culver & Huston mill, in December, 1913. This concern manufactured a buckwheat cereal.

J. W. RUDE

Is Lafayette's popular and efficient postmaster, appointed in 1898, and has made a faithful official. For over 30 years he has conducted a general store and has been in business in Lafayette longer than any other merchant. Has a fine hardware store, does plumbing, tinning and general repair work.

ARMSTRONG & DEMAREST.

One of the largest feed and grain concerns in Sussex county is that of Armstrong & Demarest, of Lafayette. Situated on a private siding of the Lackawanna Railroad, within a few hundred feet of the Lafayette depot of that road, the company enjoys unequalled facilities for handling their business. The firm is composed of Obadiah E. Armstrong and Gillam Demarest, both of Newton. The former is Secretary of the Sussex County Tax Board and the latter a member of the Mosquito Commission appointed by Governor Wilson. In addition to their feed and grain business, they manufacture the famous old Sussex Brand of Buckwheat Flour. The mill in which this is manufactured was built in 1859 and 1860 by Obadiah P. Armstrong. Power is furnished by the Paulinskill, which flows by the building. The concern handles all the approved dairy feeds, all kinds of grain, cattle salt, fertilizers, cement, poultry supplies, paints, oils, Scranton coal and fertilizer salt, and enjoys a big farm trade.

O. P. JOHNSTON,

Dealer in Dry Goods, Groceries, Boots and Shoes, store is at Lafayette, N. J., where he has been in business three years. Mr. Johnston was in business at Hackettstown, N. J. before locating here. He has a well stocked store and is enjoying a good trade.

LAFAYETTE HOUSE
R. J. BLAUVELT, Proprietor
Lafayette, N. J.

The Lafayette House is one of the attractive, home-like hotels, of the county. Modern in every detail. Most excellent in table and appointments. Mr. Blauvelt is the ideal host, and understands the business thoroughly.

THE FAIRVIEW HOUSE,   LAFAYETTE, N. J.

LYMAN A. LITTELL, Proprietor.

This is one of the popular hostelries of the county. Mr. Littell has conducted it for the past two years, and in that time has remodeled and greatly improved the surroundings. He has a fine trade, and looks carefully to the comfort of his many guests. Tourists and automobile parties accommodated at all times.

McAFEE DRIVING ASSOCIATION.

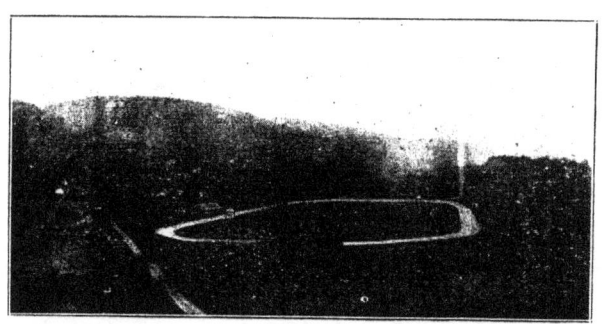

This association was organized in the spring of 1913, and the officers are the following well known business men:: R. D. Simpson, President; B. Drew, Vice President; F. A. Mingle, Treasurer and Assistant Secretary; L. C. Ruban, Secretary, and Director General; A. B. Card, Assistant Director General, and Henry Flanigan, Director. The association is doing a great work in stimulating the breeding and training of fine horses in this section. The track is one of the best in Northern New Jersey.

FRANK A. MINGLE.

An enterprising merchant of McAfee, N. J., in 1905 purchased the store of John Wright, and in 1910 the store of H. J. McDanold Co., and now operates the two stores and enjoys a good trade. Mr. Mingle is one of the town's most public spirited citizens.

SUSSEX HOTEL   L. C. RUBAN, Proprietor.

McAFEE, N. J.

Mr. Ruban has conducted the hotel three years. Has a first-class place and a large trade. Is secretary of the McAfee Trotting Association, a famous driver and trainer of horses. His training stables have such well known horses as "Blow Patch," "May Plant," "Joe Wilson" and "A. S. A."

A. R. TRUMBULL.

Conducts the general store in Glenwood. He was appointed postmaster in January, 1913. Has a well stocked, up-to-date place; carries Dry Goods, Groceries, Hardware, Farmers' Implements and Dairymen's Supplies.

J. H. SUTTON.

The subject of this sketch was born in Sparta township, Sussex county, and has lived there all of his life. In 1868 he established the general merchandise business at Monroe. In 1892 erected store and residence shown in illustration. He married Miss Mary Benjamin, Jan. 2, 1872.

Mr. Sutton was postmaster of Monroe for 25 years, served on Town Committee nine years and has been Trustee and Treasurer of the North Hardyston Cemetery Association since its organization.

R. J. KIMBLE,

Merchant miller, farmer and cider manufacturer at Monroe. Operates the old Kimble mill which has been there for a century. Mr. Kimble has remodeled and modernized the property and it is now one of the pretty places of the county. He has been in the employ of the Lehigh & Hudson Railroad 31 years, and is still their agent. He has a fine farm of 50 acres, is a Mason, Odd Fellow and Jr. O. U. A. M., and prominent in the affairs of the community.

S. R. ADAMS.

Is a native of Sussex county. Has conducted a blacksmith and wheelwright shop in Monroe for nearly 20 years. Is an expert shoer of horses, builds wagons and does all kinds of repairing. Is a member of the Jr. Order of American Mechanics.

L. R. CONGLETON.

Deputy postmaster and dealer in General Merchandise at Monroe. Born in Ogdensburg and lived in the county all his life. Farmed till six years ago, when he engaged in the mercantile business. Handles groceries, provisions, dry goods and farm implements. Is public spirited. Served as Assessor of Hardyston township. Is a Republican and a Jr. O. U. A. M.

A. ROBBINS & SON.

GEORGE BONKER.

Conducts the village smithy in Middleville. He is a native of Sussex county and has lived here all of his life. Learned his trade in Sparta. First had a shop in Baleville. Located in Middleville in 1913. Is a fine workman and enjoys a large trade. Is prominent in fraternal orders, being an Odd Fellow and a P. O. S. of A.

This firm consists of A. Robbins and V. M. Robbins. They have a general store at Middleville, N. J. and carry a fine stock of Dry Goods, Groceries and General Merchandise. They operate a cider press in season and are large shippers of Sweet Cider. Mr. A. Robbins is also a well known contractor and builder.

BRICK HOUSE HOTEL

Montague, N. J.

GOTTFRIED S. WEILAND, Prop.

Mr. M. Swartwood is the genial proprietor of the Mountain Brook Hotel at Middleville. He has conducted it for 13 years, and has a first-class, up-to-date hostelry. It is on the shores of Swartswood Lake and a favorite resort for guests at all seasons.

One of the landmarks of the county, built in 1776. The present proprietor, Mr. Weiland, has conducted the place about 13 years. In that time has modernized the building, and made a most attractive place for tourists and automobile parties. Mr. Weiland also has a large general store in Montague. He takes a keen interest in town affairs, is a prominent Mason and very popular.

NEWTON

Newton, the county seat and largest town in Sussex county, is situated on the Sussex division of the Lackawanna Railroad and is about sixty miles from New York. Prior to 1765 there was but one house at or near the location of the town. The erection of a Court House and jail by order of the colonial governor caused the erection of a number of dwelling houses, most of which were built about the present county park. From that time on the growth of the town, both in business and wealth, has been steady. Newton is built among the hills 700 feet above sea level. The air is clear and dry and the altitude causes it to be both a health resort and a residential place of unsurpassable beauty. Magnificent mountains, valleys and lakes surround it on all sides and the roads and drives through the surrounding country form scenery excelled by none in the State and by but few in the east.

Newtonians are proud of several things about their beautiful town. The excellent gravity water system from Morris Lake, situated among the hills east of Sparta, fed by sparkling mountain streams; the sewer system, considered to be one of the best in the State; a fire department composed of four companies, equipped with the best apparatus and officered by competent men; broad streets and avenues lined with stately trees; a grammar and High School, second to none; a Military Academy of high rank, and a number of thriving industries. Five religious denominations: Baptist, Catholic, Presbyterian, Episcopal and Methodist and five nicely appointed places of worship, while the Volunteers of America and the Newton Mission look after the soul welfare of those outside the churches. Fraternalism has secured a great hold in Newton and practically every lodge of any importance is represented. Among these are: Masonic, Odd Fellows, Red Men, Knights of Pythias, Royal Arcanum, Jr. O. U. A. M., P. O. S. of A., Loyal Order of Moose, Loyal Order of Buffalos, Heptasophs, Daughters of Liberty, Pythian Sisters, and kindred organizations. Another organization of which Newton is proud is her Building and Loan Association. This has just closed its 23rd year with a history perhaps never equaled by any other Building and Loan Association in the country. In all its years of existence it has never been necessary to foreclose a mortgage held by it. Two newspapers, The Sussex Register and New Jersey Herald, cater liberally to the needs of the community.

That the citizens of Newton and the surrounding country are industrious and thrifty is evidenced by the amount on deposit at the three banks of the town. According to the report made to the banking authorities under date of October 21, of this year the deposits were $3,649,258.73, with total resources of $4,820,912.82.

"Newtown," as it was at first called, was formed in 1753 as one of the four precincts of Sussex county. At that time it contained nearly all the present county east of the Blue Mountains. From time to time new precincts or townships were set off until it was reduced to its present size in 1904. The township of Newton has had no civil existence since 1864, when the town of Newton was formed.

Geographically Newton is situated a little south of the center of the county, lying in a valley between the Wallkill mountains on the east and the Kittatinny on the west. The east branch of the Paulinskill rises near the town. The elevation of Newton is 645 feet above tidewater. Who the first settler was is a question. It is claimed that the first white man's dwelling was on what is known as High street. In 1761, however, the only dwelling in the limits of the present town, was the one occupied by Henry Hairlocker, a native of Holland. His burial place is claimed to be near the present gate house of the Horton mansion.

The Indian name for the town was Chinkchewunska, or "side hill" town. Why the name was changed from the original Newtown to Newton has never been explained.

The first court held in the town granted a license to Henry Hairlocker to keep a "public house," and he was the first to keep a hotel in Sussex county. This was in 1753.

DENNIS LIBRARY.

In 1866 Alfred L. Dennis, of Newark, a former resident of Newton, announced that he would give the sum of $25,000 toward the erection and equipment of a public library building on condition that the citizens of Newton would give $5,000 for the same object. The first conference was held in November of that year, at which Mr. Dennis placed securities to the amount of $30,000 in the hands of Martin Ryerson as a pledge. In April, 1867, a special act of the Legislature was passed incorporating the Newton Library Association. The incorporators being Martin Ryerson, George H. Nelden, Franklin Smith, Thomas Anderson and others.

The work of securing subscribers for the Association was at once begun and was completed on February 4, 1868, 78 subscribers having been obtained, 201 shares of stock being taken at $25 per share, making a total, including the amount given by Mr. Dennis of $30,025. The first meeting of the stockholders was held at the Court House on May 30, 1868, the following Board of Directors being elected: Alfred L. Dennis, Robert Hamilton, Daniel S. Anderson, Joseph Coult, Samuel Johnson, George M. Ryerson, Henry C. Kelsey, Thomas Ryerson, Theodore Morford, Myron Barrett, Jonathan F. Shafer, John McCarter and Franklin Smith. This Board organized by electing Robert Hamilton, President; Daniel S. Anderson, Vice-President; Henry C. Kelsey, Secretary and Treasurer; Rev. Myron Barrett, Librarian. A building committee and committee on by-laws was also appointed. The building committee purchased a lot on High street, adjoining the Presbyterian church, for $2,500. An architect, J. V. Nichols, was engaged to draw up plans and specifications for a building. The plans were approved by Mr. Dennis and adopted by the Board of Directors on November 27, 1867. Bids were asked for, the lowest being $22,000, a sum believed to be too large for the Association. On April 26, 1869, an attempt was made to indefinitely postpone the erection of the building, but because of objections of the subscribers, this plan was not carried out and in January, 1870, bids were again asked for with no better results. New plans were drawn and on October 29, 1870, they were approved by Mr. Dennis and the Board of Directors. The building committee was directed to proceed at once and erect a building on what was known as the drug store lot, with a frontage of 66 feet on Main street, and 200 feet deep. This lot was purchased for $5,000. The contract was awarded to Baughn & Price for $18,500, the work to be completed by October 1, 1872. The work was delayed, however, and the building was publicly opened on the evening of November 28, 1872, by appropriate exercises presided over by Robert Hamilton, President of the Board of Directors.

CHURCHES
CHRIST CHURCH.

Following a meeting held in Newton on December 28, 1769, at which subscriptions were taken and the question of acquiring land on which to build a parsonage for the housing of a clergyman was discussed, a petition was presented to the proprietors of the eastern division of New Jersey on April 11, 1770, by Rev. Thomas P. Chandler, setting forth a desire on the part of "some inhabitants of the township of Newton, in Sussex county," to have an Episcopal minister residing among them, but because they were unable to purchase a "glede" they asked the assistance of the board. In response to this appeal a warrant was issued for 200 acres of land in any place unappropriated in the county of Sussex. Accordingly a farm of 200 acres, located on the Fredon road, about three and a half miles southwest of Newton, was deeded to the parish on December 16, 1774, by Cortland Skinner and John Johnston, to whom the grant was made. Prior to this 27 acres had been deeded to the parish by Jonathan Hampton

Rev. Ernest C. Tuthill.

and on this a parsonage was built. The parish was incorporated August 15, 1774, by a charter granted by Governor William Franklin, in the name and by the authority of George the Third. The rectors of the church have been as follows: the Third. The rectors of the church have been as follows:

Rev. Uzal Ogden, Jr., 1770-1774; Rev. Clarkson Dunn, 1820-1857; Rev. Nathaniel Pettit, 1857-1867; Rev. William Welles Holley, 1868-1870; Rev. William H. Moffet, 1870-1885; Rev. Samuel Edson, 1885-1892; Rev. Charles L. Steel, 1892-1910; Rev. Ernest C. Tuthill, 1910- . Between 1784 and 1820 the church passed through a long period of discouragement,

almost of dissolution. Occasional services were held by Rev. John Croes, afterward Bishop of New Jersey, and other rectors, but the church was without a resident rector. During the pastorate of Rev. Clarkson Dunn the communicants' list was increased from six to seventy-one, 358 persons were baptized and 141 were presented to the Bishop for confirmation. In 1868 the farm, under an act of Legislature passed April 4, 1867, was sold for $15,759 on May 10. A contract was entered into for the erection of a new church on the site of the old church. The cornerstone of the new building was laid Friday, August 21, 1868, the first services being held on July 11, 1869. The building was consecrated by Bishop Odenheimer on October 20th of the same year. The rectory was built the same year at a cost of $5,600. The sale of land from the parsonage lot and the sale of the old parsonage house netted the parish $17,600.

FIRST PRESBYTERIAN.

The First Presbyterian church of Newton was organized about 1780 and the first edifice was built on the present site in 1785 and fronted on Church street. The present church building of this society was dedicated on May 17, 1871, being the third church building to occupy the corner of High and Church streets. The chapel adjoining the church was built about 1885.

The first minister was Rev. Ira Condit, D. D., who was pastor from 1787 to 1793. The second minister was Rev. Halloway Hunt, who served from 1793 to 1795. There is no record at hand concerning the third pastor. The subsequent pastors were: Rev. Joseph Linn Shafer, D. D., 1812 to 1835; Rev. David M. Barber, 1835 to 1838; Rev. Joseph Linn Shafer,

Rev. Clarence W. Rouse.

D. D., 1838 to 1853; Rev. Myron Barrett, 1854 to 1859; Rev. George S. Mott, D. D., 1859 to 1869; Rev. Theodore L. Byington, D. D., 1869 to 1874; Rev. J. Addison Priest, 1875 to 1881; Rev. Eugene Olney, 1881 to 1883; Rev. Alexander H. Young, D. D., 1883 to 1891; Rev. Samuel Carlisle, 1892 to 1902; Rev. Clarence W. Rouse, who is the present occupant of the pulpit, took charge in 1903.

FIRST METHODIST.

The history of local Methodism of which the First Methodist Church of Newton, N. J., is the outgrowth begins with the year 1831. In October of that year a meeting of Methodists was held in the Court House and a Board of Trustees was elected. The triple oaths, one to support the Constitution of the United States; one to be loyal to the State of

New Jersey and one of allegiance to the Tenets of Methodism was administered by Thomas McIntire, Esq., to the following: John H. Hall, Samuel Ingersoll, James Iliff, Lewis DeCamp, Dr. Francis Moran, Azariah Davis and Ira Beach.

John H. Hall, the father and founder of The Sussex Register, was elected the first president of the first Board of

Rev. Milton E. Grant.

Trustees of the First Methodist Episcopal Church, of Newton.

In the spring of 1832 an effort was made to secure the funds with which to build a church. This was so successful that in March of that year a resolution by the Board of Trustees to build a church was adopted. Owing, however, to the financial failure of two successive contractors the building was not completed until the early spring of 1834.

This building served the purpose until 1859, when the erection of the present edifice was begun. After many tribulations and embarrassments the building was completed and dedicated March 23, 1861.

During the fifty years since its original dedication it has been remodeled and repaired from time to time as needed.

The present year the outside has been thoroughly repaired and repainted; the inside tastefully and appropriately redecorated and refurnished. A new pipe organ has been purchased and modern electric indirect reflectors have been installed. The total result is a very pleasing and commodious audience room, lecture room, class rooms, and well equipped kitchen which well serves the congregation now numbering 600 members.

A generally prosperous condition is the reward of the faithful and efficient services of the present official board. Rev. Milton E. Grant is the present pastor.

FIRST BAPTIST.

The First Baptist Church of Newton was organized about 1830 and was admitted to membership in the Warwick Baptist Association in July of that year. In 1833, at a meeting of Baptists near Newton, of which meeting Jonathan Hill was chairman, the building of a Baptist church in Newton was considered. This project was made possible about 1838 by the receipt of a bequest of several thousand dollars made by Sarah Hill. The building was begun at once and dedicated February 25, 1847. Because of the fact that a fire in the

Rev. John R. Humphreys.

basement of the store of E. A. Muir, who was the active head of the church business for many years, about fifteen years ago, destroyed all the old church records, the history of the Baptist organization between 1840 and 1900, is more or less hazy. On March 6, 1910, fire partially destroyed the building situated at the corner of Main and Liberty streets. Through the efforts of the present pastor, a new church edifice costing $12,000 was erected.

YOUNG WOMEN'S CHRISTIAN ASSOCIATION.

Ranking next to the churches of the town is the Young Women's Christian Association, with headquarters and rooms at 119 Spring street. The Association was formed in 1900 and has a membership of 346, of which twenty-six are sustaining, 283 active and thirty-seven associate. In 1913 seventy new members were admitted. The work of the Association is divided into four departments, educational, physical, social and religious, each being under the head of efficient leaders. The Association has a library of nearly 350 volumns, the tables in the room being supplied with weekly papers and monthly magazines. The physical department, started about two years ago, proved a success and among its branches are a basketball team, tennis club, captain ball club and folk dancing class. During 1913 the different committees, clubs and classes of the association held 282 meetings, which were attended by a total of 7,069. Three hundred and thirty-five calls were made and 1,316 bulletins issued.

FIRE DEPARTMENT

In the history of the fire matters in Newton, it is a fact that only one man of the original fire company is now living, viz: Alanson A. Vance, of Morristown. He was secretary of Pheonix No. 1, in the thirties. The home of this organization was a little house, not more than a shed, located on a portion of the property of Mrs. E. B. Potter, on Main street. The engine was almost a plaything, operated by iron crank arms, and its wheels were placed in a box frame with spikes to steady it when in operation.

It was not until the early fifties that another engine—a goose-neck—was brought to Newton, and the first location was in the barn of Dr. Thomas Ryerson, then located between the residence of S. H Hopkins and the Inslee home, on Main street, and directly opposite the quarters of Pheonix No. 1.

Chief Engineer Edward Hall.

Prior to the advent of Neptune No. 3, which was a most excellent piece of fire apparatus, No. 1 had been neglected, but almost as soon as the new company was organized, and it comprised the leading citizens of the town, at that time, a company was formed for No. 1. Amos Kinney and Fritz VanEtten tried to change it from a bucket to a suction engine, but it was not a great success. However, the rivalry was enough to secure a well built house for the new apparatus, fronting on Church street, and occupying a portion of the present Presbyterian church lot. The Phoenix boys were progressive, and later a new company was formed. To match the new machine and even do a little better, an engine, known as Hercules No. 4 was purchased, and housed in the old quarters on Main street. Joseph Coult was the first foreman of this company. After somewhat exciting rivalry, a younger element came in possession of old No. 3, and a larger engine, known as No. 7 was purchased from Newark. This was damaged by a fire in No. 3's house and was afterward sold almost as junk.

After this old No. 3 was stored in a room on Moran street, and for a year or two there was "a hot time" very frequently. The Fire Department was a separate organization, the town officials having no control over it, and whoever was chosen President did about as he pleased. Finally all interest seemed to be lost, and there were no organized companies, while the town was practically without fire protection, until the Fall of 1873, when a disastrous fire swept the block from the corner of Spring street to the Library building, where the flames were checked.

This was followed by a demand for fire protection, and following a house was built on High street, now occupied by Sussex Chemical No. 2, and the nucleus of the present department formed. Fire in rear of the McCarter storehouse showed unwillingness to "man the brakes," and under pressure the Town Committee purchased a steam fire engine, and Newton Steamer Company No. 1 was organized. Kittatinny Hose was also formed at the same time, and Charles Crook, who alone had exercised care of the old apparatus was elected as Chief Engineer.

With the growth of the town increased fire protection was demanded, and the double engine house on Spring street was built, accommodating Steamer No. 1 and Kittatinny Hose. Later a company was organized to care for the old hand engine, Hercules No. 3, who took the quarters on High street, and afterward developed into Sussex Chemical Co. No. 2. Old Hercules was kicked about and was nearly ruined, as was the fate of Hercules No. 4.

The necessity for fire protection in the vicinity of the shoe factory and silk mill, resulted in the formation of Newton Hose, No. 3, and the erection of a suitable fire house on Diller avenue.

NEWTON STEAMER COMPANY NO. 1.

Following the fire of September 22, 1873, which destroyed property to the amount of $85,000, the Newton Town Committee immediately took action toward the purchasing of a steam fire engine. Martin Rosenkrans, Esq., and Charles Crook, chief engineer, were appointed a committee to visit Paterson, Newark, New York and Hudson to examine engines on sale at those places, together with suitable equipments. On September 26, Mr. Rosenkrans reported to the Town Committee that the committee had bargained with Clapp & Jones, of Hudson, N. Y., for a 4th-class steam engine and 800 feet of 4-ply rubber hose, to be in Newton on or about the 8th of October, at a cost of $5,000. The report was unanimously accepted and the new engine was named the Newton No. 1. The following officers and men were appointed on September 30: Chief Engineer, Charles Crook; Assistant Chief, John R. Hemingway; Foreman, Martin R. Snyder; Assistant Foreman, Coulter Cannon; Engineer, Henry C. Bonnell; 1st Assistant Engineer, John J. Case; 2nd Assistant Engineer, Stephen Norris; 3rd Assistant Engineer, Charles S. Steele; Fireman, Charles McCollum; Assistant Fireman, John Masker, L. L. Davenport, Bowdine VanAuken, J. D. Simmons, Peter Hough, I. L. Hallock, George W. Dawkins, George W. Frace, George A. Wintermute, Wesley Trusdell, G. B. Dunning, Stephen Woodruff, William Busekist, L. F. VanEtten, J. W. Crigar, C. K. Foster, W. D. Steele, C. M. Woodruff, Thomas E. Smith, William F. Howell, A. G. Phillips, William A. Faull, George R. Leport, A. Losee, Theodore Simonson, H C. Clark, Charles Shiner.

The first meeting of the Company was held on Thursday evening, October 2, 1873. The following style of uniform was adopted, blue shirt, blue cloth cap, with rubber cover and plain black leather belt. The steamer arrived in Newton on October 9. The following day it was thoroughly tested and was accepted by the Town Committee.

The officers at the present time are: Foreman, E. Dana Ely; Assistant Foreman, M. P. Strader; Secretary, Fred Loges, Jr.; Treasurer, Albert Grover; Engineer, Charles S. Steele; Stoker, Fred Loges, Sr.

KITTATINNY HOSE COMPANY.

On October 24, 1873, twenty members of Newton Steamer Company were appointed as hose men, Wesley Trusdell being named as foreman. They were to have charge of the two-wheeled jumper to carry hose for use with the steamer. In 1878 the hose members withdrew from the steamer company and organized a separate company with George Van Gelder, Foreman; Lewis M. Morford, Assistant Foreman; Israel L. Hallock, Secretary, and John C. Howell, Treasurer. The name of Kittatinny Hose Company was adopted. In September, 1879, the company purchased a parade carriage of Humane Steamer Company of Easton, the original cost of which was $2,500.

The company is quartered on Spring street, in the same building as Newton Steamer Company, and is officered by the following men: Foreman, Fred R. Snyder; Assistant Foreman, Fred C. Smith; Secretary, Harry E. Demarest; Treasurer, Jacob Grimm; Chaplain, Rev. John R. Humphreys; Captain, Irving J. Kern.

SUSSEX CHEMICAL COMPANY NO. 2.

On June 14, 1892, the Town Committee authorized the formation of another fire company, to be known as Sussex

Engine Company No. 2, and appointed James E. Baldwin, Foreman; William Cutler, Assistant Foreman; John M. Hotalen, Treasurer; William H. Dunn, Secretary. The engine house on High street, formerly the property of Hercules Engine Company No. 2, which had disbanded, was placed in charge of the new company, together with the old hand engine, hose cart and other fire fighting appliances used by the former Company. The following persons were named to constitute the new company: James E. Baldwin, William Cutler, William H. Dunn, John M. Hotalen, Casper C. Beegle, Charles Boyd, John W. Bryant, John C. Kramer, Samuel W. Goble, Henry M. Ward, John T. Gorman, Clark Rose, Jehiel T. Beck, John S. Kintner, John R. Dunn, Harvey Brown, Abe W. Crawn, A. B. Brickner, Stephen Bowman, R. N. Talmage, Charles Jones, George Huff, Edward Braisted, Silas M. Beegle, Ira C. Moore, Samuel Cutler, William J. Williams, Bruno Hood, J. Clark Andress, Frank D. Whyms, Ed. S. Milham, Martin M. Flynn, Draper C. Maines, George Caverly, Lewis Beegle, Austin A. Pierson, David R. Hull, Jr., Jacob L. Bunnell, Charles House. The uniform adopted by the company consisted of blue shirts, caps, belts and dark trousers, each member of the company purchased his own outfit. The company did good service with the old hand engine.

In 1900 the Town Committee purchased a two tank Chemical, each tank holding 30 gallons. It was turned over to the Engine Company, taking the place of the antiquated apparatus. It was the intention that this Company should be in a position to get to a fire first and hold it in check until the arrival of the other companies or quench it entirely. The heaviness of the truck, however, has oftentimes handicapped the members of the company as it is too heavy to be pulled very fast, especially up the hills. During the time the livery stable occupied the Van Blarcom barn, horses were used whenever possible. At the present time the Town Committee realizes the handicap under which the members of this company work and the purchase of an auto chassis upon which to place the body of the Chemical is being agitated. Should this apparatus be purchased it would mean much to the Fire Department of Newton.

The present officers are: Foreman, Milton E. Bossard; Assistant Foreman, Theodore Simonson; Treasurer, Horton M. Beegle; Secretary, R. N. Talmadge. The Company has a membership of 31. There are but eight of the charter members left on the Company's roll. They are: Draper C. Maines, J. T. Beck, R. N. Talmadge, J. Clark Andress, Frank D. Whyms, William H. Dunn, A. B. Brickner and James E. Baldwin.

NEWTON HOSE COMPANY NO. 3.

In order to better protect the eastern part of the town, which because of the factory, was being rapidly built up, citizens of Sparta avenue and vicinity met on November 30, 1900, and organized a Hose Company, which on December 8th of that year became part of the Newton Fire Department. The first meeting was held at the residence of Wesley C. Puder. Twenty men joined the company as charter members. Of this number eleven are still members of the organization, three have died and six removed from Newton. The first officers elected were: Foreman, Wesley C. Puder; Assistant Foreman, John Hoffman; Treasurer, William H. Cooper; Secretary, George N. Harris. Its present membership is twenty-six and meetings are held on the second Thursday evening of each month at their parlors on Sparta avenue. The present officers are: Foreman, Robert Kerr; Assistant Foreman, Geo. O. Eagles; Treasurer, William Pullis; Secretary, Frank Nichols.

NEWTON FIRE PATROL.

The Newton Fire Patrol was organized June 7, 1875, and reorganized February 23, 1880. The present officers are: Foreman, Dr. Warren H. Smith; Assistant Foreman; W. W. Roe; Treasurer, L. S. Iliff; Secretary, Henry C. Bonnell.

NEWTON FIREMEN'S RELIEF ASSOCIATION.

The Firemen's Relief Association was organized February 24, 1876, for the financial protection of members of the Newton Fire Department injured in performing their duties. The first officers elected were: George Hardin, President; Henry C. Bonnell, Vice President; George Van Gelder, Secretary; Whitman D. Steele, Treasurer. The members were Richard F. Goodman, Charles S. Steele, John C. Howell, C. K. Foster, I. L. Hallock, C. D. Thompson, R. J. Redhead, L. M. Morford, Samuel Johnson, Wallace Myers, G. B. Dunning. In February, 1879, at the annual report of the treasurer the cash on hand was shown as $200.00. The treasurer's report for the year ending December 31, 1912, shows a balance of $13,495.64. The Association at the present time has nineteen members, three representatives from each of the Fire Companies, from the Fire Patrol, from the Firemen's Exempt Association, together with the Chief of the Department. The present officers are: President, Richard F. Goodman; Vice President, William H. Dunn; Secretary, Horton M. Beegle and Treasurer, Charles S. Steele. In this connection it may be well to note the time the present officers have served. Charles S. Steele was elected Treasurer to succeed his brother, Whitman D. Steele, in 1877 and has served continuously since that time, a period of 36 years. Richard F. Goodman has occupied the President's chair for 22 years, while William H. Dunn has been Vice President for 15 years. The youngest member of the official family is Horton M. Beegle, who was elected Secretary in 1903 and has, therefore, served but ten years.

NEWTON FIREMEN'S EXEMPT ASSOCIATION

The organization was instituted January 17th, 1889, with 39 charter members, the following officers being elected and appointed: President, I. L. Hallock; Vice President, A. F. O'Donnell; Treasurer, C. S. Steele; Secretary, D. B. Hetzel; Trustees, H. O. Ryerson, W. D. Steele, T. G. Bunnell; Standing Committee, A. A. Pierson, E. F. Beresford, J. W. Criger; Representatives to Relief Association, H. O. Ryerson, R. F. Goodman, H. C. Bonnell.

The officers at the present time are: President, Henry C. Bonnell; Vice President, Wm. H. Dunn; Treasurer, Chas. S. Steele; Secretary, William G. Drake; Trustees, William H. Nicholls, A. B. Brickner, George O. Eagles; Standing Committee, William H. Earl, Fred Loges, Jr.; Representatives, Charles S. Steele, R. F. Goodman, M. C. Siple. The association has a membership of 114.

SCHOOLS
PUBLIC SCHOOL.

Newtonians are proud, and justly so, of its schools. The High School ranks among the best in the State and its graduates are admitted to many of the larger colleges and universities without further examinations. The Newton Academy, a semi-military and preparatory school, has a country wide reputation and among its pupils are enrolled natives of a number of central and south American counties.

The first school building, of which there is any record, stood at what is now the corner of Liberty and High streets. It was constructed of logs and is supposed to have been erected about 1775. In 1825 a classical school was established on what is now the site of the Newton Academy, by Rev. Clarkson Dunn, then rector of Christ church. One of the teachers in 1828 was William Rankin, who previous to his coming to Newton, had conducted a school in the Clove Valley, near Sussex, then Deckertown. After teaching in Newton for two years, Mr. Rankin entered Yale and on his graduating in 1833 returned to Deckertown, where he established a school which became famous throughout the State.

The old academy building was erected in 1802 on land donated by Jonathan Hampton. In 1828 this property was traded with Judge John H. Hall, founder of The Register, for a property on what is now Division street. A new building was erected and the school continued there until 1868.

The erection of the present public school building was begun in 1869 and finished the following year, Messrs. Hoppaugh & Moore, of Newton, being the builders, the architect being J. D. Daly. The original building was 64x100 feet, three stories in height, exclusive of the basement, and was constructed of pressed brick and limestone, with brown stone trimmings. The cost of the building was $26,000. Furniture, heating plant and grading of the grounds cost $6,500 more. Since the erection of the first structure, three additions have been made, bringing the number of class rooms from eight to twenty-three. At the present time thirty-two teachers are engaged in the kindergarten, grammar and high schools. In order to accommodate the pupils rooms in the Park Block building are used, several of the higher grade being quartered there.

On September 19, 1903, fire starting in several places, burned off practically the entire top floor of the building.

The first principal of the new school was Elisha M. Allen, who was in charge from 1870 to 1879, his staff of teachers being as follows: Miss Kate Leport, Kittie Trusdell, Theresa Badgley, Carrie V. Hamilton, Annie J. Gustin, Agnes Hallock, Sarah Ribble and Eva Couse. The principal received the sum of $1,000 per year, while the staff received from $17.50 to $40 per month.

The present staff is in charge of Prof. Howard E. Shimer, a native of Pennsylvania and a graduate of Muhlenberg University, who came to the Newton school in 1909.

Prof. Howard E. Shimer.

PRIVATE SCHOOLS.

Private schools were also conducted by Miss Agnes McCarter, Katy Leport and the Misses Linn. The two former were discontinued when the free school system was established in 1868. The latter school was discontinued in 1861.

NEWTON COLLEGIATE INSTITUTE.

The Newton Collegiate Institute, better known as the Newton Academy, was organized April 5, 1850, being incorporated February 12, 1852, as the "Presbyterian Academy at Newton." Until 1856 the school was conducted under the direction of the Presbytery of Newton. In that year the name of the school was changed by legislative enactment to the "Newton Collegiate Institute." At the time the school was started, the buildings were on lands owned by William Beach. The Rev. James I. Helm being the teacher in charge. The school was later removed to its present location.

For a number of years Miss Lillian Rosenkrans conducted a preparatory and select school, under the name of the "Newton English and Classical School," in the Park Block building. This school was discontinued in 1907, when Miss Rosenkrans accepted the principalship of Washington College, a girls school, at Washington, Pa.

The Newton Business College was conducted in the same building for about ten years by Fred O. Hopkins. This school was removed to Dover in 1909, where it is now continuing its work.

WATER AND SEWER SYSTEMS.

Supplied from a lake which lies in such a position among the valleys on the top of the Sparta mountains that pollution is almost impossible, Newton has one of the best water systems of any town or city in the State. The source, Morris Lake, is fed by sparkling springs and is slightly over 280 feet higher than the town. From the lake to the town runs a ten inch main, capable of carrying 1,250,000 gallons every twenty-four hours. There are about twenty miles of main from the lake and through the town. The average pressure is from 100 to 120 pounds. To add to the security of the users of the town supply, the lake is guarded by a caretaker who daily patrols the waters in a motor boat.

After the question of a municipal water supply had been discussed at various times, an election was called and held on the 26th of July, 1894, to determine whether or not the town should be bonded for the building of a municipal plant. The proposition, which included the question of bonding the town for the sum of $60,000 carried by a vote of 507 for to 209 against, a majority of 298. On July 6 of that year, the town committee appointed Hiram C. Clark, Rev. Alexander Craig and Andrew J. Van Blarcom as members of the water commission. The commission organized on July 9, by electing Mr. Clark, president, Dr. Craig, secretary, and Mr. Van Blarcom, treasurer. Lewis C. Tribus, of New York, was employed as chief engineer and later Andrew H. Konkle was employed as assistant engineer. It was found that $60,000 would not build the plant desired and a second election was ordered for September 25, 1894. At this election an additional $50,000 was appropriated, and the town committee was authorized to issue bonds for that amount.

Morris Lake had been selected as the best source of supply. On November 13, 1894, the owners, the New Jersey Iron & Mining Company offered to sell to the town 350 acres of land, which included the waters of the lake, for the sum of $16,000. The offer was rejected and an agreement entered into whereby the town was to have all the water which could be run through a ten inch main, and sufficient land was purchased on which to erect a standpipe and build a house for a caretaker. No arrangements were made with the owners of water rights along the stream which flows from the lake before the building of the system was begun and the town found itself involved in a series of costly suits. Before these were all settled and the plant completed, it was found that the total cost would be about $125,000.

In 1912 the Town Committee, believing that it would be to the interests of the town, purchased sufficient land in and around the lake to give the town almost absolute control from the Wharton Steel Company at a cost of $25,000. Other small parcels have been purchased from various owners until the Town of Newton now owns about 360 acres of land and water.

In 1906 a reservoir was completed near High street, within the town limits, with a capacity of 8,000,000 gallons, the cost being approximately $10,000. The total cost of the plant to date, including this reservoir, has been $136,465.81.

There are at present 130 bonds in existence. The present members of the Water Commission and the other officials connected with the plant are as follows: President, Ruther-

CONTINUED ON PAGE 51.

ST. JOSEPH'S.

Rev. Michael J. Donnelly.

The first Catholic service was held by Rev. Richard Bolger at Newton on November 25, 1821; from that date until 1854, the Catholics of the county were entirely dependent upon visiting clergymen from Dover, from Madison, from New York, or more distant points. Among these missionaries, was the present Bishop of Rochester, the Rt. Rev. B. J. McQuaid. Catholics were to be found at Deckertown, Wawayanda, Montague, Hamburg, Vernon, Stanhope, Andover, Newton and as the mines and furnaces developed, at Ogdensburg and Franklin. In Newton, they worshipped at the house of Edward McCormick on Spring street and the home of Francis Graey, then living on Church street. In 1854, Father McMahon was appointed to the parish of Sussex county. At that time many Catholics were living at Andover, and Father McMahon hesitated whether to locate a church at that point or at Newton; he finally decided in favor of Newton. A church building was erected which is said to have been without pews, unplastered, thinly painted, and rough boarded without. In 1861 Father McMahon was succeeded by Rev. Edward McCosker, who in the nineteen years he was here, saw the church rapidly grow. He had the courage in 1870 to begin the building of the present brick church on Halsted street.

The edifice was completed and dedicated in 1871 by Rt. Rev. James R. Bayley, Bishop of Newark. The cost of the building was $19,000. A few years later a handsome parochial residence was erected on Elm street.

The present pastor is Father Michael J. Donnelly, having been appointed to the Newton parish by Rt. Rev. John J. O'Connor, Bishop of Newark, on December 1, 1909. He was ordained a priest June 4, 1898, and was for a time assistant at St. James church, New York.

Interior of St. Joseph's Church.

WATER SUPPLY—CONTINUED FROM PAGE 50.
ford Tuttle; Secretary, Horton M. Beegle; Treasurer, Harvey Snook; Clerk, Ackerson J. Mackerley; Town Plumber, Frank H. Bittenbender.

The Newton sewer system was begun October 17, 1905, and put in operation the following year, at a cost of about $100,000. The plant is in charge of the Water Commission. The plant is in two sections, the Clinton street division and the Sparta avenue division. The depth of the sewer beds is three feet six inches, and the filters cover about four acres, the amount of sewage treated averaging 250,000 gallons per day. Morford Smith is superintendent of the sewer system.

NEWTON IN 1800

Beginning with Main street, or "the road to New York," the buildings are designated by their numbers, as follows:

1. Bate's tavern, now site of Ryerson and Ewald buildings.
2. The Conover building, now site of Dennis Library.
3. Nathan Drake property, once occupied by Job S. Halsted.
4-5. Thomas C. Ryerson's house and law office.
6. Old Academy, now Newman property.
7. Gottleib house; afterward owned by Samuel Lane.
8. Job S. Halsted's law office.
9. Large house shown on east side (probably through lack of skill on the part of the original designer) was located on west side, facing Baptist church.
10. House owned by John H. Hall, originally built by Joseph Y. Miller.
11. A half log and half frame house, on site of W. M. Clark's lot.
12. House owned by Citizen Warbasse.
13-14. Episcopal rectory and school of Rev. C. Dunn.
15. Property of Col. Pemberton.
16. Supposed to be Phillips house, on Spring street. At time of William Drake's earliest remembrance there were but three log houses below this, on the same street.
17-18. Store of Bonnell M. Haggerty and small building adjacent.
19. Residence of Jeanette Morrow.
20-21. Bassett's tavern, afterwards Brittin's, and finally Cochran's.
22-23. House of Nathaniel Pettit, occupied by John Pettit.
24. John Feeny's store.
25. Occupied by John Harris, brewer and baker.
26. John Savacool's residence.
27. John Vandine's residence.
28. Presbyterian church, the only building on Church street, and only church edifice in town.
29. William T. Anderson's law office.
30-31. Residence of William T. Anderson. The two wings constituted the original structure in days of the Revolution.
32. Building occupied by Amos Bassett, now site of M. E. church.
33-34. Old County Hotel, occupied by Isaac Bassett.
35. Old County Clerk's Office.
36. The Court House, rear view.
37. Dwelling of Sarah Pemberton, later occupied by John Rorbach and William Drake.
38. Samuel Rorbach's residence and harness shop.
39. McCarter's store house.
40-41. Ephraim Green's dwelling.
42. Supposed to be Crossed Keys tavern.
43. John McCarter property.
44. George H. McCarter's house, afterward owned by David Thompson. The brick for this house said to have been made on site of old Methodist church, on Division street.
45. Log house on site of Foster property, built by John Eueh; after occupied by John Vanness, sexton of Presbyterian church; then by Polly Kerr, who sold cake and beer in the time when people did not go home between morning and afternoon church services.
46. Dunlevy house.
47. Occupied by ——— Crane; afterward by Joanna Hill.
48. Judge Johnson's law office.
49. Residence of Judge John Johnson.
50. Residence and office of Dr. Hunt.

Below the Court House the map fails to show an old store house, on site of present jail, built by Judge John Holmes, and afterward occupied by Oakley Anderson; it being the spot near where The Register was born, and where the late Edward C. Moore began his business career. Also, a log house owned by John Trusdell, and probably part of the old building adjoining residence of Mrs. S. J. Van Campen. Another was the Drake homestead, which stood near the present Sussex shoe factory. These, Mr. Drake says, comprised the buildings of Newton, as he remembers them, and by tradition. The blank spaces unnumbered on Main street represent a barn and wagon house on the Anderson property.

The first brewery in Newton was owned by Waterman & Daub, and was located on the site of L. Van Blarcom's barn.

1840   1914

The Sussex County Mutual Insurance Company

On the first day of February, 1913, this Company began its 73rd year of continuous and beneficent service.

OFFICERS.

President,
William P. Coursen,
Fredon, N. J.

Vice President,
David C. Truex,
Beemerville, N. J.

Secretary and Treasurer,
Andrew J. VanBlarcom,
Newton, N. J.

EXECUTIVE COMMITTE.

William P. Coursen,
David C. Truex,
Nathan H. Hart.

WILLIAM P. COURSEN.

DAVID C. TRUEX.

The Sussex County Mutual Insurance Company was formed by act of the New Jersey Legislature, February 22, 1840.

The members of the first Board of Directors: John H. Hall, Isaac Bunnell, John Bell, Pierson Hurd, John Strader, Walter L. Shee, Robert F. Shafer, James Evans, Andrew A. Smalley, Zachariah H. Price, Joseph Northrup, Jr., George H. McCarter, Whitfield H. Johnson, Nathan Smith, Nathaniel Drake, Reuben F. Randolph, Isaac V. Coursen, Richard R. Morris, Elias La'Hommedieu.

Mr. John H. Hall was the first president. Mr. Hall founded The Sussex Register in Newton in 1813. The subsequent presidents of the Company have been: Robert H. McCarter, Jonathan Whittaker, Dr. Franklin Smith, Thomas Lawrence and William P. Coursen.

Whitfield H. Johnson was the first Secretary and Treasurer of the Company and held office for 20 years, when he resigned to accept the office of Secretary of State of New Jersey. The subsequent Secretaries have been: Dr. Franklin Smith, Daniel S. McCarter, Obadiah Pellet, John T. Stewart, Charles P. Rorbach, Peter S. Decker, Martin E. Hough, Israel L. Hallock and A. J. VanBlarcom.

Mr. William P. Coursen has been president since 1893. His sound and conservative judgment and the esteem and confidence which he commands among all who know him have contributed in a great degree to the success of the Company.

In 1893, at the time of Mr. Coursen's election to the presidency, the value of property under the protection of the Company was $1,616,348 and the Deposit Notes covering the same was $47,451.

On November 1st of the present year, the value of the property under its protection was $3,723,800, and the Deposit Notes covering same $153,199.

The Office of the Company is Room No. 6, Park Block, Newton, New Jersey.

An Examiner of the Department of Banking and Insurance states, "This Company gives its policyholders safe insurance at a comparatively low cost."

DIRECTORS.

William P. Coursen, Fredon, N. J.
Watson R. Ayers, Andover, N. J.
James M. Stoll, Hainesville, N. J.
Martin Rosenkrans, Newton, N. J.
John N. Decker, Andover, N. J.
David C. Truex, Beemerville, N. J.
John Ayers, Andover, N. J.
John H. Sutton, Monroe, N. J.
Richard D. Wallace, Vernon, N. J.
Benjamin D. Simmons, Sussex, N. J.
Wm. H. Dalrymple, Branchville, N. J.
Lester T. Smith, Layton, N. J.
Nathan H. Hart, Newton, N. J.
Frank Smith, Flatbrookville, N. J.
Heman A. Timbrell, Stanhope, N. J.
Obadiah VanHorn, Stillwater, N. J.
A. J. VanBlarcom, Newton, N. J.

ANDREW J. VAN BLARCOM.

NATHAN H. HART.

THE SUSSEX NATIONAL BANK

The Sussex National Bank of Newton, N. J., is one of the oldest banking institutions in the United States, having been chartered as a State Bank January 31st, 1818. The first Board of Directors, elected June 18, 1818, was composed of Daniel Stuart, William T. Anderson, Job S. Halsted, James Stoll, Grant Fitch, Ephriam Green, Jr., John Gustin, John Armstrong, David Ford, Gershom Coursen and David Ryerson, all men of note.

Daniel Stuart was elected President and Samuel D. Morford, Cashier. The Bank began business August 17th, 1818. was succeeded as cashier by his son Theodore, who held that office until he was elected President October 24th, 1902, succeeding David R. Hull, deceased. Theodore Simonson succeeded Theodore Morford, who died May 26th, 1908.

The Bank was first located on Main street, where Daniel E. Sutton now resides, until 1823, when, in order to be in the business part of the town, the building on the corner of Church and High street was erected and occupied. In 1891 it moved to its present building, corner of Spring and Main streets, within a short distance of its starting point.

The first dividend of 3½ per cent. upon a capital of $27,300 was declared January 17th, 1820. The capital was increased to $41,000 in 1833 and to $67,500 in 1837 by assessment, and in 1849 an extra dividend raised the capital to $135,000 and another stock dividend in 1858 increased the capital stock to $200,000, at which it has since remained.

It became a National Bank March 9th, 1865.

The Presidents of the bank since the death of Daniel Stuart have been Ephriam Green, David Ryerson, David Thompson, David R. Hull, Theodore Morford, Theodore Simonson. Samuel D. Morford, who died April 11th, 1865,

It has been in business 95 years.

It has never stopped an instant during business hours.

It has a Surplus Fund, including Capital and Liability of Stockholders, of more than SIX HUNDRED and EIGHTY THOUSAND DOLLARS ($680,000) SOLELY FOR THE PROTECTION OF DEPOSITORS, ALL OF WHICH MUST BE LOST BEFORE ITS DEPOSITORS COULD LOSE ONE CENT.

It pays as liberal a rate of interest on Time Deposits as SAFETY WARRANTS.

1818 Sussex National Bank, Newton, N. J. 1914

INTERIOR OF BANKING HOUSE

Capital,
$200,000

Surplus & Profit,
$280,000

THEODORE SIMONSON,
President.

L. M. MORFORD,
Vice Pres. and Cashier.

CHARLES S. STEELE,
Asst. Cashier

THEODORE SIMONSON, President

DIRECTORS:

Andrew J. VanBlarcom,
Theodore Simonson,
Nathan H. Hart,
Luther Hill,
William W. Roe,
John Wills,
Lewis M. Morford,
Henry C. Kelsey,
Rolland T. Hull,
William H. Earl,
Walter F. Whittemore.

THE H. W. MERRIAM SHOE COMPANY

A MANUFACTURING CONCERN THAT HAS MADE NEWTON FAMOUS—OCCUPIES 90,000 SQUARE FEET OF FLOOR SPACE—GIVES EMPLOYMENT TO 550 PEOPLE—ANNUAL PAY ROLL $275,000—SALES OVER $1,000,000.00 EACH YEAR.

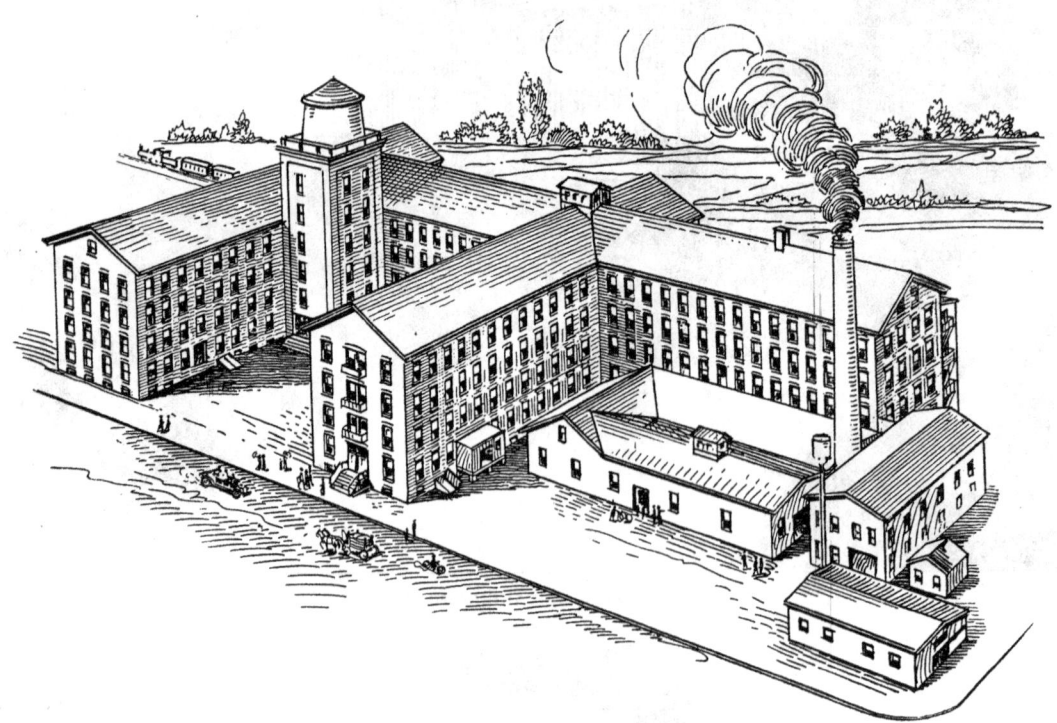

In the year 1864 the following item appeared in one of the newspapers:

"Messrs. Hall, Southwick & Co., and Mr. H. W. Merriam carried on a most extensive business, the two establishments furnishing, it is supposed, one million of pairs per annum. Both had reduced their stocks on hand pretty well when Lee's surrender took place. Prices are fully as good as they were a year ago, with labor at about the same rates and a decrease in the cost of materials. Indeed, the business has probably never been more prosperous than now. There is an enormous stock of quartermasters' stores on hand in New York, Philadelphia and Cincinnati, probably twenty millions worth in this city alone, if we include knapsacks and other accoutrements, as well as shoes and clothing."

Mr. Merriam, whose name appears in this notice, was in the year mentioned, manufacturing shoes in New York city. Recognizing the advantage of manufacturing in a small town where space and fresh air were more plentiful, he was induced through the efforts of an organization of business men to remove his business to Newton, and a new factory building was erected in 1873 on the present site, which forms a part of the plant now occupied by The H. W. Merriam Shoe Company. The records show that the first pair of shoes made in this factory were finished on June 12th of the same year, which date placed Newton on the map as one of the industrial towns of the State.

The business was started in a moderate way with only fifty employees on the pay roll and a daily output of 150 pairs. As the majority of successful enterprises start from small beginnings, this was no exception, and because of the superior quality and style of shoes manufactured, a foothold was secured and the business gradually increased. Mr. Merriam as the sole owner of the business, was ably assisted by Mr. W. L. Dutcher, who was a most efficient business man, and to him was assigned the responsibility of selling the product, and Mr. W. H. Palmer acted in the capacity of superintendent. Through the combined efforts of these men, the business continued to expand and in the year 1882 a stock company was organized under the name of the H. W. Merriam Shoe Company, with a cash capital of $80,000.00. In 1889, the company had outgrown its capital and it was increased to $200,000.00 and Mr. Merriam was made President and Treasurer and Mr. Dutcher, Vice President and Secretary. After this reorganization, Mr. Merriam continued to give the business more or less attention, but on account of failing health, he was obliged to retire from active management, and his death occurred on October 26th, 1900.

At this juncture it seems most fitting to say, that Mr. Merriam was a man not only in close touch with his own business which had much to do with its success, but he was continually looking out for the welfare of others. During his life time he made three cash distributions to his employees which totaled more than $18,000.00 besides giving largely of his means to the churches and all other good causes, and it can be truly said, that the world is better for his having lived in it.

After the death of Mr. Merriam, a large part of the responsibility fell upon Mr. Dutcher, who was well fitted for the task, but the management was shared with Mr. John Tozer, who had been associated with the company since 1895, and in whom Mr. Dutcher found a faithful assistant.

A reorganization followed on May 6th, 1901, and Mr. Dutcher was elected President and Treasurer, Mr. John Tozer,

Vice President, and J. E. Warbasse, Secretary. The management continued along well defined lines with conservative but progressive methods, which are sure to bring success to any business venture.

On March 26th, 1901, the factory of the Sussex Shoe Co. was purchased and refitted to manufacture a line of shoes which were in great demand, but through lack of room could not be made at the main factory. This plant, which was known as Factory B, was under the supervision of E. Merriam Dutcher, and continued in operation until 1910. It became apparent to the company that it would be advantageous in many ways to have the entire business under one roof, and in 1910 a large addition was made to the main plant, sufficient in size to carry out the proposed plan of consolidation. Factory B building remained closed until January 1st, 1913, when it was leased to The Standard Towel Company, who are now the occupants.

There were no important events to chronicle in the affairs of this company until the death of Mr. Dutcher, which was on February 8th, 1908. This loss was keenly felt not only by the officers and stockholders of the company, but by the community in general. At the reorganization which followed Mr. Dutcher's death, Mr. John Tozer was elected President, E. Merriam Dutcher, Vice President, G. L. Dutcher, 2nd Vice President, E. W. Merriam, Treasurer, J. E. Warbasse, Secretary.

No further changes to note until the death of Mr. Tozer, which occurred on September 27th, 1910. On October 19th, 1910, a meeting of the stockholders of the company was held and the following officers were elected:

President..................E. W. Merriam
Vice President.............G. L. Dutcher
2nd Vice President.........H. F. Merriam
Treasurer..................E. Merriam Dutcher
Secretary..................J. E. Warbasse

The present officers are all active in the business except H. F. Merriam, and because of the many years of association with the business, they are well qualified to meet the exigencies which are continually arising in a business of this magnitude. Many additions have been made to the plant and it now contains 90,000 square feet of floor space. The building is equipped with modern machinery and all best known methods are used in the manufacturing of shoes. To meet all requirements the equipment includes for fire protection, a sprinkler system, also fire alarm signals and an organized fire department on each floor. For the convenience of the managers and heads of departments, a private telephone system is installed and in fact no expense has been spared to make the plant equal in all respects, to the larger factory buildings in other states.

The actual output of the concern is 3,500 pairs every working day in the year, 550 employees are on the pay roll and the State statistics show that more hands are employed by this company than any other similar industry in New Jersey. The volume of business annually is in excess of $1,000,000.00 and the present business year, which ends November 1st, will show larger sales than any previous year. The entire product is sold direct to the retailer and nine salesmen are employed, who cover their respective territories twice each year, and in nearly all the larger towns and most of the smaller ones, can be found some dealer who is selling Merriam's Shoes. The line of shoes manufactured comprises a variety of 450 different styles in Welt, McKay and Turn, which commence with Infants and end with sizes for Growing Girls. It is well known among the shoe retailers that no other line quite fills the place in a shoe department like Merriam's shoes, and scarcely a day passes that the mails fail to bring one or more requests from dealers in all sections, to forward samples or have representative to call and show the line.

Strangers visiting the town are much amazed to see the well kept homes owned by the employees of The H. W. Merriam Shoe Company, which denote thrift and prosperity, and from the fact that a majority of the employees have been with the company from five to thirty years, is convincing proof of the harmony which exists between employees and employers.

In conclusion, we cannot refrain from saying, that The H. W. Merriam Shoe Company has not only done much to make Newton what it is in reputation, but rather what the town is in fact.

Mrs. J. Beatty
MILLINERY
139 Spring Street
OPP. HOTEL WALDMERE   -   NEWTON, N. J

THE NEWTON TRUST COMPANY
NEWTON, NEW JERSEY

OFFICERS.

LEVI H. MORRIS, President.

BRUNO HOOD, Vice President.

EDWIN W. MERRIAM, Vice President.

LOUIS A. DALRYMPLE, Secretary-Treasurer.

FLOYD C. DEVORE, Assistant Secretary-Treasurer.

DIRECTORS.

CLARENCE G. APPLETON,
Comptroller Fidelity Trust Co., Newark, N. J.

UZAL H. McCARTER,
President Fidelity Trust Co., Newark, N. J.

J. W. C. CARBER,
Merchant, Newton, N. J.

EDWIN W. MERRIAM,
President H. W. Merriam Shoe Co., Newton, N. J.

DR. BRUNO HODD,
Physician, Newton, N. J.

LEVI H. MORRIS,
Counselor at Law, President of the Company.

EDWARD KANOUSE,
Treasurer of The Prudential Insurance Co. of America.

JAMES H. SHACKLETON,
Secretary and Treasurer Fidelity Trust Co., Newark, N. J.

The Newton Trust Company was opened for business April 1st, 1902, having temporary quarters in the Park Block store, during the erection of its present building, at 30 Park Place. A cash capital of one hundred thousand dollars was paid in, and a surplus exceeding fifty thousand has since been accumulated. Total deposits have grown until they are now in excess of one million dollars.

The advent of the institution inaugurated a new era in banking in this section of the State, it being the pioneer of Sussex county to pay interest to its depositors. Although established less than twelve years ago, it has developed into one of our largest banking institutions, ranking third in total assets, and its rapid growth is due in part to the fact that it successfully launched this co-operative system. This movement was followed by other banks, and to-day all Sussex county Banks are uniform in this respect, except as to rates of interest and dates of crediting. Though criticised more or less twelve years ago, the plan has proven successful in "Old Sussex," as it had previously in counties south of us, and our people have profited to the extent of nearly a million dollars, the Trust Company alone having distributed over two hundred thousand dollars in interest to its depositors. In addition the saving habit has been encouraged, our people have grown more thrifty, business has been stimulated by the increased supply of money, and it is conceded that we have all been benefited, directly or indirectly.

During the early years of the Trust Company, 3½ per cent. per annum was paid on Time Deposits, but opportunities afforded through its connection with the Fidelity Trust Company of Newark, New Jersey, the largest and strongest banking institution in the State, with which it became affiliated during 1910, it was enabled to advance the rate to 4 per cent., which has been successfully maintained since December of that year. Interest is reckoned from the first of every month and is credited and compounded four times a year, on the first days of January, April, July and October.

On Commercial accounts, 2 per cent. per annum is paid, based on the average daily balance when in excess of $100, and the advantage of receiving interest on Checking Accounts has been strongly demonstrated to its depositors. The State of New Jersey makes use of the Company as a depository, and is paid 2 per cent. also, the established rate on State Funds.

About two years ago, extensive improvements were made upon the vault, a new three ton set of individual lock boxes installed, and the Company enjoys the distinction of having one of the best equipped Safe Deposit Departments in the community. The vault is constructed of concrete and fire brick, and with its drill proof steel lining and massive doors, absolute protection is afforded. The boxes rent from $2 per annum up, according to size.

In addition to the Banking and Safe Deposit departments a Trust Department is maintained which shows great possibilities in this county. The Company is chartered to serve in numerous capacities of trust, acting as executor, administrator, trustee, assignee or receiver, and as double security, it is required to furnish bonds like the individual, but differs in the fact that a trust company never dies, hence it is rightly termed "An ideal trust official."

The Directors of the Company are successful and experienced business men, many of whom are trained and expert bankers.

The Company is now one of our best equipped financial institutions and the growth of its business is strongly indicative of the confidence placed in its management and conservative policies.

Hon. Theodore Simonson

Conceded the leading lawyer at the Sussex County Bar, and one of the ablest members of the profession in the State. He was born in Vernon township April 26, 1848, son of Thomas T. and Mary Hynard Simonson. Educated in Warwick Academy, the Collegiate Institute and Poughkeepsie, N. Y. Read law with Hon. Robert Hamilton and Hon. Thomas Anderson, of Newton. Admitted as an attorney in February, 1876, and in 1883 was made a Counsellor and also admitted in U. S. Courts. Began practice in Newton, where he has ever since resided. His honesty, ability and industry soon made an impression, and in a short time he had won the confidence of the public and the Bar. Governor Ludlow appointed him Prosecutor of the Pleas. Governor Green reappointed him and Governor Werts appointed him in 1893 for a third term. His duties in the office were marked by impartiality and signal ability. His law business grew rapidly, and embraced much of the important litigation of this section. In addition he has taken a keen interest in civic and political matters. In 1892 he was a Presidential Elector and cast his vote for Grover Cleveland. In 1905 was made a member of the State Board of Equalization of Taxes by Governor Stokes, and held the position till 1911, in which service he became distinguished for his fairness and wide knowledge of affairs.

Politically he is a Democrat, but above all he is a citizen whose interest in the community and his fellow man rise above and extend beyond party obligations.

He is president of the Newton Library Association, President of the Sussex National Bank, Junior Warden of Christ Episcopal church, and is identified with every movement for the advancement of the county. Has resided in Newton over forty years, where he is regarded as one of our best types. Courteous, able, and of the highest character he has the esteem of all who know him.

March 10, 1881, he was united in marriage to Miss Fannie Townsend, of Newton. Their residence is one of the pretty homes of our city. Fraternally Mr. Simonson is a Mason, member of Harmony Lodge and Baldwin Chapter.

Residence of Hon. Theodore Simonson, 63 High Street, Newton, N. J.

Soldiers Monument, Newton.

Public Square, Newton, N. J.

McMurtrie Memorial Fountain.

Morris Lake.

Newton Public School.

Old Market Scene.

James E. Baldwin.

Entrance to Newton Cemetery.

Court House and County Park.

Drake's Pond.

Rutherford Tuttle,

JOHN ILIFF.

The subject of this sketch is engaged in the Furniture and Undertaking business, also sells a large number of pianos to pleased customers.

He has just completed a new brick building of three stories on Spring street, in the center of Newton, where he resides and carries on business. Educated in Newton Collegiate Institute and Coleman Business College of Newark. He is taking an active interest in public school affairs and is president of Board of Education, also active member of volunteer fireman. Member of M. E. church and one of its trustees. Stands high in the community as business man and public spirited citizen.

JUSTICE J. E. WHITNEY.

Our Police Magistrate, to which place he was appointed in October, 1913. Born in Hoboken, N. J., May 29th, 1844. Served in the Civil War in the 47th New York National Guard. Is serving his third term as Justice of the Peace, and while a resident of New York State, served many years in the same position. Stands very high as a citizen and town official.

NEWTON EMBROIDERY WORKS.

This enterprise was established in Newton seven years ago. The proprietor is Mr. J. Hermann. The plant is a modern three story brick structure of ample size and well appointed. The business is that of manufacturing embroideries and laces. Their market is New York, where they maintain offices in the Flat Iron Building. They give employment to forty people, and the industry is one of the important as well as beneficial to our city, as the pay roll is large and regular.

MARTIN WARD, JR.

This gentleman is one of Sussex county's successful business men. His business of that of a grower of Cut Flowers, Potted Plants, all kinds of Nursery Stock, Shrubbery and Vegetable Plants. He is also an expert and artistic landscape gardner and a designer of cemetery work and funeral mementoes.

Mr. Ward's green houses and offices are located at 15 Foster street, Newton, N. J. He began business in 1904. Has a large and growing trade. Has just constructed a new green house and has everything up-to-date. Can furnish anything in floral work at the shortest notice. Is the largest designer of funeral work in the county. He also furnishes green vegetables the year round.

THE DECORATIVE ART AND LADIES' SHOP.
15 Main Street, Newton, N. J.

One of Newton's unique and popular places, noted for its rare collection of Art Needle Work, Embroideries, Painted Novelties, Laces, Dainties in Neckwear, Stamping in endless designs, Ladies' Furnishings, Gift Articles and Worsteds for embroidery work, and such a splendid assortment of ladies' goods not found in other stores. Madame Anna D. Longcor, a genius in her line, is the proprietor. She established the store six years ago and enjoys a large and growing trade.

LEO. MANN.

Newton's well known and successful manufacturer of and dealer in Cigars and Tobacco. Embarked in business four years ago, in the old stand, 99 Spring street, which has been a tobacco store for more than 75 years. Mr. Mann has the only exclusive shop of the kind in the county. His "99" is one of the best nickel cigars on the market, and in high favor with smokers. Mr. Mann has an up-to-date store and everything for the smokers.

SPRINGDALE MILLS.

This is one of the oldest mills in the county. It is still a burr mill. It has been in operation more than a century. The present proprietor, Mr. S. B. Hendershot, who does custom grinding, runs a saw and cider mill, dealer in all kinds of feed, grain, and chicken "Scratch." Deliveries in Newton daily. The mill is located on the Andover pike, 2 miles south of Newton. Mr. Hendershot is a native of the county.

THE STAR STUDIO
M. F. Wintermute, Proprietor,
ARTISTIC PHOTOGRAPHY

Photographs, Crayon Portraits, Views and Enlargements, Amateur Finishing, Photo Jewelry, Picture Frames, Picture Mats, Card Board, French Picture Glass, Glass and Mats cut square, round or oval; Picture Wire, Hooks, etc.

47 Spring Street   NEWTON, N. J.

W. A. STOREY
Dealer in Crockery and Glassware
166 Spring St.,   Phone 181
NEWTON, N. J.
A Specialty of Novelties and Holiday Goods.

JOHN KALLBERG
MERCHANT TAILOR
Cleaning, Pressing and Repairing.
114 Spring St.,   NEWTON, N. J.

HENRY DAVID COUSE.

Born in Newton, N. J., January, 1860, attended private schools of Miss Maggie Anderson and the late Agnes McCarter until the opening of our present public school; leaving public high school attended Newton Collegiate Institute for two years. In 1879 entered business in the employ of the late Samuel Johnson, remaining five years. Then worked several months in a department store in Newark, N. J. Being of a mechanical trend decided to try a business where this trait would help to lead to his success and entered the employ of the late W. D. Wright to learn the jewelry, watchmaking and optical business; leaving his employ commenced business for himself January, 1887, on High street and continued in that location until April, 1892, when he moved to the present location, 79 Spring street. Prior to the time of this removal, feeling the need of a better knowledge in optics, spent some time in New York taking a course of lectures and practical instruction in fitting of glasses and adjustment of same, and this has been a prominent and successful part of his business to the present time, and hundreds who read this anniversary edition of The Sussex Register, will read through glasses fitted by the subject of this sketch.

Served on Board of Education three years, and on Town Committee 1910 to 1912, inclusive, 1910 and 1911 having charge of the street department; 1912 acting as chairman of committee. Mr. Couse is one of our enterprising citizens and enjoys the confidence of all.

HILLSIDE HOME.

This is one of Newton's important as well as attractive institutions. The Hillside is a rest retreat for convalescents, and as such has all the charms of a home with the advantages of a modern sanitarium. The Home is located at 79 High street, a choice residential location of Newton. It is equipped with every accessory for comfort, electric lights, baths and all modern conveniences. The Home was established eight years ago by Mrs. S. V. Straley and enjoys a wide popularity. The capacity is taxed to the utmost, usually, and guests find rest, relief, and complete health restoration under the care of the manager, and the board of physicians connected with the place. The food is wholesome, fresh from the farms.

MRS. L. H. PIERSON.

Dealer in Staple and Fancy Groceries at 78 Sparta avenue, Newton, N. J. Established the business fifteen years ago, has a fine store and enjoys a large and growing trade.

WILLIAM H. NICHOLLS.

The subject of this sketch is one of Sussex county's well known citizens and a prominent business man of Newton. He learned the printer's trade, and for twenty-one years was with the New Jersey Herald. Is active in Democratic politics, and enjoys the distinction of having served on the Town Committee, as Chairman, Town Treasurer and Custodian of School Funds all at the same time. In 1889 he established his present business at 71 Spring street, where he has a large stock of fine China and Cut Glass, Novelties, Sporting Goods, Toys, Stationery, Books and Magazines. He also has a modern, well equipped job printing plant where he is prepared to execute all styles of fine printing, engraving and visiting cards.

Mr. Nicholls enjoys a large and growing trade. He takes a keen interest in civic, social, religious affairs, and for ten years has been a Vestryman in Christ Episcopal church.

JOHN C. LOSEY.

A rising member of the Sussex County Bar and proprietor of an extensive General Insurance Agency. Born June 5, 1882, on a farm in Stillwater township. Is a son of William and Charlotte Losey. Graduated from the Newton High School in 1900. Read law under Levi H. Morris. Admitted to the Bar in 1907. Has held a position in the postal service since 1900. Married Miss Jessie G. Roe, daughter of Charles Roe, in 1907. Is Worshipful Master Harmony Lodge, F. & A. M., No. 8; Assistant Superintendent of the Presbyterian Sunday school. Has a rapidly growing practice and stands high in the community.

Phone No. 76.　　　　　　　　Opp. Fountain, Spring St.
Established 1887.
A Good Record for Grocers.
Agents for Columbia Flour.

The flour that satisfies. Makes more bread to the barrel than any other brand of flour on the market. Therefore the cheapest to use.

MEXICAN BLEND COFFEE.

A high grade Coffee at a low figure for cup quality and price can not be equalled. Just a trial pound will convince you of its merits.

VAN CAMPEN BROS.

CHAS. GRAEY

HARNESS AND SADDLERY GOODS

HAND MADE HARNESS

OVER HOWELL'S HARDWARE STORE

NEWTON, N. J.

At the age of eighteen, when most boys are still playing ball, the subject of this sketch was making his own way in the world by teaching school in the rural districts during the winter and helping on his father's farm for his summer vacation.

Later he decided to make teaching his vocation and attended the Trenton Normal. Here he came under the instruction of that noted penman, D. H. Farley, who instilled in him the principles of penmanship so thoroughly that his name to-day stands for Penmanship and Fountain Pens by all who know him. He taught school eighteen years, being principal at Lafayette, Andover, Hamburg and Pequannock. As a teacher he was successful. Many of his pupils became teachers. As many as forty teachers in this county received their first teachers' certificate under his instructions.

Ten years ago he entered the business world and at present is conducting a Stationery and Sporting Goods Bazaar, known throughout this county as the Busy Store. The name is well placed, as it is one of the busy spots in this town. However busy, he now and then looks over the political field and is in touch with the politics of the county.

F. C. BURHARD

HARNESS AND SADDLERY

Hand made Harness a specialty. All kinds of Horse Furnishings and Repairing.

No. 11 Spring Street,　　　Opposite Hotel Newton,
NEWTON, N. J.

FRED BAYER
Maker of
Awnings and Tents, Canvas Wagon and Engine Covers and Flags
Professional Bunting Decorator.
Tents for Sale and for Rent
Pleased to Show Samples and Give Estimates.
Sussex Telephone No. 104　　　　NEWTON, N. J.

Established 1881.

For 32 years the following lines of goods have been sold by us: Adriance Buckeye Harvesting Machinery, New Way Gasoline Engines, Doylestown Threshers, South Bend Plows, Planet, Jr. Horse Harrows and Cultivators, sherwin-Williams Paints, H. B. Smith Co. Steam and Hot Water Heaters, Fuller & Warren "Stewart" Stoves, all "best by test." Full line of all kinds hardware sold here.

W. F. HOWELL　　　　　　　Newton, N. J.

LAUNDRY.

High Grade Work.
Quick Service.
SUSSEX LAUNDRY,
Telephone 147,　　　　　　　NEWTON, N. J.

ROOF'S LIVERY

The Oldest and Best Equipped Stables in Sussex County

123½ SPRING STREET

NEWTON, New Jersey

SAFE, STYLISH and FINE ROADSTERS

CAREFUL and ATTENTIVE DRIVERS

New and Up-to-date Rubber Tire Vehicles

Handsome Coaches for all Social Functions

Also for Sale Large Variety of Wagons, Buggies and Surries

James Roof, Proprietor.

HART & ILIFF COMPANY

NEWTON, N. J. - LONG DISTANCE PHONE 43

N. H. HART, President.

The place to buy Coal, Feed, Rough and Planed Lumber, Doors, Sash, Blinds, Lead, Oil and Sun-Proof Paints House Finishings and Builders' Supplies.

Inspection Invited. Right Prices, and Satisfaction Guaranteed.

MISS EMMA C. STRADER
MILLINERY
Tailored and Trimmed Hats
The newest and smartest designs
Your last season's hat cheerfully remodeled.

MRS. HARRIET E. DEMAREST,
ARTISTIC MILLINERY

The Latest Modes, Trimmings, Feathers
and all Accessories.

Imported and Domestic Novelties. Your
patronage requested and inspection
Invited.

17 SPRING STREET, NEWTON, N. J.

WATCHES
DIAMONDS
CLOCKS
JEWELRY
SILVERWARE
CUT GLASS

THOMAS E. MURRAY

JEWELER AND GRADUATE OPTICIAN
55 SPRING ST. - NEWTON, N. J.

M. KLEPACKY

LADIES' AND GENTS' TAILOR

201 SPRING STREET - NEWTON, N. J.

Established 1887   Incorporated 1904.
MILLIKEN-KELLAM CO.,
Successors to George A. Williams Co. and John P. Milliken Co.

Manufacturers of High Grade Fly Screens for windows, doors and porches. Fine cabinet work, mill work and specialties.

NEWTON, - - - - - NEW JERSEY.

THOMAS SMALE
MERCHANT TAILOR.

9 Spring Street, Newton, N. J.

Suits to order $14 up.   Cleaning, Pressing, Repairing.
Prompt Service and Satisfaction Assured.

MISS MAUDE L. KISHPAUGH
A COMPLETE LINE OF MILLINERY
Prices to suit all
Inspection invited.

255 Spring street,   Next door to Hart & Iliff Co.,
NEWTON, N. J.

A gift to please those you would favor with a mark of your esteem—your portrait.
Nothing could be more appropriate.
Make the opportunity to-day.

THE JACKSON STUDIO,
67 Spring Street, NEWTON, N. J.

J. O. BISSELL
Dealer in

FANCY GROCERIES

Provisions, Feed, Flour and Grain.

Sole Agents for
CHASE & SANBORN'S FAMOUS TEAS and COFFEES.

We carry the following well known brands of Canned
and Packed Goods—
Blue Knot Coffee
White Rose Brand
Mistletoe Brand

J. O. BISSELL,   178 Spring St.,   NEWTON, N. J.

Improved Machinery   Latest Type Faces
LEWIS J. KISHPAUGH
Ideal Job Printer
All Orders Receive Personal Supervision
Telephone No. 117

26 Park Place   NEWTON, N. J.

CORNS AND BUNIONS.

When your Electric Corns and Gas Bunions hurt tell us. We can and will help you. We believe we can help you more than your friend (?) He is looking for something.

WHAT?

NEWTON GAS & ELECTRIC COMPANY.

J. S. FICHTER, Grocer.
47 Sparta Avenue,   Newton, N. J.
SUSSEX PHONE 146.

Carber's Store

111 SPRING ST. - NEWTON, N. J.

The Leading Dry Goods Store of Sussex County

This business was established in 1870 by F. M. Hough, Mr. Carber serving nine years as learner under him, seventeen years at Sussex, N. J., and now twelve years as present owner of the business, making thirty-eight years continuous experience in the Dry Goods business in Sussex county. It is the policy of this store to keep every department thoroughly stocked in all the latest, up-to-date merchandise and to cater to the every day wants of all the people. Every attention is given to the smallest detail of the business, courteous treatment, prompt and willing service to all by experienced helpers.

J. W. C. CARBER

ASSISTANTS
L. H. Willson   John Quackenbush
Amelia E. Julier   Luna Kymer
Lulu A. Shotwell

W. EARL NICHOLLS

PLUMBER   STEAM FITTER

See Me for Installaion of Modern Baths and Lavaories.

149 SPRING ST. - NEWTON, N. J.

Horse Shoeing a Specialty   Rubber Tire Work

CHARLES M. OAKES
NEWTON, N. J.

Wheelwrighting and Blacksmithing
Gasoline Engines   Farm Machinery
Columbia Veterinary Remedies   Reliance Roofing

C. E. McCRACKEN
Blacksmithing and Wheelwrighting
Horse Shoeing a Specialty
Expert on Crippled Horses   General Repairing
258 Spring Street,   NEWTON, N. J.

A. H. Decker   Theo. AUBLE.

DECKER & AUBLE
Books, Stationery, Crockery and Novelties.

11 Main Street   NEWTON, N. J.

Interior View of the Boss Clothing Store.

The Boss Clothing Store

61 Spring Street
Newton, N. J.

Headquarters for everything to wear. Newton's Most Up-to-date Outfitters.

W. D. BOSS, Prop.

SPRINGDALE HOTEL

T. J. CUFF, Proprietor

A popular and well-known hostelry on the Andover and Newton Boulevard, about half way between the two places. Established by Mr. Cuff, who built the hotel and has added to it from time to time till he now has a roomy, up-to-date establishment. Everything to eat and drink of the best.

For 26 years Mr. Cuff was general foreman with the L. & H. R. R. Co.

L. VAN BLARCOM

ATTORNEY AT LAW

41 HIGH STREET - NEWTON, N. J.

EDWARD I. JENSEN

CLEANSER AND DYER

23 HIGH STREET - NEWTON, N. J.

Make your Dollars have more Cents

TRADE AT

RYERSON'S PHARMACY

The Rexall Store

NEWTON - N. J.

MISS SARAH E. DOYLE

Proprietor of Newton's Well Known Pure Food Bakery —A Type of One of the County's Successful Business Women.

Exterior of Store.

Miss Sarah E. Doyle established a Bakery in Newton in 1881, in a small way, at first, but perseverance and a determination to give her patrons fine bread and wholesome pastry enabled her in a short time to enlarge the plant and greatly improve her facilities.

When the pure food laws became effective she was the first to equip her bakery with the latest sanitation methods and the most modern machinery, and is the pioneer in this county in the effort to have an establishment that is in every way worthy the name it now enjoys Miss Doyle has built up a large trade, and has in every way made her business a conspicuous success, and expert work given the products of the Pure Food Bakery have made them popular in every home, and the many patrons are assured that bread, pies and cake made at Miss Doyle's bakery are not surpassed for wholesomeness and cleanliness anywhere.

Interior of Store.

GEORGE H. SAVACOOL,
BOX MANUFACTURER, NEWTON, N. J.

Office Interior.

Residence.

This is one of Newton's important industries. Its proprietor is Mr. George Savacool, who established the enterprise 25 years ago, having a small plant, and employing six girls and two boys, who turned out about 1,000 boxes daily. He now employs thirty people and the output is nearly 8,000 boxes a day. The plant is most complete, having been enlarged several times. Modern in equipment. Shoe, shelf, corset, candy boxes and everything of that nature are turned out promptly and cheaply. Mr. Savacool is one of Newton's highly esteemed men.

One of our prominent ladies recently remarked that E. J. Quinn's Clothing and Furnishings surpass all others in quality and price. It is good to be thus appreciated by the best judges. If you want further information come and investigate. It will, without doubt, convince the most skeptical.

E. J. QUINN
Successor to M. P. Tully
Merchant Tailor, Clothier, Hatter
and Gents' Furnisher
Newton, N. J.

George Peatfield

Storage Warehouse

Piano and Furniture Moving and all kinds of Hauling.

Automobile Moving Van

Phone 148 for Estimates
Go Anywhere
Move Anything
NEWTON, N. J.

Standard Towel Company

This company was incorporated at Newton, N. J., July, 1907. They started business in a small way at the corner of Water and Clinton streets, having only twelve looms and employing five hands. The business rapidly increased and in December, 1912, they moved to their present location on Spring street, where they have 44 looms and employ 40 hands at good wages. They manufacture Turkish Towels and Terry Fabrics, the market being large department stores in New York and Boston, Mass. The officers are William H. Mellor, President, and J. Bertram Mellor, Secretary and Treasurer.

NEWTON IN 1880.

BRICKNER BOTTLING WORKS

High Grade Mineral Waters

All Flavors.

KRUEGER EXPORT BEER

SCHLITZ. **MILWAUKEE.**
For Family Use. For the Trade.

Office at

THE WALDMERE,
Spring Street.
A. B. BRICKNER,
Newton, N. J.

THE PEOPLE'S BAKERY

Makers and Distributors of the Famous

"HOME MADE SPECIAL"

A bread that is both light and wholesome. The family favorite. Try it and you will always BUY IT.

27 Spring Street   Newton, N. J.

B. FISHER and N. FOGELSON, Proprietors

Pies and Cakes of All Kinds.

James G. English.   Patrick J. English.

JAMES ENGLISH'S SONS,

BLACKSMITH and MACHINISTS

HORSESHOEING

General Machinery Repairing

NEWTON, N. J.

Engines, Boilers, Pumps, Pulleys, Hangers, Shaftings, Etc.

SUSSEX MARBLE AND GRANITE WORKS.

JACOB BENZ, Proprietor

277 Spring Street   NEWTON, N. J.

Opposite D., L. & W. R. R. Station.

LEHMAN & CO.

Interior View of store.

Up-to-date Grocery, Meat and Provision Market.   Headquarters for Everything Good to Eat.

PARK BLOCK - NEWTON, NEW JERSEY

An appetite for good things to eat is born in one. If that appetite is not properly cared for, nothing will "taste right". Good foods, prepared from the Fresh, Clean Groceries we sell, will tempt the most jaded appetite. Try a sample order and prove to yourself that all the appetizing points of Good, Sweet, Clean Food are carefully preserved at This Grocery.

Established in 1899.

A. P. Vansickle
GROCER

SUSSEX PHONE 31 - NEWTON, N. J.

THE MERRIAM HOME.

HENRY B. DeKAY.

THE QUALITY DRUG STORE
ALLINSON & HENDERSHOT
PHARMACISTS
NEWTON, N.J.
→ PHONE 159 ←

ROBERT T. JOHNSON.

WILLIAM TOWNSEND
GROCER

Best Butter a Specialty

"SUNBEAM" and "CARMELO" Brands Canned Goods.
Distributed by Austin, Nichols & Co., Inc.

GOLD MEDAL FLOUR

A TRIAL WILL CONVINCE YOU

ORDER AND DELIVERY SERVICE

233 SPRING STREET — TEL. CONN.
FORMERLY DEMAREST'S STORE

OGDENSBURG.

SWEENEY'S HOTEL.

This is one of the popular Hotels of Sussex county, at Ogdensburg, and enjoys a fine reputation. Mr. John Sweeney, Jr. is the accommodating proprietor, and has kept the hotel 11 years, served on the School Board 18 years, and is a prominent Odd Fellow.

The Hotel is modern, and makes a specialty of fine dinners for tourists.

J. P. MADDEN.

A well known merchant and fruit grower. Postmaster at Ogdensburg, to which position he was appointed in 1898. Active in civic affairs, a Republican in politics, member of the County Committee, served on the School Board and conducts an extensive Fire Insurance Agency, owns the Ogdensburg Opera House, and is one of the hustlers of the community. Very popular, and has a fine up-to-date store in the village.

P. J. DOLAN.

A prominent merchant of Sussex county, located in Ogdensburg where he has conducted a general store more than 35 years. Takes a keen interest in civic and other affairs. Is a member of the School Board and one of the influential citizens of that section of the county.

RAYMOND CASE.

Is the genial proprietor of the Ogdensburg House, one of the attractive Hotels of the county, located in Ogdensburg. Mr. Case is entering his fifth year as proprietor, and enjoys a fine trade. He is prominent in the affairs of the town, a member of the School Board, member of the order of Red Men, and a popular hotel keeper.

H. A. BEIERLE.

Dealer in Stationery, Confectionery, Ice Cream, Fruits, Tobacco, Cigars and Choice Family Groceries, at Ogdensburg, N. J. Established the business in 1910, enjoys a good trade and is one of the enterprising citizens of Ogdensburg.

JACOB LIPSKY.

Conducts a fine Clothing and Shoe Store in Ogdensburg. He carries a large line of Ladies' and Gents' Furnishing Goods, Notions, Boots, Shoes, Rubbers, Curtains and Children's ready-to-wear articles.

B. C. GORDON.

Wholesale and Retail Baker of Ogdensburg, N. J.

Wagon delivers daily fresh Bread, Rolls, Pies and Cake. A specialty is made of supplying churches, festivals and picnics at reasonable rates. His goods are in great favor with households and his business improves year by year.

Moses Bigelow, President.   George R. Swain, Treasurer.

WHITE LIMESTONE CO.,
OGDENSBURG, N. J.

Manufacturers Crushed Road Stone, Ground Limestone for the land and Crystalline Grit for poultry.

PAPAKATING.

W. F. DePUY.

Conducts an up-to-date blacksmith and woodworking shop at Papakating where he located two years ago. Is an expert in the art of horseshoeing. Has a fine growing trade, Is prominent in fraternal circles, being a Mason, K. of P. and Jr. O. U. A. M. Mr. DePuy stands high in the community.

ALFRED D. SNOOK.

An enterprising citizen of the county, and postmaster at Papakating. Is a native of Sussex county, and was reared on the farm. Began his mercantile career April 1st, 1912, by purchasing the store at Papakating. Carries a full line of general merchandise and dairymen's supplies. Has a fine trade, is a Mason fraternally, and enjoys the confidence of all.

SPARTA.

The reputation of Sparta as a leading summer resort is deservingly high and year after year the permanent residents are doing more to increase the attractiveness. City people in large numbers are buying lots and building summer homes in the town or in its immediate vicinity. The climate of the region in which Sparta is situated is exceptionally healthful, the air pure and invigorating and the natural scenery equal in attractive picturesqueness to the finest elsewhere within or without the State. The town is situated on the New York, Susquehanna & Western Railroad. The population of the township in which Sparta is situated is 1579, of which Sparta has between 400 and 450. The town has one public school and two churches, the Methodist and Presbyterian. There is also a Village Improvement Society.

The place was settled about the year 1770. At one time an immense amount of iron was forged in the village. Six forges were kept continually supplied. A large number of ship anchors were annually manufactured there. Most of the ore was supplied from the Ogden mine near Ogdensburg.

Soldiers' Monument, Sparta.

H. C. DODGE

Dealer in General Merchandise, Sparta, N. J. Established the business five years ago and enjoys a good trade.

SHUMAN BROS.

The house of Shuman Bros., Undertakers and Embalmers, of Sparta, was established by Jacob H. Shuman 45 years ago. H. J. and W. L. Shuman are now the proprietors, and took over the business about nine years ago. Both are natives of the county. H. J. Shuman is Town Clerk. W. L. Shuman is a prominent Mason and Odd Fellow. They are licensed Embalmers and have all the accessories required for their work.

J. W. MASEKER.

A prominent and successful merchant of the county in Sparta, where he has done a thriving business for nearly a quarter of a century. Deals in General Merchandise and is an extensive buyer and shipper of Eggs, Potatoes, and other Country Produce.

JAMES CONDON.

Is Sparta's well known and long established blacksmith and wheelwright. He is a native of Sussex county, and began business in Sparta thirty years ago. Has a fine up-to-date shop, is an expert farrier and a wagon maker of high repute. Does general repairing and does it with skill and promptness.

THE GLEN HOUSE.

One of the county's favorite Hotels, located in Sparta, and conducted by Mr. David Goble, the ideal host, who has presided over the place for more than thirty years. The Glen is open all the year. Tourists and automobile parties will find this one of the most attractive places in this section. The best to eat and drink. The Hotel is remodeled and up-to-date in every detail.

JOSEPH M. DECKER.

Is the enterprising Wheelwright and Blacksmith at Sparta. He has an up-to-date shop, builds wagons and sleds, does general repairing, keeps auto supplies, gasoline and accessories. Established his business in 1904. Enjoys a fine trade and the confidence of all who know him. Is a Jr. O. U. A. M. and active in the civic and social life of Sparta.

GEORGE B. FISHER.

One of the prominent business men of Sussex county. Manufacturer of fine hand made Harness at Sparta, where he has been since 1870. Has worked at his calling 58 years. Served as justice twenty-one years, as notary twenty years. His harness are famous in many states. He is a prominent Odd Fellows, and is one of Sparta's most substantial and revered citizens.

H. W. FOLK.

Residence of H. W. Folk, Sparta, N. J., was erected by his father, Henry Folk, and was the family homestead for many years.

Mr. H. W. Folk conducts a general merchandise business at Sparta. The enterprise was established by his father about 30 years ago.

Mr. Folk is one of the prominent and well known business men of Sussex county, and enjoys the confidence of all who know him.

GEONERVROE INN,

One of Sparta's Popular Hotels.

This beautiful and up-to-date Hostelry was established twenty-one years ago by its present manager, Mrs. Minerva Roe. It is a great favorite with summer tourists. Has accommodations for forty. Farm dairy and poultry yards attached supply guests with the freshest of fruits, vegetables, eggs, milk and cream.

MAPLE GROVE INN,

EUGENE SMITH, Proprietor.

Sussex county has no more attractive summer hotel than Maple Grove Inn of Sparta. It is thoroughly up-to-date in equipment, conveniences and furnishings. Delightfully situated and able to accommodate fifty guests. Mr. Eugene Smith, the proprietor, has conducted the place six years, and his cordial hospitality has endeared him to all. Mr. Smith is the manager of a large fire insurance agency, representing the leading companies.

CHARLES HALSEY.

Is the popular postmaster of Sparta. Born in the town and has lived there all of his life. Learned harness making in Newton. Was town Assessor three years and Commissioner of Deeds thirty years. Was appointed postmaster eight years ago. Is a prominent Republican, and is one of Sparta's enterprising citizens.

Auto Parties Catered to
CENTRAL HOTEL
Sunday Specialties
CHICKEN AND BEEFSTEAK DINNERS
GEORGE B. MAINES Proprietor.
SPARTA   New Jersey

PRIDE GELSCHE NO. 151155.

An Auray Farms show cow. Daughter of Sir Gelsche Walker Segis. A. R. O. record at 2 yrs, 5 mos, 20 days. Butter 7 ds: 15.62, milk 7 ds: 397.20 At 5 yrs. record just completed. Butter 7 ds. 25.56, milk 7 ds. 564.6.

GELSCHE SEGIS NO. 111683.

The $1300 daughter of King Segis, for whose unborn calf, by the King of the Black and Whites, $1000 was offered and refused. A granddaughter of Prilly, and one of the stars at Auray Farms.

AURAY FARMS

PURE BRED HOLSTEIN-FRIESIAN CATTLE

F. M. AVERY   SPARTA, SUSSEX CO., N J   IRVING M. AVERY

A few great-grandsons of King of the Pontiacs, King Segis and Pontiac Korndyke from A. R. O. daughters of some of the greatest Holstein-Friesian sires always on hand to select from.

NO FEMALES AT PRIVATE SALE

PEDIGREES, PHOTOS AND DETAILED INFORMATION ON REQUEST

STIDWORTHY BROTHERS

Fire-Proof Garage

Repairs, Supplies and Storage

Telephone 18 Netcong

NETCONG,   NEW JERSEY.

THE FRANKLIN HOUSE
Chris. Kelly, Proprietor.   John W. Kelly, Manager.

STANHOPE, N. J.

Rates $2.00 per day.   Telephone No. 54

Phone 6-W—Stanhope   Prompt Attention to all orders

STANHOPE BOTTLING WORKS
Peter J. Kelly, Proprietor.

Beer, Ale, Porter and Soft Drinks, Wines and Liquors.

STANHOPE, N. J.

R. M. INSCHO.
STANHOPE, N. J.

Dealer in Meats, Groceries and Vegetables. Established eighteen years.

A. A. KING

Sussex County Distributor for

Chase Trucks.

NETCONG,   Netcong, N. J.

S. H. CHAMBERLAIN,

REAL ESTATE and INSURANCE

Rents Collected, or Loans Negotiated.

Bank Building,   NETCONG, N. J.

The new, up-to-date market recently erected by Mr. Inscho.

H. HANOVITZ SONS'.
Stanhope, N. J.

Exclusively Clothiers and Haberdashers. Everything in the newest modes and styles. Kirchbaum Clothes and Stetson Hats.

NELDEN'S PHARMACY

This well known establishment has been doing business in Stanhope since 1897. The proprietor is Dr. H. H. Nelden. This is one of the model stores of Sussex county, in which may be found all kinds of Drugs, Proprietary Medicines, Toilet Articles, Confectionery, Novelties, Stationery, and everything usually carried in a first class pharmacy.

R. M. SMITH,

Dealer in

GRAIN,

FLOUR,

FEED,

CUSTOM GRINDING,

COAL,

ETC., ETC.

SPARTA, New Jersey.

STANHOPE.

Stanhope, situated in the extreme end of the county, and separated from Netcong by the Morris canal, is one of the thriving boroughs of Sussex, its present population being about 1,300. The railroad station (Stanhope-Netcong) on the Lackawanna, is in the Netcong section, about three-quarters of a mile from the center of the town. Netcong also affords the banking facilities. The Singer Sewing Machine Company have one of their foundries here. The borough has an excellent water system, electric lights furnished by the Willsbrook plant and has the main thoroughfare macadamized. There is an excellent public school and two churches, Methodist and Presbyterian.

JOHN WILLS
Dealer in Lumber, Coal and Building Material
STANHOPE, N. J.

Up-to-Date Delivery Truck.

J. O. BISSELL.

A prominent and enterprising business man of Sussex county, operating grocery stores in Newton and in Stanhope. His establishments are well known and popular trading places for the people of the county. They are up-to-date, and stocked with the freshest of goods.

The Stanhope store carries a fine supply of fresh and Salt Meats, and to its management, Mr. Bissell gives his personal attention, his son, Mr. L. A. Bissell is the active manager of the Newton store. Mr. Bissell is a native of the county, and is interested in civic affairs, is a prominent Republican and for many years has served as vice chairman of the Republican County Committee.

HOTEL STANHOPE
STANHOPE, N. J.

F. P. KISZ Proprietor.

Modern in every detail.
The Best to Eat and Drink.
Tourists and automobile parties given special attention.

View of Hotel Stanhope Stables.

H. A. TIMBRELL.

An enterprising merchant of Stanhope, N. J. Established the general merchandise business there twenty-five years ago. Has been District Clerk of Board of Education for twenty years and is Vice President of the Bank of Netcong and Vice President of the Building and Loan Association of Netcong.

SUSSEX BOROUGH.

About the year 1870, a man by the name of Peter Decker, a Hollander by descent, passed over the Kittatinny or Blue Mountains from the settlement along the Navisink River, made in the latter part of the seventeenth century, in search of good land on which to settle. Coming down through what is now Wantage township, he located near what is now the corner of Main and Bank streets. Others followed him and a small village or settlement was the result, it taking the name of Deckertown, in honor of its first settler. The name was changed in 1900 to Sussex. The town is situated along the Clove Creek, sixty-nine miles from New York, on the New York, Susquehanna & Western Railroad. The Lehigh & New England Railroad also enters the town. According to the census of 1910, it had a population of 1,212. Sussex has an excellent gravity water system, the water coming from Lake Rutherford on the top of the Blue Mountains above Colesville, seven miles distant. Fire protection is afforded by a well equipped and well manned fire department consisting of a hose company and a hook and ladder company. The high and grammar school is of the best and there are four churches, Methodist, Presbyterian, Baptist and Catholic. Two newspapers, the Sussex Independent and the Wantage Recorder cover the news field fully. The Masons, Odd Fellows, Royal Arcanum, Foresters, Junior Mechanics and Granges have lodges in the town. Sussex is the center of a big farming country and thousands of quarts of milk are shipped from the three creameries in and near the town. Among the industries in the town are a towel mill, dairy machinery company, woodworking establishment, fruit evaporating plant and several smaller establishments. The merchants are highly progressive and the homes of the residents are neat and well kept. Four hotels, all modern and up-to-date, furnish accomodation for the traveler.

HON HENRY C. HUNT.

Born in Blairstown, N. J.; father Marshall Hunt, for many years a partner of John I. Blair; mother, Sarah A. Shipman. Educated at Blair Academy and graduated from Lafayette College, class of 1877; read law with Charles D. Thompson in Newton and was admitted to the bar in November, 1882, and afterward as a counsellor; practiced in Newton until September 1894, and from that time in Sussex, and has an office in Newark, where he is associated with John D. Anderson. Was appointed Judge of the Sussex county courts in 1902, and served until 1906, when he was appointed member of the County Tax Board, and was elected its president and served until 1909, when again appointed Judge and served until 1911. Was nominated by the Republicans for the office of Senator in 1909. Married Etta McCoy, daughter of Samuel McCoy, of Newton, in 1887, and has eight children; the oldest, Marshall Hunt, being a graduate of the class of 1912 Lafayette College, and now a student in his father's office. Judge Hunt stands high at the bar, and enjoys the esteem of all who know him.

HUGH C. BALDWIN.

A rising member of the Sussex county Bar, born in Newton in 1887, son of J. E. and Anna F. Baldwin. Educated in the High and English and Classical School of Newton and New York Law School, graduating in 1909, degree L. L. B., the youngest in a class of 250. Studied law under Charles D. Thompson, Jersey City, and Thomas Kays, Newton. Admitted to the Bar in 1911. Practiced in Newton and in 1913 located in Sussex. Is counsel for S. P. C. A., and recently appointed Master in Chancery by Chancellor Walker, and is the youngest Master in Chancery in the county. Mr. Baldwin enjoys a fine practice, and is regarded very highly by all who know him.

HARRY R. MENSCH.

Born on a farm in 1882, near Wilkes-Barre, Pa., son of Stephen A. and Sarah Mensch. Educated in the Forty Fort High School, State Normal, East Stroudsburg, and in Harvard University. Principal Forty Fort, (Pa.) Grammar School 1904 to 1907. Principal of Fairview High School three years. Came to Sussex in 1910 as principal of the High School. Has an enrollment of 270 students and ten subordinates. Professor Mensch will make teaching his life work, and has been very successful. Is a member of the County and State Teachers' Institutes. Married Miss Maud G. Stroh in 1905. One daughter, Audrey, blesses the union. A Mason fraternally, member of the M. E. church and choir leader.

HAROLD M. SIMPSON.

The youngest member of the Sussex county Bar, born in McAfee in 1886, son of Ora C. and Magdaline Simpson. Educated in the Newton Public Schools, the English and Classical School, Princeton and Lehigh Universities. Studied law under Hon. Theodore Simonson, and being admitted to the Bar located in Sussex, where he is counsel for Wantage township and enjoys a fine practice. Is a Democrat politically, takes a keen interest in the county's affairs, and is regarded very highly as one of our rising lawyers.

DR. CAROLINE WALLIN.

A prominent Osteopathic Physician of the county, located in Sussex. Doctor Wallin is a graduate of the American School of Osteopathy of Kirksville, Mo. She holds a certificate of the State Board of Medical Examiners of the State of New Jersey, and is therefore recognized by the Commonwealth as a regular physician.

The practice of Osteopathy has become more popular year by year, as people understand the logic as well as the simplicity of the art. It is to-day the recognized drugless method of healing disease and restoring the afflicted to a normal condition. It's application is attended by no disastrous effects, and a very slight investigation will convince the most skeptical of its beneficent results.

LAWRENCE & HARDEN COMPANY.

This is one of the important enterprises of Sussex, N. J. The business was established in 1869 and incorporated in 1905. The officers are S. H. Lawrence, President; H. M. Kernick, Secretary, and Ora Harden, Treasurer. The company are dealers in Feed, Grain, Flour, Coal, Lumber, Hardware, Paints and Building Material of all kinds. The plant is opposite L. & N. E. depot, Sussex, and they have a branch store at Pellettown, N. J.

THE MANNING COMPANY,
SUSSEX, N. J.

Are dealers in Lumber, Coal, Feed, Fertilizers, Salt, Lime, Cement and Building Materials. They are also manufacturers of the famous "Gold Medal" Flour, a flour very popular with the housewife in this section. Give it a trial and you will be convinced. Your patronage solicited; right prices and satisfaction guaranteed.

WILSON'S BAKERY.

This business was established nineteen years ago at Sussex, N. J., by Mr. Frank Wilson, the present proprietor. The bakery is modern and up-to-date in every way—and the best of Bread, Cakes and Pies are for sale.

Mr. Wilson enjoys a large and growing trade which he richly deserves.

A. W. BEDELL,
Postmaster, Sussex.

Born in Frankford township, Sussex county, and has always resided therein. Attended school in the old Academy in Deckertown, and later took a course in higher branches of learning under the late Dr. Joseph H. Morrison. He then adopted the profession of teaching, continuing for five years.

May, 1889, accepted the assistant postmastership at Deckertown, serving five years. Resumed his profession of teaching, and continued until March, 1898, when he became assistant postmaster and served till March, 1911, when he was appointed postmaster by President Taft.

Served as member and President of Sussex Council. Three terms as member of the school board. Is an ardent Republican, an authority on all postal matters, advocate of good government, is public spirited and takes a keen as well as active interest in the welfare of the community.

DECKER & SIMMONS.

The firm of Decker & Simmons, Sussex, N. J., is composed of E. H. Decker and J. D. Simmons. The business is that of dealing in Feed, Flour, Grain, Hay, Straw, Coal, Brick, Lumber, Shingles, Lath, Doors, Blinds, Mouldings, Lime, Cement, and Builders' Material. The business was established in 1888 and has always enjoyed a good trade.

ABOUT WAGONS AND WHERE TO GET THEM.

We help you to get what you require and provide an easy price on what you must buy. Our way of serving you will surely satisfy. This stand has been in the wagon business for 35 years and what makes our wagon sales easy are the satisfied customers that return to us every year.

We are not experimenters in the wagon business. It is our business all the year round, not once in awhile in the spring. A blacksmith always on hand for changes and repairs.

WRIGHT'S MILLS,
Clove Road,   SUSSEX, N. J.
W. S. Wright, Prop.

W. F. MORRISON,
Proprietor Hotel Morrison,

SUSSEX, N. J.

A native of Dublin, Ireland, came to America a child. Located in Sussex in 1880. Established the Morrison Hotel in 1903. Has a modern up-to-date place, where everything to eat and drink may be had. Is secretary of the Sussex County Hotel Men's Association, and steamship agent. A popular and public spirited citizen.

J. R. MOORE,

A prominent merchant of Sussex engaged in the Clothing, Shoes and Men's Furnishing business. Has an up-to-date store which he established in 1910. Carries a fine line of Haberdashery, Hats, Ties, Shirts and the latest in Clothing. Mr. Moore is a native of the county, and is a young man of sterling business qualities.

SUSSEX FEED STORE.

Mr. W. Scott Martin is the enterprising proprietor of this establishment. He has been in business in Sussex eleven years and deals in the most popular brands of Feed, Allentown Portland Cement and Poultry Food. Give him a trial when you need anything in this line and you are sure to receive courteous treatment as well as the best goods.

A. E. WOLFE,
Granite Monuments,
SUSSEX, N. J.

Only the best domestic and foreign Granite used. Up-to-date designs. Inspect my stock. Prices low as consistent with first-class work.

FARMERS NATIONAL BANK,
SUSSEX, N. J.

Capital Stock $100,000.00
Surplus 1,00,000.00

Solicits your accounts and does a general Banking business. Resources over $1,000,000.00.

Officers—F. W. Margarum, President; Frank Holbert, Cashier.

Directors—Charles G. Wilson, A. Watson Slockbower, Theodore F. Northrup, Frank Holbert, Samuel S. Vandruff, Elihu Adams, William A. Roy, James R. Kincaid, F. W. Margarum.

Notary Public   Commissioner of Deeds

A. C. TULLY,

Fire Insurance of every description in Stock and Mutual Companies.

LOANS AND REAL ESTATE.

THE UNION HOUSE,
SUSSEX, N. J.

F. U. Dickson   Proprietor.

o ——— o

One of the most up-to-date hotels in this section of the State. Recently refitted and refurnished. Modern in all details. Table unsurpassed. The best to drink. Popular prices and every consideration.

DR. J. D. HAGGERTY,
Dentist,
SUSSEX, N. J.

THE CENTRAL GARAGE
D. S. Haggerty, Proprietor.
Selling Agents for
OVERLAND AND FORD CARS
General Repair Work, Oils, Gasoline and Necessary Supplies
SUSSEX, N. J.

DR. I. B. LOWE,
Dentist,
SUSSEX, N. J.

SMITH & WELLS,
Livery and Sale Stable,
Opposite Union Hotel,   SUSSEX, N. J.

Up-to-date rigs. Safe horses. Careful drivers. Social functions supplied.

G. DYMOCK
Planing and Moulding Mill
Builders' Supplies.

SUSSEX, N. J.

H. N. Havens   F. B. Vandruff

SUSSEX GARAGE
Machine and Electrical Work

Agency Studebaker Cars "25," "35," "Six."

SUSSEX, N. J.

New concrete construction. Thoroughly up-to-date Storage, Repairs and Supplies. Local and Long Distance Telephones.

STILLWATER.
REV. T. W. MARVIN.

The subject of this sketch is a native of Monroe county, Pa., being born there June 21, 1870. Came to Sussex county with his parents when six years of age. He was educated in the public school and Allegany College, from which he obtained a degree of B. A. For several years he was employed with the H. W. Merriam Shoe Co., of Newton, and for fifteen years more or less engaged in evangelistical work. He then became pastor of the First Baptist church of East Stroudsburg, Pa. After which he was identified for one year with his father in the mercantile business at Bartonville, Pa.

January, 1913, he began the Mercantile, Real Estate and Insurance business at Stillwater, N. J., where he has a fine trade, and enjoys the confidence of the community.

The Stillwater Mill

Stillwater, N. J.
A. D. CORNELL, Proprietor

JOHN W. EARL.

A well known contractor and builder, residing in Stillwater since 1894. Built the new public school building and the Presbyterian church. Is a prominent member of the Grange, an Odd Fellow and P. O. S. of A.

LAKE HOUSE,
Swartswood, N. J.

EDWARD M. HILL, Proprietor.

Mr. Hill has conducted this up-to-date hostelry since April, 1912. He is ably assisted by Mrs. Hill and they are making the Lake House a splendid home-like retreat.

D. S. AND M. B. WINTERMUTE.

These gentlemen compose the firm of Wintermute Bros., Merchant Millers and Sawyers. They have a well appointed grist and saw mills at Middleville, N. J. The grist mill is over a 100 years old. They deal in Flour, Feed, Sprouts, Grain and manufacture a superior brand of roller process Buckwheat Flour, which is in great demand locally, and in other counties. They are both natives of the county, enterprising and public spirited. Both are Odd Fellows and Jr. O. U. A. M. and popular in the trade.

W. H. ELLETT.

A native of Sussex county and now a well known merchant of Walpack Centre, where he conducts a general store, and is assisted by Mrs. Ellett, who is also postmistress. Mr. Ellett began business in Walpack Centre in September, 1912, purchasing the Elmer T. Roe store. He carries Dry Goods, Groceries, Provisions, Drugs, Oils and Patent Medicines, and is an extensive shipper of country produce.

I. L. LABAR.

TRANQUILITY, N. J.

General Store and Feed Store,

Mr. LaBar established the general merchandise business at Tranquility thirteen years ago. He deals in Dry Goods, Groceries, Notions, Boots, Shoes, Rubbers, Harness, Hardware, Flour, Feed and Cement. He was appointed postmaster in 1900, is a native of Sussex county and enjoys a large trade.

S. S. COLEMAN,

TRANQUILITY, N. J.

Mr. Coleman is a native of the county. Is agent for the Lehigh & Hudson Railroad and conducts a large general store. Deals in Feed, Flour, Coal, Cement, Hardware, Groceries, Dry Goods, Boots and Shoes, and buys country produce. Has served as Town Committeeman, is a director of the cemetery and a prominent Democrat. Enjoys a fine trade.

Residence of S. S. Coleman, Tranquility, N. J.

WILLIAM H. LABAR.

A well known citizen of the county, formerly a carpenter and builder, now a wheelwright at Tranquility. Born in Pennsylvania in 1833, and never uses glasses at work or reading. Has conducted his business in Tranquility for about six years. Is a staunch Republican. Has taken The Sussex Register sixty-five years. Trustee of the M. E. church and keenly interested in civic affairs.

A. L. CASSEDY.

Is the postmaster at Waterloo. He was appointed in 1898. He keeps the village store and has been in business there twenty-two years. Is a member and president of the Board of Education of Byram township. Mr. Cassedy has a fine general store, enjoys a large trade and is one of the popular citizens of the county.

Store and Residence, Vernon, N. J.
R. D. WALLACE.

THE VERNON HOUSE,
Vernon, N. J.

JOSEPH BURROWS,   Proprietor.

Modern, steam heat, best of everything to eat, drink and smoke. Mr. Burrows has conducted the hotel thirty years. He is now assisted by his son, Joseph. Both are vry popular with the trade.

Is the popular postmaster of Vernon, to which position he was appointed September 13, 1898. Takes an active interest in civic matters. Served as Township Collector six years. Conducts a fine store and deals in general merchandise, Flour, Provisions, Hardware and Agricultural Implements. Is the agent for the Travelers Insurance Company, both ordinary and accident. Mr. Wallace enjoys a fine trade and the confidence of all who know him.

THE VERNON GRANGE STORE
Vernon, N. J.

Dealers in Dry Goods, Groceries, Flour, Feed, Hardware, Coal, Agricultural Implements. Established in 1908, and enjoys a fine trade. A S. Drew, General Manager.

Officers and Directors—President, N. D. House; Vice President, T. B. Storms; Secretary and Treasurer, A. S. Drew; Samuel A. Williams, Willard Forshee, L. R. Martin, Jr., E. C. Burrows, F. A. Mott, A. P. Shaw.

The company does a large business and is very successful.

R. V. NORTHRUP.

Conducts the largest general store in Vernon. Is a native of Sussex county and has been in business in Vernon three years. Has a large and growing trade; deals in General Merchandise, Flour Feed, Coal, Hardware, Groceries, Dry Goods, Cigars and Confectionery.

THEODORE VAIL.

The popular postmaster and Erie Railroad agent at Quarryville, N. J. Has been agent for the railroad company thirty years, and served as postmaster more than fifteen years, being first appointed in 1883, serving until 1895. Reappointed in 1911. Was school trustee for Wantage township twelve years. A big minded, conscientious gentleman and a faithful as well as most efficient official.

THE ROGERS STORE,

Quarryville, N. J.

COURT AND COUNTY OFFICERS.

Supreme Court Justice—James F. Minturn, Hoboken.
Circuit Judge—Charles C. Black, Jersey City.
County Judge—Allen R. Shay, Newton, term expires 1916.
Prosecutor of Pleas—William A. Dolan, Newton, term expires 1917.
State Senator—Samuel T. Munson, Franklin Borough, term expires 1915.
Member of Assembly—Henry T. Kays, Newton.
County Clerk—Harvey S. Hopkins, Newton, term expires 1917.
Deputy County Clerk—H. Clarence Cole, Newton.
Surrogate—Emmet H. Bell, Newton, term expires 1918.
Deputy Surrogate—Sayre S. Martin, Newton.
Sheriff—Edward C. Maines, Newton, term expires 1914.
Deputy Sheriff—Albert T. Lyons, Newton.
Coroners—George Peatfield, Newton, term expires 1915; Joseph G. Coleman, Hamburg, term expires 1915; Edward P. Uptegrove, Vernon, term expires 1914.
Clerk of Grand Jury—Lewis VanBlarcom, Newton.
Superintendent of Public Schools—Ralph Decker, Borough Sussex, term expires 1915.
Superintendent of Weights and Measures—William D. Willson, Sussex.
Game and Fish Warden—J. B. Hendershott, Newton.
Board of Freeholders—William Iliff, term expires 1914; Frank Coe, term expires 1915; John J. VanSickle, term expires 1916; Clerk, R. Lee Slater.
County Engineer—Harvey Snook, Newton.
County Counsel—Levi H. Morris, Newton.
County Supervisor of Roads—Seymour R. Pullis, Sparta.
County Collector—Lewis S. Iliff, Newton.
Steward of Almshouse—Floyd Dickison.
Almshouse Physician—Dr. Edgar A. Allen, Lafayette.
Board of Taxation—J. Frank Quince, President, Sussex; Martin W. Bowman, Sussex, Robert T. Johnson, Newton; O. E. Armstrong, Newton, Secretary.
Board of Elections—Marshall Hunt, Sussex; Raymond Case, Ogdensburg; Robert T. Smith, Andover; S. E. Ingersoll, Lafayette.
Almshouse Chaplain—Rev. Fletcher S. Garis, Branchville.
Jury Commissioner, William F. Howell, Newton.

TOWNSHIP AND BOROUGH OFFICIALS.

Town Clerks.

Andover Borough—Frank N. VanSyckle, Andover.
Andover—Charles W. Roof, Newton, R. D. No. 3.
Branchville Borough—George W. Roe, Branchville.
Byram—Frank W. Spranger, Andover, R. D. 1.
Frankford—Jesse W. Fountain, Branchville.
Franklin Borough—M. M. Dolan, Franklin Borough.
Fredon—Edson P. Warner, Newton, R. D. 2.
Green—Clarence Cooke, Newton, R. D. 1.
Hampton—Charles Emmons, Halsey.
Hardyston—Abram B. Rude, Hamburg.
Hopatcong Borough—David W. King, Landing.
Lafayette—William H. Benson, Lafayette.
Montague—Bruce A. Penney, Port Jervis, N. Y., R. D. 1.
Newton—William E. Decker, Newton, 40 Mill street.
Sandyston—James J. Black, Hainesville.
Sparta—Henry J. Shuman, Sparta.
Stanhope—George C. Valentine, Stanhope.
Stillwater—Victor M. Robbins, Middleville.
Sussex Borough—Harry E. Wells, Sussex.
Vernon—William D. Parker, Vernon.
Walpack—Nathaniel VanAuken, Flatbrookville.
Wantage—James A. Wilson, Sussex.

Assessors.

Andover—William Iliff, Newton, R. D. No. 3.
Andover Borough—William E. Willson, Andover.
Branchville Borough—George W. Roe, Branchville.
Byram—George M. Prickett, Andover, R. D. 1.
Frankford—George W. Smith, R. D. 1, Augusta.
Franklin Borough—Philip W. Henderson, Franklin Boro.
Fredon—William N. Westbrook, Newton, R. D. 1.
Green—I. L. Labar, Tranquility.
Hampton—John W. Thompson, Newton.
Hardyston—Nicholas Farber, Hamburg.
Hopatcong Borough—Peter E. Boomer, Landing.
Lafayette—William S. Vought, Lafayette.
Montague—George McCarty, Port Jervis, N. Y., R. D. 1.
Newton—A. V. B. Mackerley, Newton.
Ogdensburg Borough—Halsey Hoppaugh, Ogdensburg.
Sandyston—Warren H. VanSickle, Layton.
Sparta—David F. Kinney, Sparta.
Stanhope Borough—William C. Best, Stanhope.
Stillwater—O. VanHorn, Stillwater.
Sussex Borough—Charles E. Willson, Sussex.
Vernon—R. D. Simpson, McAfee.
Walpack—Joseph W. Bunnell, Walpack Center.
Wantage—Simeon M. Parcel, Sussex.

Collectors.

Andover Borough—Harry A. Stackhouse, Andover.
Andover—George M. Hendershot, Newton R. D. No. 3.
Branchville Borough—Alfred J. Canfield, Branchville.
Byram—Frank W. Spranger, Andover, R. D. 1.
Frankford—Jacob N. VanAuken, Beemerville.
Fredon—Harry G. Wilson, Newton, R. D. 1.
Green—Howell Hamilton, Newton, R. D. 1.
Hampton—Willard A. Yetter, Halsey.
Hardyston—Jonas S. Woods, Hamburg.
Hopatcong Borough—Gustave Reinberg, Landing.
Lafayette—Charles E. Mackerley, Lafayette.
Montague—Fred Reinhardt, Port Jervis, N. Y., R. D. 1.
Newton—Norman B. Anderson, Newton.
Ogdensburg Borough—David L. Dolan, Ogdensburg.
Sandyston—Frank McKeeby, Layton.
Sparta—David L. Dolan, Ogdensburg.
Stanhope Borough—John D. Coursen, Stanhope.
Sussex Borough—Peter V. Hammond, Sussex.
Stillwater—William S. Huff, Middleville.
Vernon—Andrew S. Drew, Vernon.
Walpack—Charles P. Haney, Flatbrookville.
Wantage—Frank T. Snook, Papakating.

Township Committees, Mayors and Councilmen.

Andover—Clark M. Kinney, Benjamin Fritts, Aaron Masaker.
Andover Borough—Mayor, Robert T. Smith; Councilmen, Charles A. Meyer, Joseph Ackerson, Andrew L. Dobbins, Henry N. Hinds, George O. Young, O. A. McPeek.
Branchville Borough—Mayor, William C. Cook; Councilman, George E. Knox, Benjamin F. Rosenkrans, Victor E. Bevans, Isaiah Hornbeck, William H. Dalrymple, W. F. Dye.
Byram—Augustus McMickle, Hiram Stone, Geo. P. Hart.
Frankford—Victor Compton, George B. Titman, George F. Clark.
Franklin Borough—Mayor, D. W. McCarthy; Councilmen, E. D. Shuster, Dr. F. P. Wilbur, J. A. Herzenberg, F. N. Shepard, G. L. Shaw, Watson Littell.
Fredon—Peter E. Garris, Alfred C. Snook, Jesse M. Budd.
Green—D. H. Longcor, E. E. Cooper, A. Hull.
Hampton—Isaac Williams, John A. Sigler, W. H. Quince.
Hardyston—George W. Lewis, Thomas D. Edsall, Caleb Farber.
Hopatcong Borough—Mayor, Hon. R. L. Edwards; Coun-

cilmen, Thomas B. Atterbury, Theodore A. Gessler, Philip W. Oetting, Frederick Schwanhausser, Hudson Maxim, R. S. Baker.

Lafayette—Edward Ackerson, John D. Ackerson, Michael Tidaback.

Montague—Alfred Hartrim, Henry J. Schneider, George Hooker.

Newton—William Townsend, Charles S. Steele, E. Merriam Dutcher.

Sandyston—D. M. Johnson, Ira Stoll, W. H. VanSickle.

Sparta—Benjamin C. Gordon, Walter D. Byram, William Huffman.

Stanhope Borough—Mayor, John Wills; Councilman, Amos J. Almer, Lorenzo McKinney, William Niper, George McMickle, Daniel Inscho, Augustus Woodruff.

Stillwater—Eugene Huff, William P. Struble, Charles Westbrook.

Sussex Borough—Mayor, Frank Holbert; Councilmen, Walter L. Bird, Frank B. Ewald, Henry N. Havens, William Smith, Daniel E. VanEtten, Frank Wilson.

Vernon—L. F. Kinney, N. P. Ryerson, Monroe Houghtaling.

Walpack—Eugene Rosenkrans, Lester J. Fuller, Emmet B. Struble.

Wantage—Jason C. House, Walter J. Hait, Frank A. Meddaugh.

MUNICIPAL OFFICERS OF THE TOWN OF NEWTON.

Town Committee.

William Townsend, Charles S Steele, E. Merriam Dutcher.
Chairman—William Townsend, 191 Spring street.
Treasurer—Charles S. Steele, 12 Elm street.
Custodian of School Funds—Charles S. Steele, 12 Elm St.
Town Clerk—William E. Decker, 40 Mill street.
Assessor—A. V. B. Mackerley, 93 Madison street.
Collector—Norman B. Anderson, 24 Madison street.
Street Commissioner—Harvey Snook, 125 Spring street.
Town Attorney—Henry T. Kays, 6 Park Place.
Town Engineer—Harvey Snook, 125 Spring street.
Overseer of Poor—J. Wesley Randall, 16 Stuart street.

Water Commission.

Rutherford Tuttle, President, 61 Spring street.
Horton M. Beegle, Secretary, 18 Union Place.
Harvey Snook Treasurer, 27 Maple avenue.
Ackerson J. Mackerley, Clerk, 93 Madison street.
Morford Smith, Supt. of Sewers, 16 Orchard street.
Frank Bittenbender, Plumber, 11 Mill street.

Police Department.

Officers—Arthur T. Byram, 203 Main street; Charles Straway, 15 Shady Lane.

Police Justice.

John E. Whitney, 19 High street.

Fire Department.

Edward Hall, Chief Engineer, 248 Spring street.
Jacob Grimm, Assistant Chief, 164 Main street.
Fred R. Snyder, Foreman Kittatinny Hose, 44 Trinity St.
E. Dana Ely, Foreman Steamer No. 1, 131 Spring street.
Theodore Simonson, Foreman Sussex Chemical, 38 Mill St.
Robert Kerr, Foreman Hose No. 3, 86 Madison street.
Warren H. Smith, Foreman Fire Patrol, 91 Main street.

Board of Health.

Warren H. Smith, M. D., President, 91 Main street.
A. V. B. Mackerley, Secretary, 93 Madison street.
Roswell McPeek, Inspector, 216 Spring street.
Charles S. Steele, William Townsend, E. Merriam Dutcher.

SUSSEX COUNTY BOARDS OF EDUCATION.

Andover Township.

President, O. P. Case; Vice President, Millard E. Parliman; Clerk, William Iliff; Lee R. Fritts, George M. Hendershot, Wm. Ackerson, Marshall Burd, Clark N. Kinney, Lewis O. Willson.

Branchville Borough.

President, John A. McCarrick; Vice President, M. L. Bond; Clerk, George E. Knox; C. H. Crisman, E. M. Smith, J. C. Price, M. D., Wilbur F. Dye, Wm. P. Ellett, William C. Cook.

Franklin Borough.

President, C. R. Ricker; Vice President, E. D. Shuster; Clerk, M. M. Dolan; Joseph A. Herzenberg, W. M. Boynton, Michael J. Hyde, Wm. C. Nestor, Joseph P. Quinn, James C. Stephens, William Stephens.

Hopatcong Borough.

President, Thomas B. Atterbury; Vice President, David W. King; Clerk, Theodore A. K. Gessler; Gustave Reinberg, Alva Nelson, Frederick Schwanhausser, John P. Muller, R. L. Edwards, Charles F. Muller.

Ogdensburg Borough.

President, P. J. Dolan; Vice President, Raymond Case; Clerk, W. N. Harris; William Osborne, H. R. Collins, Reuben Stidworthy, Dr. L. C. Burd, Fowler J. Casterline, Nelson Washer, John Sweeney.

Stanhope Borough.

President, Amos J. Almer; Vice President, A. S. Van Arsdale; Clerk, H. A. Timbrell; John H. Slaght, George C. Valentine, John D. Coursen, Robert M. Inscho, Herbert K. Salmon, N. A. Woodruff.

Sussex Borough.

President, William D. Wilson; Vice President, A. C. Tully; Clerk, John E. Stickney; Fritz H. Nilsson, Robert Burns, Winfield S. Martin, Samuel S. Vandruff, Parker S. McCoy, George W. Sutton.

Byram Township.

President, Jesse L. Roleson; Vice President, James Sutton; Clerk, Frank W. Spranger, Hiram Stone, George P. Hart.

Frankford Township.

President, Robert V. Armstrong; Vice President, Geo. B. Titman; Clerk, Boyd S. Ely; J. W. Fountain, Thomas C. Roe, J. E. Dickerson, George O. Kymer, Joseph F. Rutan, James H. Ayers.

Fredon Township.

President, Charles M. Gruver; Vice President, Joseph E. Huff; Clerk, Frank Emmans; Clinton R. Hardin, David A. Manley, George W. VanHorn, W. R. Morris, A. C. Snook, J. Hampton Roy.

Green Township.

President, Fred R. Labar; Vice President, Howell Hamilton; Clerk, Clarence Cooke; I. F. Straley, James Coates, Daniel H. Longcor, Theodore Hunt, Jr., E. E. Lambert, Sidney Hull.

Hampton Township.

President, Jacob R. Ackerson; Vice President, John Thompson; Clerk, Frank N. Kelleger; John A. Van Atta, Nathaniel Jones, Andrew J. Hendershot, Charles J. Hendershot, Charles Van Horn, Harry Vail, Dennis Morris, John Fields.

Hardyston Township.

President, W. H. Ingersoll; Vice President, Caleb Farber; Clerk, Smith Simpson; John L. Woods, H. S. Potter, Grant Edsall, Raymond Dymock, Milton A. Bird, Thos. P. Renouf.

Lafayette Township.

President, Fred M. Pellet; Vice President, Arthur A. Edwards; Clerk, William S. Vought; Fred Snook, J. H. Iliff, Peter Simmons, W. E. Plotts, W. J. Vought, C. E. Mackerley.

Montague Township.

President, Joseph Shimer; Vice President, Harry Cortright; Clerk, John Middleton; Bruce A. Penny, Daniel Smith, Joseph Martin, Jacob McCarty, Henry Schneider.

Newton.

President, Harvey S. Hopkins; Vice President, Warren H. Smith; Clerk, R. Tuttle; W. H. Sherred, Whitfield Gray, Fred R. Snyder, Henry W. Huston, John Iliff, William Hutt.

Vernon Township.

President, T. B. Storms; Vice President, F. A. Mott; Clerk, W. L. Rohn; N. P. Ryerson, Jesse Barrett, L. R. Barrett, L. R. Martin, F. A. Mingle, Whitfield Davenport, B. F. Paddock, Theodore Hunt.

Walpack Township.

President, Charles P. Haney; Vice President, Wesley Garris; Clerk, Edward Darrone.

Wantage Township.

President, A. D. Hough; Vice President, A. J. Davenport; Clerk, Jason C. House; L. B. Dunn, S. M. Parcell, Dolson Ayers, Frank B. Compton, Edward Layton, W. W. Titsworth.

CHURCHES.

Frankford Plains Methodist Episcopal Church.

This church was undoubtedly the first church of any denomination in Sussex county. While the first settlers were contending with the Indians for possession of northern New Jersey, the people living in what is now the township of Frankford and Wantage, met and worshipped in a little log church standing in one corner of what is now the Frankford Plains cemetery. This church was built in 1710 and from the names of some of the pastors it was evident that it belonged to some branch of the German churches. The log church was replaced by a frame structure in 1750, being built by the same society that built the log church. In 1787 the control of the church passed to the Methodist society and Rev. Thomas Merrill, an officer in Washington's command, who was converted at Valley Forge, was the Methodist pastor, licensed by Bishop Asbury. In 1800 this church was torn down and the lumber used in constructing a barn on a nearby farm. A third church known as the old "Plains Church" was built in 1800 alongside the highway. The timber used in constructing the frame was sawed from logs grown on the farm now owned by Lynch Wyker and the carpenter work was done by James Hamilton. This church stood until 1860, when it was sold. When the church was built one side extended a few feet on the land of an adjoining farmer, with his consent. This caused the church people a great deal of trouble and in order to prevent the Free Church party from moving the building the Methodists fastened it with lock and chain to a tree, while the Free Church party to prevent the Methodists from moving it, fastened it with lock and chains to a post set in the ground on the other side of the line. The trouble was only settled by the sale of the adjoining farm. This church edifice was sold in 1860 and a fourth Plains Church was erected and dedicated on January 31, 1861. The cornerstone having been laid in June, 1860. The building of a church near Deckertown in 1830 drew some of the congregation away from Plains Church and the building of other churches in parts of the community drew still more, and when in 1840 a church was built at Lafayette the two churches were placed under one pastor and services were held in the Plains Church in the afternoon. In 1866 Frankford Plains and Branchville were set off as a separate charge, being thus associated together until 1893, when the Plains Church became a separate charge. Since that time it has been supplied by students from Drew Theological Seminary. In 1911 the church was repaired and the interior greatly changed.

The third church built in 1800 was ceiled with pine boards and painted white. The seats were also of pine boards, those on the right being reserved for the ladies and on the left for the men. The church was heated by two box stoves, one on either side and a pipe from each stove led to a drum near the center of the church, while from this drum a pipe ran about thirty feet to the center of the roof. The pulpit was about eight feet high, the floor being supported by a single post in the center.

On quarterly meeting days it is estimated that 1,500 people were sometimes crowded in the church and as many more remained on the outside. The services commenced with a love feast at nine o'clock, with preaching and communion services at ten o'clock. The present pastor of the church is E. R. Graham.

Stillwater M. E. Church.

Methodism was introduced in Stillwater in 1801. In that year James Egbert, a resident of Stillwater, visited his former home in Hunterdon county and heard Rev. Elijah Woolsey preach. He invited Mr. Woolsey to come to Stillwater and preach there. The first sermon was preached in the house of Jacob Maines. The novelty of a Methodist minister in the neighborhood drew a large crowd. The sermon resulted in the organization of a class of 12 members, probably the first Methodist class formed in Sussex county. For several years services were held either in the open air or in the Maines home. Stillwater was made a regular appointment of the Flanders circuit in 1802. For a time services were held in a barn opposite the home of Martin Kishpaugh. At the time Stillwater was made an appointment there were only eleven appointments in the State with less than 4,000 members. The Flanders circuit embraced about one-half of the State. The preachers in the appointment had about 75 appointments, travelling on horse back from one to the other, being absent from home seven weeks at a time.

In 1832 Stillwater was transferred to the Warren circuit and at the close of the year subscriptions were taken for the building of a church edifice, which was erected early in 1833, under a contract given to Thomas A. Dildine for $1,350. The church was dedicated in the fall of that year by the Rev. Isaac Winner. A Sunday school was formed in 1834. In 1889 Stillwater was separated from the Swartswood church and made a pastoral charge alone. In 1862 under the pastorate of Rev. I. N. Vansant 100 people joined the church, and in 1875, 100 more were added. In addition to the pastors named above, the following have served at that church: Rev. J. C. Hall, Frederick Bloom, E. W. Bice, W. H. Whitte, H. B. Allen, R. H. Schoonover, DeWitt A. Berry, Seth W. Longacre, James McClintock, A. J. Sunderland and William H. Sloat. The present pastor is the Rev. Frederick S. Benson.

Sparta M. E. Church.

Although Methodism was introduced in Sparta in the year of 1820, it was not until 1842 that a church was built. The building was erected on the lot now occupied by the residence of William G. Palmer. This building was sold in 1868 and the present church edifice and parsonage built on Newton avenue. The present pastor is Rev. J. G. Lytle, who was installed in 1912.

Baleville Christian Church.

The Baleville Christian Church was founded in 1826 at Branchville by Revs. Simon Clough and J. S. Thompson. The church edifice was erected at Baleville in 1836 and was remodeled in 1906. The present pastor is Rev. E. E. Hoffman. He has served the church for the past two years.

Tranquility Methodist Episcopal Church.

The Tranquility Methodist Episcopal Church was built in 1828 following the holding of meetings at Long Bridge. In 1866 the original building was removed to Quakertown and is now used as a school house, the upper part long having been used for preaching services. A new edifice was erected the same year. Rev. John Talmadge was pastor in 1828, the Rev. Isaac Van Sant being the first pastor after the building of the new church in 1866. Since the building of the first church in 1828, over fifty pastors have served the congregation. Rev. S. O. Rusby is the present pastor.

First Presbyterian Church of Beemerville.

was founded in 1834 by the Presbytery of Newark. The church edifice was erected at once and dedicated on January 4, 1835. The building has been remodeled a number of times; the last time in 1912. The first pastor of the church was Rev. Edward Allen. The subsequent pastors being: Rev. Peter Kanouse, Rev. Robert Crossette, Rev. Nathan Leighton, Rev. Ambrose C. Smith, Rev. Stephen D. Noyes, Rev. Andrew Tully, Rev. William F. Arms, Rev. Charles E. Burns, Rev. Charles P. Clover, Rev. Glenroie McQueen, Rev. Alex M. Higgins, Rev. Joseph Dixon. The present pastor is Rev. William G. Westervelt, who has been in charge of the congregation for the past ten years.

The church officers are as follows: Elders, Barret A. Van Auken, Merritt L. Hockenberry, Henry S. Phillips, E. Willis Clark, John B. Compton.

Lafayette M. E. Church.

was founded December 9, 1837. The first meeting for the organization of the church was held at the home of Isaac Van Gilder, at which time trustees were elected. For a time meetings were held at the homes of various members of the congregation. The church edifice was erected in 1841. It was remodeled in 1859. It was burned and rebuilt in 1898.

Warren C. Nelson was the first pastor on record, being in charge of the church in 1843. The first quarterly conference recorded in the church minutes was July 13, 1844. The present pastor is Rev. William C. Casperson. The trustees are as follows: J. W. Hagerman, Joseph Slaughter, James Iliff, Michael Tidaback, Arthur Edwards, Martin Mabie, William Hopper. The stewards are: J. D. Ackerson, J. E. Jones, Brice Stanton, Ford Ackerson, Jacob Losey, Frederick Snook, William F. Runion.

First Presbyterian Church of Franklin

was erected in 1837 and remodeled in 1894. The first pastor was Rev. George B. Crawford, Rev. Edwin C. Holman is the present pastor, having been in charge of the church since Jan. 1, 1910. The church officers are: James May, Samuel Rowe, Frank Edwards, Thomas J. Treloar.

First Presbyterian Church of Stanhope.

The first Presbyterian Church of Stanhope was founded June 11, 1838, by Rev. Asa Hillyer and Elder Silas C. Byram, the first pastor being Rev. John Ward. The first church edifice was built in 1844 and has since been remodelled twice, once in 1867 and again in 1901. The present pastor is Rev. N. P. Crouse, who began his pastorate there on March 1, 1905. Since the closing of Rev. Mr. Wards' pastorate there have been 13 men to fill the pulpit as follows: Rev. Ashel Bronson, Rev. Oliver W. Norton, Rev. Robert Crossett, Rev. O. H. P. Deyo, Rev. Charles Milne, Rev. James Morton, Rev. John J. Crane, Rev. Joseph W. Porter, Rev. S. W. Boardman, Rev. I. H. Condit, Rev. E. K. Donaldson, Rev. B. J. Morgan, Rev. N. P. Crouse. The present church officers are: Session, A. B. Cope, Orren W. King and Silas E. King.

Monroe Christian Church.

The Monroe Christian Church was founded in 1850 by Rev. Abigail Roberts. The church edifice was built at once. The building was remodeled in July, 1885. The first pastor was Rev. D. W. Moore, his successors being Rev. W. M. Pitman, Rev. W. M. Bothwick and Rev. J. C. Emerson. The present pastor, Rev. E. French, took charge in September of last year. The present church officers are: R. D. Smith, Oscar Stoll, J. H. Sutton, Stephen Smith and Joseph Van Blarcom.

Andover First Methodist Church.

The first church in Andover was erected by the Baptists in 1834, assisted by a provision in the will of a Miss Hill. The congregation was small and after an effort of nearly twenty years to sustain the church, the building was sold to William M. Iliff, who resold it to Judge Azariah Davis. Judge Davis deeded the building to the trustees of the First M. E. Church of Andover in 1854, that denomination having organized in 1853. The first pastor was Rev. Reuben Van Syckle, who was assisted by Rev. T. H. Smith, of Newton. The church edifice was remodeled in 1859. The building as it stands at present was built early in 1893 and dedicated during June of that year.

The first Board of Trustees elected consisted of: Judge Davis, William T. Hunt, J. V. Van Syckle, James L. Northrup, William McConnell, Peter VanNess, Samuel Hibler and Reuben Van Syckle. The Rev. Benson S. Crowcroft is at present pastor of the church. The official board consists of: W. R. Ayers, President; Dr. J. C. Clark, Secretary and Treasurer; William H. Valentine, E. N. Reed, Frank McDavit and A. O. Ayers.

Swartswood M. E. Church.

This church was built in 1856, being dedicated on October 14th of that year. The dedicatory ceremony was preached by Rev. William P. Corbett. The first pastor was the Rev. Geo. A. Carmichael. Until 1891 the church was connected with the Harmony M. E. Church and in that year it was made a separate organization. The present pastor is Rev. James Howe, who was installed in October, 1912.

Waterloo Methodist Episcopal Church.

The Methodist Episcopal Church of Waterloo stands largely as a monument to the religious zeal, generosity and loyalty of the late Peter Smith and his family. The society was organized in the house of Peter Smith on March 24, 1859. The first board of trustees was composed of Peter Smith, James C. Ayers, Samuel W. Stackhouse, John Burrell, William M. Bryan, Hon. Samuel T. Smith, Abraham L. Clark, George W. D. White and Benson S. Clark. The Rev. George T. Jackson was the first pastor. In the spring of 1904 the Waterloo charge was taken from the Stanhope charge and has since been served by the following pastors: Charles W. Collard, W. W. Millard, L. B. McMickle, W. F. Hunter and J. A. Hills, all students from Drew Seminary. Morris T. Gibbs, who served the charge four years when it was connected with Stanhope, is the present pastor. The officers of the church are: S. R. Smith, Lewis Smith, Peter D. Smith, A. L. Cassidy,

Abram B. Force, Miss Melissa Cassidy, Mrs. Frank Smith, Philip Dolan, John R. Mooney and George Ball. Legacies for the support of the church and other benevolences have been left by John Smith, father of Peter Smith; Peter Smith, Samuel T. Smith and Mrs. Frances L. Hetzel. These legacies are in the care of S. R. Smith, President of the Hackettstown National Bank. Mr. Smith is also treasurer of the church.

First Methodist Church of Branchville.

Prior to 1864 Branchville belonged to the Lafayette charge, which included the townships of Lafayette and Frankford. In the spring of 1864 the Methodists of Branchville and vicinity decided to build a Methodist Church and a celebration was held on July 4th of that year for the purpose of securing funds. The net receipts of this celebration amounted to $700. On July 16th a meeting was held in the Academy, a society was organized and trustees elected. William H. Bell deeded a lot to the society upon which was to be erected a Methodist Episcopal Church. The lot fronted on South Main street, as Broad street at that time was a meadow and only open as far as the dwelling now owned by Mrs. S. R. Crane. The ground for the new church was broken on Saturday, August 13th, and the cornerstone was laid on October 20th. $501.37 was raised by subscriptions. The frame for the church was drawn by the citizens from the north side of the Blue Mountains, about three miles from Tuttles' Corner. The mason work was let by contract for $500 and the carpenter work, exclusive of the f ame, for $3,000. The size of the building was 40x60 feet. The building was raised and partially enclosed when a heavy gale of wind blew it down. This left the society in debt to the amount of $1,300.

The following spring the charge was divided and the Rev. J. H. Runyon was given the charges of Branchville and Frankford Plains, and $90 missionary money was apportioned to the charge to aid in his support. On May 4th, 1865, the trustees and a number of others met and took down the broken timbers and disposed of same. On this sale they realized $175. This money, to which funds were added from time to time, was used to liquidate the indebtedness. During this period the lot had been sold, the walls partially taken down and a blacksmith shop had been erected upon the spot. From 1865 to 1878 the society worshipped in halls and school houses. In August, 1878, the society decided to build again. Mrs. Aseneth Bedell left, in her will, $100 to the society providing they built within a certain time. On July 10, 1879, the audience room was dedicated. Rev. Dr. C. N. Sims preaching the dedicatory sermon. About $600 was raised leaving a debt of about $1,100. The debt was reduced gradually until in 1882, when Rev. M. T. Gibbs became pastor it was decided to procure a bell. In order to have a solid foundation it was thought best to start the spire from the ground, thereby enlarging the church and making a more attractive edifice. This was done at an expense of $1,000. This amount was raised by subscription and money, leaving the society as before the undertaking, $600 in debt. In the meantime one of the leading trustees died, H. J. Bedell, and by his will he left the society $300. The balance of indebtedness was raised and all indebtedness was cancelled during the pastorate of Rev. C. M. Anderson. In 1890, during the pastorate of Rev. J. W. Ryder, the walls were handsomely decorated in oil colors. In 1892 the basement was neatly finished and paid for together with a small floating debt. Rev. W. A. Knox was pastor at that time. In 1889 a lot adjoining the church was procured and a parsonage erected. In 1906, during the pastorate of Rev. W. C. James, the auditorium was remodeled, also new pews and carpet were put in, new windows, the floor was elevated and the rear entrance to the basement was changed to a front entrance. This was done at a cost of $3,300. During the pastorate of Rev. F. G. Willey, 1911-1913, the church underwent extensive repairs, both inside and out. The church has also enjoyed a marked religious growth.

St. Thomas Roman Catholic Church.

This church was founded in 1881 at Ogdensburg by the Rev. A .M. Kammer, who was the first pastor. The church edifice was built at once. It was later burned and rebuilt, the new building being remodeled some years later. In August, 1912, the new church was dedicated. The first pastor lived at Franklin Furnace. Since that time the priests in charge at Franklin go to Ogdensburg and hold services. The lay trustees are John Brachen and Henry Epple. Rev. W. V. Dunn is now pastor of St. Thomas Church, having served for about one year.

Colesville M. E. Church.

Colesville M. E. Church was erected in 1887 by members of that denomination living at Colesville and in the immediate neighborhood. The first pastor was Rev. L. F. Bowman. This church also includes Libertyville, where preaching services are held Sunday afternoons. The pastors who have served the church since Mr. Bowman are: Rev. J. W. Ryder, Henry C. Thompson, Samuel O. Rusby, William B. Cuonic, William Reberzer, Gerhard J. Schilling, David P. Weidner, M. L. Andaniere, E. H. Atwood, F. C. Raymouth, E. W. Kelley, Clyde E. Baker, D. D. Smalley, the present pastor being Rev. William Martin. The church officers are: C. C. Meddaugh, R. S. Coursen, Jonas Simpson, Elmer Slate, P. P. Swarts, H. D. Hoffman, W. W. Harden, Joseph Ayers, Charles Ayers, Peter Hockenberry, August Beechlotz, William J. Howell, Levatus Wilson.

Magyar Reformed Church, Franklin.

Magyar Reformed Church, of Franklin, was founded in 1909 by Hungarians of that place who, with the help of the New Jersey Zinc Company, erected a church building opposite the public school building. The parsonage was built in 1912. Rev. John Ambrus has been in charge of the church since its organization. To assist in the maintenance of the church and its working, the New Jersey Zinc Company donates $500 yearly. The officers of the church are: President, Bertie Barta; Presbyters, Alex Helmecri, George Times, Mike Szoto, and Tmre Jaeac.

GRANGES.

The Patrons of Husbandry, otherwise known as the Grange, is one of the strongest semi-secret organizations in the county, and the most potent organization for the benefit of the farmer. Scattered around the county, in practically every town and village, are thirteen subordinate Granges, with a total membership of about 900. Until of recent years the Grange was merely an organization, the members of which met weekly or semi-monthly, as the case might be, for the purpose of passing a social hour. Lately, however, the farmer has come to realize that to insure proper recognition for himself and his products, he must organize the same as any other trade or profession. To-day the meetings of the Grange are filled with the discussion of how to better grow and enlarge the crops produced, and with addresses by experts along different lines of farm work. The work of the housewife is also given attention, for the farmer's wife and daughter are live, working, integral parts of the organization and life of the Grange.

In the Grange work there are seven degrees, the first four being worked by the subordinate Grange, the fifth by the Pomona Grange, the sixth by the State Grange and the seventh by the National Grange. Of the 872 members in Sussex county, 339 have taken the fifth degree, about 200 the sixth, and 28 the seventh. The first Grange in the county was organized over forty years ago, at Branchville, with thirty-seven members. Following this Granges were organized at Lafayette,

Hamburg, Layton, Deckertown, (now Sussex), Walpack, Andover and Fredon. For a time the organization prospered and on June 4, 1875, pursuant to a call issued by County Deputy Daniel Wyker, of Branchville, delegates from the various granges assembled in Library Hall, Newton, for the purpose of organizing a Pomona Grange. The representatives were: Branchville, No. 23, Jacob A. Coursen, Daniel Wyker, Sarah Wyker, Z. H. Price, L. H. S. Martin and Sarah Martin; Lafayette, No. 33, Sylvester Slater, Mary Slater, Raymond Snyder and Dr. Franklin Smith; Hamburg, No. 47, W. H. Edsall, L. W. Pellett, John P. Wilson and Sarah Wilson; Layton, No. 72, Elias H. Roe, William Clark, Stewart Layton, Ophelia Layton and Huldah Roe; Deckertown, No. 78, Abiah Wilson, Lebeus M. Martin, J. S. DeWitt and Kate Titsworth; Walpack, No. 82, J. H. Wood, J. W. Bunnell and Josephine Wood; Andover, No. 83, Albert Puder, John Ayers, Lydia Hart and William Iliff; Fredon, No. 94, was not represented.

After a short preliminary meeting these officers were elected: Master, Dr. Franklin Smith; Overseer, Sylvester Slater; Lecturer, John H. Wood; Steward, Jacob A. Coursen; Assistant Steward, J. W. Bunnell; Chaplain, Albert Puder; Treasurer, Daniel Wyker; Secretary, L. H. S. Martin; Gatekeeper, Elias Roe; Ceres, Sarah Wyker; Pomona, Huldah Roe; Flora, Ophelia Layton; Lady Assistant Steward, Sarah Martin. Mortimer Whitehead, Master of the New Jersey State Grange and staff, were present, and conferred the fifth degree on the delegates. The first executive committee was as follows: Z. H. Price, Raymond Snyder, W. H. Edsall, William Clark, Lebus Martin, I. S. Rundle and John Ayers. The second meeting was held at Branchville on June 23, 1875, and a large class was initiated. For two years the work progressed rapidly and then for some unknown cause interest was lost. At the meeting at Lafayette on June 1, 1878, only three Granges were represented, and it was decided to discontinue the Pomona Grange in the county.

The various subordinate Granges also lost in membership and finally but one Grange with a membership of forty-nine was left in the whole county. For a number of years nothing was done in Grange affairs. Richard M. Holly was made county deputy by the State body. Working day and night Holly succeeded in again interesting the farmers, and during his terms as deputy he organized eleven subordinate Granges and the present Sussex County Pomona Grange, which was organized June 7, 1905, thirty years to the day from the time of the organization of the first Pomona Grange.

The present Pomona Grange started with fifty-three charter members, its present membership being nearly 400. Since its organization it has lost by death ten members and by demit three. The Masters since 1905 have been: 1905, R. M. Holly; 1906, J. Linn Quick; 1907, A. P. Shaw; 1908, E. W. Clark; 1909, W. B. Hough; 1910-1911, Thomas W. DeKay; 1913-1914, R. L. Everett. George E. Hursh, of Layton, was the first secretary until 1908, when he was succeeded by Geo. C. Smith, of Hamburg. In January, 1909, full regalia was purchased by the organization. The present officers are: Master, Robert L. Everett; Overseer, Sanford J. Crawn; Steward, Ira Stoll; A. S., J. M. Willson; Lecturer, Frank Stoll; Chaplain, R. M. Holly; Treasurer, Alex. A. Watt; Secretary, George C. Smith; G. K., James M. Shay; Ceres, Mrs. R. V. Armstrong; Pomona, Mrs. C. L. Giveans; Flora, Mrs. D. C. Howell; L. A. S., Rose Reinhardt; Alternate to the State Grange, H. W. Gilbertson.

Wantage, No. 78.

Master, Eugene Slaughter; Lecturer, Mrs. Brice Roy; Secretary, Mrs. Evi Vandruff.

Vernon Valley, No. 134.

Master, Charles L. Giveans; Lecturer, Rev. Hiram G. Conger; Secretary, Emma P. Giveans.

Mt. View, No. 137.

Master, S. LeRoy Tuttle; Lecturer, Elinor Perry; Secretary, Mrs. D. Ayers.

Montague, No. 140.

Master, John Scheels; Lecturer, C. Reinhardt; Secretary, H. E. Courtright.

Delaware Valley, No. 143.

Master, Ira Stoll; Lecturer, Frank Stoll; Secretary, Geo. E. Hursh.

Lafayette, No. 158.

Master, Brice B. Stanton; Lecturer, Mrs. Fannie Runion; Secretary, Anna Everett.

Frankford, No. 160.

Master, Andrew Sherred; Lecturer, Mrs. Thomas C. Roe; Secretary, Mrs. Bertha P. Conover.

Hardyston, No. 164.

Master, John S. Katzenstein; Lecturer, Mrs. E. K. Martin; Secretary, George C. Smith.

Enterprise, No. 165.

Master, W. W. Roy; Lecturer, Louis N. Hunt; Secretary, C. M. Crawn.

Swartswood Lake, No. 176.

Master, B. T. Hill; Lecturer, Mrs. T. Hill; Secretary, A. W. Huff.

Stillwater, No. 177.

Master, John W. Earl; Lecturer, O. Van Horn; Secretary, William C. Earl.

Pequest, No. 178.

Master, James S. Coates; Lecturer, Mrs. Grace Stickles; Secretary, C. Cooke.

FRATERNAL ORGANIZATIONS.

Harmony Lodge, No. 8, F. & A. M., Newton.

Worshipful Master, Frank D. Whyms; Senior Warden, Jacob Herman; Junior Warden, William H. Cooper; Treasurer, Past Master Abram P. Van Sickle; Secretary, Henry C. Bonnell; Senior Deacon, Floyd C. Devore; Junior Deacon, Martin J. Cox; Senior Master of Ceremonies, Wilbur D. Boss; Junior Master of Ceremonies, George H. Moore; Chaplain, Rev. Ernest C. Tuthill; Senior Steward, Sherwood D. Van Campen; Junior Steward, Harry F. Clark; Marshal, Andrew J. VanBlarcom; Tyler, Svante Swanberg; Trustee for three years, Richard F. Goodman; Auditing Committee, Past Master Lester Layton, F. C. Devore and Past Master J. Victor Rosenkrans; Representative to Grand Lodge, Philetus R. Van Horn.

Baldwin Chapter, No. 17, Royal Arch Masons, Newton.

High Priest, A. P. Van Sickle; King, Harvey S. Hopkins; Sojourner, Richard F. Goodman; Treasurer, Andrew J. Van Blarcom; Secretary, Henry C. Bonnell; C. of H., Jacob Herman; P. S., Ora C. Simpson; R. A. C., Howard E. Shimer; Trustee three years, Warren H. Smith; two years, Richard F. Goodman; one year, Fred R. Snyder; Grand Master 3rd Veil, William F. Hazelton; 2nd Veil, Martin J. Cox; 1st Veil, Chas. A. Boss; Chaplain, Rev. John R. Humphreys; Tyler, Svante Swanberg; Standing Committee, Harvey S. Hopkins, Charles Fredenburg, Levi H. Morris.

FRATERNAL ORGANIZATIONS.

Kittatinny Lodge, No. 164, F. & A. M.

W. M., Lewis Ike; Sr. W., J. Martin Couse; Jr. W., Ole M. Whitaker; Treasurer, William C. Cook; Secretary, George W. Roe; Chaplain, Rev. F. G .Willey; Sr. D., Robert Shotwell; Jr. D., Burson C. DePue; Sr. M. of C., Marcus L. Bond; Jr. M. of C., William Gould; Tyler, Frank R. Dalrymple; Auditing Committee, John A. McCarrick, P. M., Burson C. Depue; Trustees, A. J. Canfield, T. J. McDanolds.

Owassa Chapter, No. 14, O. E. S., Branchville.

Worthy Matron, Mrs. Mary E. McCarrick; Assistant Matron, Mrs. Elizabeth Fair Riddell; Secretary, Mrs. Mary F. Depue; Treasurer, Mrs. Linnie Cook; Conductress, Mrs. Hannah Roe; Associate Conductress, Mrs. Minnie Ellett; Marshall, Mrs. Alfred Struble; Chaplain, Mrs. Cynthia McNeilie; Adah, Mrs. Amanda Rosenkrans; Ruth, Mrs. Bertha Parcelle; Esther, Mrs. Sarah Silvers; Martha, Mrs. Flora M. Lantz; Electa, Mrs. Rosa Ike; Warder, Mrs. Irene McNeillie; Sentinel, Charles H. Crisman; Organist, Mrs. Cora McDanolds; Trustee, Mrs. Flora A. Lantz; Financial Committee, Mrs. Martha Struble, Rosa Ike, J. Martin Couse, P. P.

Musconetcong Lodge, No. 151, F. & A. M., Stanhope.

Worshipful Master, Robert Mershon; Senior Warden, William Sickles; Junior Warden, Dr. H. G. McElroy; Treasurer, James Powers; Secretary, A. B. Cope; Chaplain, H. A. Timbrell; Senior Master of Ceremonies, Charles H. Timbrell; Junior Master of Ceremonies, John Cooper; Tyler, Lorenzo McKinley; Trustees, Thomas J. Knight and Isaac Kinnicutt; Representative to Grand Lodge, Frank Stackhouse; Trustee of Masonic Realty Association of Stanhope, G. H. Lunger.

Samaritan Lodge, F. & A. M., Sussex Borough.

Worthy Master, Robert Burns; Senior Warden, Harry Harden; Junior Warden, William Stephens; Treasurer, Seymour H. Lawrence; Secretary, J. J. Coons; Trustee, C. A. Potter.

Ivy Lodge, No. 221, I. O. O. F.

Past Grand, William Iliff; Noble Grand, Frank W. Lord; Vice Grand, Charles P. Demarest; Recording Secretary, Geo. O. Eagles; Financial Secretary, Peter M. Knight; Treasurer, Lewis J. Kishpaugh.

Estella Rebekah, Newton.

Noble Grand, Rose East; Vice Grand, Edna Kerr; Recording Secretary, Florence Grover; Financial Secretary, Sadie Linden; Treasurer, Mary Braisted; Right Support to Noble Grand, Margaret Savacool; Left Support to Noble Grand, Amelia Grimm; Right Support to Vice Grand, Florence Rodimer; Left Support to Vice Grand, Bertha Coates; Warden, Jennie Howell; Conductor, Ada Kishpaugh; Outside Guardian, Minnie Robeson; Inside Guardian, Minnie Dickinson; Chaplain, Ida Maines.

Cupid Encampment, No. 7, I. O. O. F.

Chief Patriarch, Lewis J. Kishpaugh; High Priest, William Iliff; Senior Warden, Willis M. Howell; Junior Warden, Leonard Minnikin; Scribe, Charles A. Walker; Treasurer, Albert Grover.

Culver Lodge, No. 133, Branchville.

Noble Grand, Conrad F. Lockburner; Vice Grand, Geo. E. Knox; Recording Secretary, Ole M. Whitaker; Financial Secretary, Gabriel S. Crone; Treasurer, Louis Steibig; Warden, Isaiah Hornbeck; Conductor, Richard M. Kimball; R. S. S., Nelson Van Orden; L. S. S., Harry Dalrymple; R. S. N. G., Burson C. DePue; L. S. N. G. Charles Gould; R. S. V. G., Arthur Bowman; L. S. V. G., William Hooey; Chaplain, Rev. William C. Perez; Inside Guardian, Roy Hamm.

Olive Lodge, No. 41, I. O. O. F., Stanhope.

Noble Grand, S. G. Wilgus; Vice Grand, Max Lezette; Treasurer, A. J. Almer; Recording Secretary, Peter Hummer; Financial Secretary, William H. Mowery.

Mescal Rebekah Lodge, No. 60, I. O. O. F., Branchville.

Noble Grand, Mrs. Elizabeth Ingersoll, re-elected; Vice Grand, Mrs. Mary Skinner; Recording Secretary, Mrs. H. E. Ridell; Financial Secretary, Mrs. Gabriel Stone; Treasurer, Miss Mae Ingersoll.

Washington Camp, No. 18, P. O. S. of A., Newton.

President, Wm. H. McPeek; Past President, Fred Berry; Vice President, Anthony Pflug; Master of Forms, Cecil O. Bell; Recording Secretary, John D. Kinney; Financial Secretary, James L. Kymer; Treasurer, Charles M. Oakes; Conductor, Hector Saunders; Inspector, Roy Condit; Guard, Richard W. Hawkey; Trustee, Alonzo Stevens.

Washington Camp, No. 18, P. O. S. of A., Branchville.

Past President, William B. Kays; President, R. W. Kimball; Recording Secretary, H. J. S. Struble; Financial Secretary, B. F. Rosenkrans; Master of Forms, George Williams; Guard, A. C. Struble; Inspector, Martin W. Everitt; Chaplain, O. D. Ellett; Treasurer, B. F. Rosenkrans; Trustee, Edward M. Smith.

Washington Camp, P. O. S. of A., Stillwater.

Past President, William C. Maines; President, Eugene Huff; Vice President, Charles Vanstone; Master of Forms, Hiram L. Beegle; Financial Secretary, Robert Snyder; Secretary, Charles M. Garris; Treasurer, Schooley J. Huff; Inspector, Obadiah Van Horn; Conductor, George Campbell; Outer Guard, Charles Chamberlain.

Washington Camp, No. 24, P. O. S. of A., Stanhope.

President, Mrs. Elizabeth Hummer; Assistant President, Mrs. Alice Lance; Vice President, Miss Josephine Lance; Assistant Vice President, Miss Amy Hulmes; Secretary, William Niper; Financial Secretary, Mrs. Maggie Mallay; Treasurer, Mrs. Susan Chamberlain; Past President, Mrs. Jennie Angus; Assistant Past President, Mrs. William Niper; Conductor, Mrs. Helen Wolverton; Guard, Mrs. Peter Best; Sentinel, Miss Pearl Lance; Trustees, Mrs. William Niper, Mrs. Arabella Anders and Mrs. Alice Lance.

Normanock Tribe, I. O. R. M., Newton.

Sachem, Levi Tice; Senior Sagamore, Walter R. Taylor; Junior Sagamore, George B. VanAuken; Prophet, Lewis O. Dreher; Chief of Records, George M. Keepers; Collector of Wampum, Lorenzo E. Dobbins; Keeper of Wampum, William A. Miller; First Sannap, George Coates; Second Sannap, Alvah Hissam; First Warrior, Joseph Werner; Second Warrior, Floyd Cosner; Third Warrior, Arthur Stoll; Fourth Warrior, William Green; First Brave, Harry Vale; Second Brave, Bert Bale; Third Brave, Claude Condit; Fourth Brave, William Stoll; Guard of Wigwam, Cecil Bell; Guard of Forest, Lester Bowman.

Newton Council, No. 259, Jr. O. U. A. M.

Councilor, Harry Tice; Vice Councilor, Harry Masters; Recording Secretary, J. D. Kinney; Assistant Recording Secretary, James L. Kymer; Financial Secretary, Howard Rodimer; Treasurer, Charles M. Oakes; Conductor, Edgar

Hough; Warden, Claude Condit; Inside Sentinel, Wm. McPeek; Outside Sentinel, Richard Hawkey; Jr. Past Councilor, Cecil O. Bell; Trustee, Ivan McPeek; Representative, John W. Dobbins.

Musconetcong Council, Jr. O. U. A. M., Stanhope.

Councilor, Jesse Campbell; Vice Councilor, George E. Saunders; Recording Secretary, Charles Hull; Assistant Secretary, Roy Hull; Financial Secretary, Robert Lewis; Treasurer, William Niper; Conductor, Charles Fluke; Warden, Roy Lance; Inside Guard, Russell Smith; Outside Guard, Harold Saunders; Trustee, Thomas Haggerty.

Newton Lodge, No. 41, Knights of Pythias.

Chancellor Commander, Raymond E. Byram; Vice Chancellor, John LaForge; Prelate, F. Ernest Wallace; M. of W., Frank H. Nickels; K. of R. and S., Martin J. Cox; M. of F., J. Rusling Cornell; M. of E., Morris C. Siple; M. at A., Moses Strader; I. G., Cyrus Muir; O. G., Fred Nickels.

Pythian Sisters, No. 12.

Past Chief, Mary Howell; Most Excellent Chief, Helen Dobbins; Excellent Sr., Jennie Gunn; Excellent Jr., Margaret Nickels; M. of F., Hattie Barber; M. of R. & C., Edna Kerr; Manager, Amelia Slaght; Protector, Mrs. M. J. Dunlap; Guard, Mabel Washer; Trustees, Jennie Gunn and Margaret Hutton; Grand Representative, Nellie Wallace; Alternate, Minnie Johnston; Pianist, Nellie Wallace; Captains of Degree Staff, Margaret Hutton; Julia La Forge.

Whittier Council, No. 1313, Royal Arcanum, Newton.

Past Regent, Philip Friedman; Regent, Philip S. Wilson; Vice Regent, Edgar Hough; Collector, John W. Bryant; Treasurer, James Roof; Secretary, Winfield Coe; Guide, T. S. Stone; Orator, Harry H. Hendershot; Chaplain, William H. Jones; Sentry, Andrew Snover; Warden, Wm. Lavene.

General Kilpatrick, No. 1631, Royal Arcanum, Sussex.

Regent, C. E. Tuttle; Vice Regent, R. Decker; S. P. Regent, A. W. Bedell; Orator, C. L. Rutan; Secretary, R. F. Gordon; Collector, N. VanDine; Treasurer, L. Potter; Chaplain, A. Snook; Guide, H. C. Peterson; Warden, E. Wilson; Sentry, J. P. Cosh; Trustee for three years, C. A. Potter.

Newton Tent, No. 9, Knights of Maccabees.

Past Commander, M. J. Boyer; Commander, Cecil O. Bell; Lieutenant Commander, J. Belcher; Finance Keeper, Charles Straway; Chaplain, William E. Snook; Sergeant, Samuel Pierson; Master-at-Arms, Harry Perry; 1st Master of Guards, Russell Hopper; Sentinel, C. Drake; Picket, Evi Shay.

Newton Camp, No. 14,807, Modern Woodmen.

Past Consul, Benjamin Hornick; Consul, Raymond E. Smith; Advisor, Frank Babcock; Banker, C. J. Hinds; Clerk, Joseph H. Kithcart; Escort, Charles L. Roe; Watchman, Thomas Everett; Sentry, Roy Armstrong; Chief Forester, F. Ernest Wallace.

Newton Lodge, No. 654, Loyal Order of Moose.

Dictator, Theodore Simonson; Vice Dictator, Arthur Beegle; Prelate, Condit B. Roy; Treasurer, Joseph Straulina; Inside Guard, Foster Pierson; Outside Guard, Wilson R. Porter; Trustee three years, John Moffat; Representative to Supreme Lodge, Lewis O. Dreher.

Olympia Conclave, No. 572, Improved Order Heptasophs.

Archon, H. E. Shimer; Secretary, E. J. Quinn; Financier, J. Grimm; Treasurer, L. H. Willson; Prelate, J. W. Poole; Sentinel, H. I. Beemer; Provost, William Knox.

Loyal Order of Buffalos, Newton Herd, No. 18.

Commander, Ivan McPeek; Vice Commander, George Wolf; Past Commander, Collins T. Brown; Prophet, C. Warner; Recording Secretary, Ernest Teets; Financial Secretary, Collins T. Brown; Treasurer, Arthur Beegle; Inside Guard, E. Brown; Outside Guard, A. Bonker.

Newton Ruling Fraternal Mystic Circle.

Newton Ruling No. 629, Fraternal Mystic Circle, was organized January 27, 1897, with 85 charter members. This is an insurance order paying sick and death benefits. Total and partial disability benefits and old age benefits to men and women between the ages of 18 and 49 years. The meetings are held monthly on the last Tuesday evening of each month at 125 Spring street. The present membership is 70. The officers are as follows: A. P. Van Sickle, W. R.; Jacob Grimm, Collector and Secretary; A. C. Van Auken, Treasurer; James Roof, V. R.

Marquette Council, No. 588, K. of C., Franklin.

Grand Knight, Robert H. Collins; Deputy Grand Knight, Henry Epple; Chancellor, Leon Dolan; Warden, William McEntee; Recording Secretary, William Dolan; Financial Secretary, George Selmes; Treasurer, Thomas O'Malley; Inside Guide, Thomas Condon; Outside Guide, Owen Corrigan; Lecturer, James C. Hyde; Trustees, Wm. McEntee, James C. Hyde, John O'Malley.

MISCELLANEOUS ORGANIZATIONS.

Republican County Committee.

Chairman, Frank Armstrong; Vice Chairman, John O. Bissell; Secretary, Harry E. Wells; Treasurer, Charles S. Steele.

Democratic County Committee.

Chairman, George N. Harris; Vice Chairman, W. Frank Hazelton; Secretary, Robert T. Smith; Treasurer, S. Frank Quince.

Young Men's Republican Club of Sussex County.

President, J. Rusling Cornell; Vice President, George L. Dutcher, Philip S. Wilson, John C. Losey; Secretary, E. A. Shay; Treasurer, Louis A. Dalrymple; Board of Trustees, George L. Dutcher, Morris C. Siple, Lewis Van Blarcom, Isaac M. Rundle, Wilbur D. Boss, Herbert W. Bentley, J. Rusling Cornell; Vice Presidents representing the voting districts are: Andover Borough, Joseph Ayers; Andover township, Ira Case; Branchville, D. L. B. Smith; Byram, Hiram Stone; Frankford, Theodore M. Roe; Fredon, William R. Morris; Green, Edward E. Lambert; Hampton, J. Martin Couse; Hardyston, 1st, Reeve Harden; Ogdensburg, J. P. Madden; Sparta, South, Eugene Smith; Stanhope, John Wills; Stillwater, A. D. Cornell; Sussex, Ford W. Margarum; Vernon, Thomas W. DeKay; Walpack, William N. Harris; Wantage, North, Frank Armstrong; Wantage, South, David C. Truex.

Newton League of the Sussex County Suffrage Association.

President, Miss Anna E. Dunn; Vice Presidents, Mrs. Shepard Voorhees, Mrs. John Iliff, Mrs. Harry Snyder; Secretary, Mrs. Allen R. Shay; Treasurer, Mrs. William Sherred.

Newton Board of Trade.

Was organized in May, 1897. The organization meets the first Monday evening in each month in the rooms of the Newton Club. Following are the officers: President, Richard F.

Goodman; Vice President, Thomas E. Murray; Secretary, Edwin M. Quick; Treasurer, Lewis S. Iliff; Trustees, T. W. Bentley, N. H. Hart, C. J. Hinds, H. D. Couse, Theodore Simonson; Committees, Finance, C. J. Hinds, L. H. Wilson, W. H. Nicholls; Transportation, Thomas W. Bentley, Lewis S. Iliff, R. F. Goodman; Town Affairs, J. W. C. Carber, James Roof, E. H. Bell; Industrial, W. W. Roe, N. H. Hart, Theodore Simonson, R. H. Snook, E. A. Shay, W. H. Earl and Fabian Weiss.

Sussex County Historical Society.

President, Nathan A. Stackhouse; Vice President, Ralph Decker; Recording Secretary, Miss Anna E. Dunn; Corresponding Secretary, Charles E. Stickney; Treasurer, Andrew J. VanBlarcom; Trustee, Samuel Warbasse.

Sussex County Bible Society.

President, N. A. Stackhouse, Andover; Vice Presidents, Rev. S. W. Powell, Sussex; Rev. B. S. Crowcroft, Andover; Secretary, F. N. Van Syckle, Andover; Treasurer, J. W. C. Carber, Newton; Depositary, William H. Sherred, Newton.

Epworth League Newton M. E. Church.

President, Charles Downing; Vice Presidents, Frank Perry, Miss Helen Burres, Miss Florence Steele, Mrs. William Morris; Secretary, Miss Kathryn Taylor; Treasurer, William Polhemus; Organist, Mrs. Louise Kindred.

Womans' Auxiliary Christ Church.

President, Mrs. Lester Layton; Vice Presidents, Miss Mary Hall, Miss Eleanor Hall, Miss Virginia Morford; Secretary, Mrs. W. L. Keplinger; Treasurer, Mrs. George Wilshire; Treasurer Unitarian Offering, Mrs. John Jackson.

Brotherhood Newton Presbyterian Church.

President, E. Merriam Dutcher; Vice President, Jacob Herman; Secretary and Treasurer, E. A. Shay.

Woman's Society Newton Presbyterian Church.

President, Mrs. Andrew Konkle; 1st Vice President, Miss Helen Clark; 2nd Vice President, Mrs. Edgar Layton; Secretary, Mrs. Louise Ballou; Treasurer, Mrs. Frank Roe.

Chautauqua Association of Sussex County.

President, William W. Woodward, Jr.; Vice President, Rev. E. C. Tuthill; Secretary, Frank B. Boss; Treasurer, Roland T. Hull.

The Sussex County Ministerial Union.

President, Rev. Milton E. Grant; Vice President, Rev. Ernest C. Tuthill; Secretary and Treasurer, Rev. N. S. Becker.

Sussex County Nature Study Club.

President, Mrs. William G. Drake; Vice Presidents, Miss F. Blanche Hill, Mrs. John Farrell; Secretary, Mrs. William Wilson; Treasurer, Miss Anna E. Dunn.

The Newton Club.

President, Thomas M. Kays; Vice President, W. H. Mellor; Treasurer, Levi H. Morris; Secretary, Geo. P. Matthews; Trustees, L. S. Iliff, W. L. Keplinger, N. H. Hart, Thomas E. Murray, Dr. W. H. Smith, James Roof, E. J. Quinn.

Newton Athletic Club.

President, Henry T. Kays; Vice President, William H. Nicholls; Secretary, Herbert Bentley; Treasurer, Floyd C. Devore; Executive Committee, Thomas W. Bentley, J. W. C. Carber, George L. Dutcher, Nathan H. Hart, Lewis S. Iliff.

Captain Griggs Post, G. A. R.

Post Commander, Benjamin F. Herrick; Post Adjutant, Samuel G. Barnes; Senior Vice Commander, John Campbell; Junior Vice Commander, John Emory; Quartermaster, J. W. Randall; Chaplain, J. E. Whitney; Officer of the Day, James Johnson; Surgeon, Martin Hughes.

Sussex County Branch S. P. C. A.

President, Richard F. Goodman; First Vice President, E. A. Shay; Second Vice President, Mrs. George A. Smith; Third Vice President, Rev. John R. Humphreys; Treasurer, Charles S. Steele; Secretary, Mrs. H. L. Voorhees; Executive Committee, Prof. Philip S. Wilson, Chairman, Prof. Howard E. Shimer, Rev. John R. Humphreys, Rev. Ernest C. Tuthill, Miss Mae Morford, Jacob Beatty.

Sussex County Automobile Club.

President, Thomas W. Bentley; Vice Presidents, E. Merriam Dutcher, Reeve Hardin, Ford Margarum; Secretary, E. A. Shay; Treasurer, Edwin M. Quick.

Newton Cornet Band.

President, Alvah S. Keen; Secretary and Treasurer, Reuben N. Talmadge; Leader, A. B. Brickner.

Newton Tennis Club.

Was organized in 1908 and incorporated in 1911. Meetings are held monthly. President, Lewis Van Blarcom; Vice President, George L. Dutcher; Secretary, Henry W. Huston; Treasurer, Frank B. Boss; Trustees, Miss May M. Morford, Miss Floy Iliff, William L. Keplinger, William A. Dolan, R. T. Hull.

Branchville Tennis Club.

President, John A. McCarrick; Vice President, Wilbur F. Dye; Secretary, Miss Allan Ayers; Treasurer, Miss Frances Roe; Trustees, three years, Leonard Roe, Marcus L. Bond, Ernest Roe; two years, Mrs. Ernest Roe, Miss Mae Ingersoll; one year, Miss Virginia Mott, William Harden.

Franklin Athletic Association.

President, Stephen M. Case; Vice President, Clayton R. Ricker; Secretary, M. M. Dolan; Treasurer, Joseph P. Quinn.

Primrose Social Club.

President, Ralph Frace; Vice President, Alfred T. Booth; Secretary, F. Ernest Wallace; Treasurer, Harold Coriell.

Delaware Club, Newton.

President, Norman Anderson; Vice President, Fred James; Secretary and Treasurer, Frank Nickels.

Green Township Vigilant Society.

President, C. F. Ayers; Vice Presidents, John N. Decker, E. E. Lambert; Secretary, George A. Cooper; Treasurer, C. L. Cooke; Pursuers, C. F. Ayers, I. L. Labar, A. O. Ayers, G. O. Young, James A. Toomath, John N. Decker, C. L. Cooke, W. S. Phillips, John Roe, Eugene Coleman, E. E. Lambert.

Sussex County Medical Society.

President, Dr. Blase Cole; Vice President, Dr. Thomas R. Pooley, Jr.; Secretary, Dr. Fred P. Wilbur; Treasurer, Dr. E. Morrison.

Newton Gun Club.

President, Ora C. Simpson; Vice President, N. H. Hart; Secretary, A. B. Brickner; Treasurer, Lewis M. Morford.

Chinchewunska Chapter, Daughters of the American Revolution

Regent, Mrs. Frank Arthur Roe; Vice Regent, Mrs. Henry Huston; Recording Secretary, Mrs. Samuel B. Van Stone; Corresponding Secretary, Miss Ardelia H. Allen; Treasurer, Miss Lillian Walker; Registrar, Miss Sarah E. Doyle; Historian, Mrs. John R. Fields.

Sussex Society of New York.

President, Justice Swayze; Vice Presidents, Edgar D. Johnson, N. E. Drake; Harold H. Phillips; Executive Committee, George E. Bedell, William S. Bennet, Wayne Dumont, Michael Dunn, Dr. William M. Dunning, Mrs. Loton Horton, Martin R. Kays, E. S. Lewis, Frank H. Little, Jesse G. Roe, Dr. A. A. Smith, Mrs. Ella O'Gorman Stanton.

Wallkill Valley Sportsmen Association.

President, H. J. Woodward; Vice President, Irving M. Avery; Secretary and Treasurer, William N. Harris; Captains, Park Washer, W. D. Wild.

Lafayette Vigilant Society.

President, William R. Case; Secretary, Brice B. Stanton; Treasurer, Nelson R. Ackerson.

North Jersey Poultry Association.

President, C. W. Longdon; Vice President, W. J. Morris; Secretary, Henry J. Woodward; Treasurer, D. K. Marshall.

Woodlawn Driving Park.

President, Jacob S. Wise; Secretary, Sayre S. Martin; Treasurer, James Roof.

Wantage Driving Park Association.

President, John L. McCoy; Vice President, William R. Edsall; Secretary, Frank U. Dickson; Treasurer, William D. Wilson; Directors, Samuel D. Sprague, Chris. N. Stanton, Thomas E. Campbell.

Sussex County Principals' Association.

President, D. Fred Aungst; Vice President, Howard E. Shimer; Secretary and Treasurer, Harry R. Mensch.

Southern Branch Sussex County Teachers' Club.

President, Miss Ellen Connell; Vice President, Miss Eleanor V. Bosch; Secretary, Mrs. Margaret Willis; Treasurer, Miss L. Mae Emmons.

Northern Branch Sussex County Teachers' Club.

President, W. N. Harris; Vice President, Miss Anna Heller; Secretary, Miss Jennie Kistler; Treasurer, Miss M. V. Driesbach.

Western Branch Sussex County Teachers' Club.

President, Mrs. Edna Day; Vice President, Miss Lura L. Depue; Secretary, Miss Asenath Skinner; Treasurer, Arthur G. Wood.

Alumni Association Newton High School.

President, Frank Farrell; Vice President, Mrs. John C. Losey; Secretary, Miss Mae Horner; Treasurer, Floyd C. Devore.

Sussex County Cow Testing Association.

President, W. S. Phillips; Vice President, Arthur Danks; Secretary, Thos. E. Inslee; Official Tester, Fred L. Champion.

Tri-County Medical Society.

President, G. Wyckoff Cummins, M. D., of Belvidere; Vice Presidents, E. A. Ayers, M. D., Branchville, Dr. Britton D. Evans, Morris Plains; Treasurer, Frederick W. Flagge, M. D., Rockaway; Secretary, C. B. Smith, M. D., Washington; Executive Committee, F. J. LeRiew, M. D., Washington; Shepard Voorhees, M. D., Newton, John Walters, M. D., Wharton; Finance Committee, H. V. Kice, M. D., Wharton, E. Morrison, M. D., Newton, C. M. Williams, M. D., Washington.

Branchville Water and Improvement Company.

George N. Ingersoll, President; E. A. Shay, of Newton, Secretary, and A. J. Canfield, Treasurer. William C. Cook and William H. Dalrymple were elected auditors, and Isaiah Hornbeck Superintendent of the company's plant

Branchville Hose Company, No. 1.

Foreman, John A. McCarrick; Assistant Foreman, Chas. Gould; Secretary, Ole M. Whitaker; Treasurer, George Van Ness.

Branchville Firemen's Relief Association.

President, John H. Nelden; Secretary, O. M. Whitaker; Treasurer and Collector, Howard W. Dye.

Hamburg Firemen's Relief Association.

The Hamburg Firemen's Relief Association was organized April 6, 1911, receiving its charter on April 27 of that year. The membership is forty-nine. Meetings are held on the first Thursday evening of April, August and December, in Jr. O. U. A. M. Hall, Hamburg. The present officers are: President, I. D. Chardavoyne; Vice-President, H. J. Corwin; Secretary, George C. Smith; Treasurer, Jonas S. Woods

Fire Wardens, Sussex County.

Byram, Edward Niper, Roseville; John S. Hammell, Waterloo; Frankford, Asher E. Snook, Culver's Lake; Hardyston, Claude Birdsell, Stockholm; Jaques Beleit, Beaver Lake; E. F. Williams, Hamburg; Hopatcong, Philip Reule; Montague, Thomas Dutton, Duttonville; Joseph Martin, Brick House; W. P. VanSickle, High Point; Sandyston, H. C. C. Snook, Hainesville; Henry Steffen, Normanock; Sparta, W. A. Current, Ogdensburg; Seymour Pullis, Sparta; Wm. Riker, Sparta; Stillwater, Lester VanHorn, Wintermute; Wilbert Lambert, Middleville; Vernon, Joseph Burrows, Vernon; E. M. Utter, Kampe; S. E. Williams, Glenwood; Walpack, H. L. Trauger, Flatbrookville; Robert Robbins, Walpack Center; Wantage, W. N. VanSickle, Unionville.

Newton Cemetery Co.

President, W. W. Roe; Vice President, Theodore Simonson; Secretary and Treasurer, H. O. Ryerson; Directors, W. W. Roe, Theodore Simonson, H. O. Ryerson, Levi H. Morris, W. W. Woodward, N. H. Hart, William I. Young.

The North Hardyston Cemetery Association.

President, H. S. Potter; Vice President, Caleb Barber; Secretary, Robert Smith; Treasurer, John Sutton; Trustees, three years, Robert Smith, H. S. Potter.

Vaughan Cemetery Association.

President, Richard Vaughan; Vice President, Judson V. Vaughan; Secretary, C. A. Kinney; Treasurer, Edward Ackerson; Mahlon J. Reed and Jacob Reed.

L. S. ILIFF, Pres. - H. N. CRANE, Sec'y and Treas.

The L. S. Iliff Company

Dealers in COAL, FEED, GRAIN and BUILDERS' SUPPLIES.

OPPOSITE D., L. & W. PASSENGER DEPOT
NEWTON, N. J.
TELEPHONE NO. 32

The
EFFICIENCY UTILITIES COMPANY
REAL ESTATE DEPARTMENT

Because of its having representatives in the big cities, is better able to handle your real estate business than any other concern in Sussex county. Let us prove it to you.

ROOMS 5 & 6 QUICK BUILDING, NEWTON, N. J.
NEW YORK OFFICE
23 EAST 26th STREET.

IF YOU WANT ANYTHING IN

HARDWARE
CHARLES A. WALKER

SPRING ST.   -   NEWTON, N. J.

is able at all times to supply you.

The largest, most varied and up-to-date line in the county from which to select. In fact, everything.

J. B. HENDERSHOTT   J. C. HENDERSHOTT
Residence Telephone 153-R   Residence Telephone 107-L

Real Estate

The largest handlers of Real Estate in Sussex County. List your farm or property —no charge unless sale is made.

Insurance

We represent 16 of the largest Fire Insurance Companies, also write Accident, Liability, Plate Glass, Boiler, Tornado, Live Stock, Burglary, Automobile and Rent Insurance.

J. B. HENDERSHOTT & SON
REAL ESTATE and INSURANCE

Park Block, Room 9   Newton, New Jersey

OFFICE TELEPHONE 17

When you buy dry goods you go to a dry goods store, groceries at a grocery store, shoes at a shoe store.

Why not use the same judgment and buy your Flour, Feed, Grain, Hay and Poultry Supplies where these goods are specialties.

All our Grain and Feeds are bought direct from the large elevators. Our Flour direct from the miller for cash and sold at the very lowest possible price.

We are mill agents for "Webster Star," "White Elephant" and "Cream" Flour.

There is no better Flour made in the United States than these three brands, besides the price is always low because we buy in large quantities for cash. Don't fail to include one of these flours when ordering from your grocerer. If they can't supply you send your order direct to us.

Our Specialties are: Dried Brewers Grains, Malt Sprouts, "Larro" Dairy Feed, "best on earth," Full Grain Horse Feed, Cut Hay, Grain of all kinds, a full line of Poultry Supplies.

Always be sure to get our prices before purchasing.

Lunger Grain & Elevator Co.

Wholesale and Retail Dealers

NETCONG   -   N. J.

Storage House near Station. Office near G. H. Lunger's house, Mechanic street, where a full line of goods are always on hand. Business established since 1891.

Sixty Years of continuous business at the same old stand has made Hull's one of the best known stores in Sussex county. It has also given us a reputation for square dealing and business honesty of which we are justly proud.

Fifty years ago, when your fathers and mothers bought their goods at David R. Hull & Co.'s store, they were getting full value for every dollar invested. That has always been our first thought.

Now Our Specialties are :

CARPETS,

      RUGS,

           LADIES' SUITS

                and FURS

which are always here for your inspection.

DAVID R. HULL & CO.
NEWTON, N. J.

INDEX

This index lists all names found in the text.

ACKERSON, Edward 88 96 Ford 90 J D 90 Jacob R 88 John D 88 Joseph 26 87 Nelson R 96 Wm 88
ADAMS, Charley 25 Elihu 83 Ellsworth 40 S R 44
ALLEN, Ardelia H 96 Edgar A 87 Edward 90 Elisha M 50 H B 89
ALLINSON, 74
ALMER, A J 93 Amos J 88
AMBRUS, John 91
ANDANIERE, M L 91
ANDERS, Arabella 93
ANDERSON, 52 C M 91 Daniel S 45 John D 81 Maggie 64 Norman 95 Norman B 87 88 Oakley 52 Thomas 6 9 45 60 William T 52 54
ANDRESS, J Clark 49
ANGUS, Jennie 93
APPLETON, Clarence G 58
ARMS, William F 90
ARMSTRONG, 42 Bradford C P 23 Frank 94 John 54 Mrs R V 92 O E 23 87 Obadiah E 23 42 Obadiah P 42 Robert V 88 Roy 94
ARNOLD, Gen 18
ARVIS, Sheriff 24
ASBURY, Bishop 89
ASHWORTH, Chris 30
ATTERBURY, Thomas B 88
ATWOOD, E H 91
AUBLE, 68
AUNGST, D Fred 96 Grace 33
AVERY, F M 78 Irving M 78 96
AYERS, A O 90 95 Allan 95 Anna 23 C F 95 Charles 91 Dolson 89 E A 96 James C 90 James H 88 John 53 92 Joseph 91 94 Mrs D 92 W R 26 90 Watson R 26 53
BABCOCK, Frank 94
BADGLEY, Theresa 50
BAILEY, J S 8
BAKER, Clyde E 91 R S 88
BALDWIN, Anna F 81 Hugh C 81 J E 81 James E 7 49 62
BALE, Bert 93 Henry 42
BALL, George 91
BALLOU, Louise 95
BARBER, David M 46 Hattie 94
BARLOW, J L 8
BARNES, Samuel G 95
BARRETT, Jesse 89 L R 89 Myron 6 45 46
BARTA, Bertie 91
BASSETT, 52 Amos 52 Isaac 52

BATE, 52
BAUGHN, 45
BAYER, Fred 65
BAYLEY, James R 51
BEACH, Ira 47 William 50
BEATTY, Jacob 95 Mrs J 57
BECK, J T 49 Jehiel T 49
BECKER, N S 95
BEDELL, A W 82 94 George E 96 H J 91 Mrs Aseneth 91
BEDLE, Gov 18 Joseph D 10
BEEBE, Gilbert J 9
BEECHLOTZ, August 91
BEEGLE, Arthur 94 Casper C 49 Hiram L 93 Horton M 49 51 88 Lewis 49 Silas M 49
BEEMER, 29 H I 94 Henry 27
BEIERLE, H A 75
BELCHER, Gov 13 14 J 94 Jonathan 12
BELEIT, Jaques 96
BELL, Cecil 93 Cecil O 93 94 E H 95 Emmet H 20 87 John 29 53 Robert 20 Sarah 20 William H 9 15 91
BENJAMIN, Mary 43
BENNET, William S 96
BENSON, Frederick S 89 William H 87
BENTLEY, Herbert 95 Herbert W 94 T W 95 Thomas W 95
BENZ, Jacob 72
BERESFORD, E F 49
BERG, Walter G 18
BERK, Sarah 20
BERKELEY, John 12
BERRY, Dewitt A 89 Fred 93
BEST, Mrs Peter 93 William C 87
BEVANS, Victor E 87
BICE, E W 89
BIGELOW, Moses 75
BIRD, Milton A 89 Walter L 88
BIRDSELL, Claude 96
BISHOP, Samuel 29
BISSELL, J O 67 80 John O 94 L A 80
BITTENBENDER, Frank 88 Frank H 51
BLACK, Charles C 87 James J 87
BLAIR, John I 81
BLAUVELT, R J 42
BLOOM, Frederick 89
BOARDMAN, S W 90
BOLGER, Richard 51
BOND, M L 29 88 Marcus L 29 93 95

BONKER, A 94 Emery 26 George 44
BONNELL, H C 49 Henry C 9 48 49 92
BOOMER, Peter E 87
BOOTH, Alfred T 95 T F 39
BOSCH, Eleanor V 96
BOSS, Chas A 92 Frank B 95 W D 69 Wilbur D 92 94
BOSSARD, Milton E 49
BOTHWICK, W M 90
BOWMAN, Arthur 93 George J 29 L F 91 Lester 93 Martin W 22 87 Stephen 49
BOYD, Charles 49
BOYER, M J 94
BOYLAN, J H 36
BOYLES, Alexander 42
BOYNTON, W M 88
BRACHEN, John 91
BRADY, D J 36
BRAISTED, Edward 49 Mary 93
BRICKNER, A B 49 72 95
BRITTIN, 52
BRODERICK, Virgil 14
BRONSON, Ashel 90
BROWN, Collins T 94 E 94 Harvey 49
BRYAN, William M 90
BRYANT, John W 49 94
BUDD, Jesse M 87
BUNNELL, Isaac 53 J W 92 Jacob L 9 49 Joseph W 87 T G 49 Thomas G 9
BURD, L C 88 Marshall 88
BURHARD, F C 65
BURNS, Charles E 90 Robert 88 93
BURR, Aaron 10
BURRELL, John 90
BURRES, Helen 95
BURROWS, E C 86 Joseph 86 96
BUSEKIST, William 48
BYINGTON, Theodore L 46
BYRAM, Arthur T 88 Raymond E 94 Silas C 90 Walter D 88
CALVIN, Bartholomew S 12
CAMP, Lemuel D 26
CAMPBELL, George 93 Jesse 94 John 95 Thomas E 96
CANFIELD, A J 16 29 93 96 Alfred J 29 87
CANNON, Coulter 48 Uncle Joe 23
CANON, Joe 23
CARBER, J W C 58 68 95
CARD, A B 40 43
CARLISLE, Samuel 46
CARMICHAEL, Geo A 90
CARTERET, Philip 12 George 12
CASE, Ira 94 John J 48 O P 88 Raymond 23 75 87 88 Stephen M 33 95 William R 96
CASKEY, William K 25
CASPERSON, William C 90
CASSEDY, A L 85
CASSIDY, A L 90 Melissa 91
CASTERLINE, Fowler J 88
CAVERLY, George 49

CHAMBERLAIN, 93 S H 79 Susan 93
CHAMPION, Fred L 96
CHANDLER, Thomas P 45
CHARDAVOYNE, I D 96
CLAPP, 48
CLARK, Abraham L 90 Benson S 90 Champ 18 E W 92 E Willis 90 George F 87 H C 48 Harry C 41 Harry F 92 Helen 95 Hiram C 50 J C 90 Jeptha C 26 John Y 41 W M 52 William 92
CLAY, Henry 5
CLEVELAND, Grover 60 Pres 23
CLOUGH, Simon 90
CLOVER, Charles P 90
COATES, Bertha 93 George 93 James 88
COBB, George T 6
COCHRAN, 52
COE, Carrie 19 Frank 87 Frank J 19 Winfield 94
COIT, C S 6
COLE, Blase 95 George B 10 H Clarence 20 87 Jackson 20 Mrs Jackson 20
COLEMAN, Eugene 95 J G 39 Joseph G 87 S S 85
COLLARD, Charles W 90
COLLINS, H R 88 Robert H 94
COMPTON, Frank B 89 John B 90 Susan 8 Victor 87
CONDIT, Claude 93 94 Dr 26 I H 90 Ira 46 Roy 93
CONDON, James 76 Thomas 94
CONGER, Hiram G 92
CONGLETON, L R 44
CONNELL, Ellen 96
CONOVER, 52 Bertha P 92
COOK, Linnie 93 William C 87 88 93 96
COOKE, C L 95 Clarence 87 88 Oliver W 14
COONS, J J 93
COOPER, E E 87 George A 95 John 93 Mr 15 William H 30 49 92
COPE, A B 90 93
CORBETT, William P 90
CORIELL, Harold 95
CORNELL, A D 84 94 J Rusling 94
CORNINE, Ludlow S 26
CORRIGAN, Father 36 George W 36 Owen 94
CORTRIGHT, Harry 89
CORWIN, H J 96
COSH, J P 94
COSNER, Floyd 93
COULT, 29 Eliza 6 Frances A 6 Hannah 6 Joseph 3 6 45 48 Joseph Jr 6 20 Lillian 6 Margaret 6 Mr 3 6
COURSEN, Gershom 54 Hannah 6 Isaac V 53 Jacob A 92 John D 87 88 R S 91 Raymond S 31 William P 53
COURTRIGHT, H E 92
COUSE, David 24 Eva 50 H D 24 95 Henry 24 Henry David 64 J Martin 94 Martin 93 Mary 24 Minnie 24
COX, Anna 19 Charles C 23 John 25 Lucy 23 Martin J 9 92 94
CRAIG, Alexander 50
CRANE, 52 Christie 33 J I 33 John J 90 John W 29 Mrs S R 91
CRATE, John 26
CRAWFORD, George B 90

CRAWLEY, Ellen 33
CRAWN, Abe W 49 C M 92 Sanford J 92
CRIGAR, J W 48
CRIGER, J W 49
CRISMAN, C H 29 88 Charles H 93
CROES, John 46
CRONE, Gabriel S 93
CROOK, Charles 48
CROSSETT, Robert 90
CROSSETTE, Robert 90
CROUSE, N P 90
CROWCROFT, B S 95 Benson S 90
CROWELL, 4
CUFF, T J 25 69
CULVER, 42
CUMMINS, G Wyckoff 96
CUONIE, William B 91
CURRENT, W A 96
CUTLER, Samuel 49 William 49
DALRYMPLE, Frank R 93 Harry 93 Louis A 58 94 William H 87 96 Wm H 53
DALY, J D 50
DANKS, Arthur 96
DARRONE, Edward 89
DAUB, 52
DAVENPORT, A J 89 L L 48 Whitfield 89
DAVIS, Azariah 47 90
DAVISON, Calvin K 26
DAWKINS, George W 48
DAY, Edna 96
DECAMP, Lewis 47
DECKER, 68 Alice R 21 Amelia 21 E H 82 Helen A 21 James L 10 John Jr 31 John N 53 95 Joseph M 76 Martin 21 Peter 81 Peter S 23 53 R 94 Ralph 21 87 95 Sarah E 21 William E 87 88
DEKAY, Henry B 74 Thomas W 92 94
DELAFAYETTE, Marquis 42
DEMAREST, 42 Charles P 93 Gillam 42 Gilliam 23 Harriet E 67 Harry E 21 48 J 21 Mrs J 21
DENEE, Jep 26
DENNIS, Alfred L 45
DEPUE, Burson C 93 Lura L 96 Mary F 93
DEPUY, W F 75
DEVORE, F C 92 Floyd C 58 92 95 96
DEWITT, 29 J S 92
DEYO, O H P 90
DICKERSON, J E 88
DICKINSON, Minnie 93
DICKISON, Floyd 23 87 Mrs Floyd 23
DICKSON, F U 83 Frank U 96
DILDINE, Thomas A 89
DIXON, Joseph 90
DOBBINS, Andrew 26 Andrew L 87 Helen 94 John W 94 Lorenzo E 93
DODGE, H C 76
DOLAN, David L 87 Leon 94 M M 87 88 95 P J 75 88 Patrick J 20 Philip 91 William 94 William A 20 87 95

DONALDSON, E K 90
DONNELLY, Michael J 51
DORAN, John 36
DOW, John 8
DOWNING, Charles 95
DOYLE, Sarah E 70 96
DRAKE, 26 52 C 94 Mrs William G 95 N E 96 Nathan 52 Nathaniel 53 Victor M 9 William 26 52 William G 49
DREHER, Lewis O 93 94
DREW, A S 39 86 Andrew S 87 B 43
DRIESBACH, M V 96 Matilda V 33
DRYDEN, 15 John F 9
DUKE, Of Newcastle 12 Of York 12
DUMONT, Wayne 96
DUNLAP, Mrs M J 94
DUNLEVY, 52
DUNN, 8 Anna E 94 95 C 52 Clarkson 46 49 John R 49 L B 89 Michael 96 W V 36 91 William H 49 Wm H 49
DUNNING, G B 48 49 William M 96
DUTCHER, E Merriam 57 88 95 G L 57 George L 94 95 W L 56
DUTTON, Thomas 96
DYE, Howard W 96 W F 87 Wilbur F 88 95
DYMOCK, G 83 J 40 41 Raymond 89
EAGLES, Geo O 49 93 George O 49
EARL, 3 John W 84 92 W H 95 William C 92 William H 49 55
EAST, Rose 93
EDISON, 29
EDSALL, B B 3 25 Benjamin B 3-5 Benjamin Bailey 5 Grant 89 Mr 3 5 6 Thomas D 16 39 87 W H 92 William R 96
EDSON, Samuel 46
EDWARDS, Arthur 90 Arthur A 89 Frank 90 R L 87 88
EGBERT, James 89
ELLETT, Minnie 93 Mrs 84 O D 93 Oren D 29 W H 84 Wm P 29 88
ELY, Boyd S 88 E Dana 48 88
EMERSON, J C 90
EMMANS, Frank 88
EMMONS, Charles 87 L Mae 96
EMORY, John 95
ENGLISH, James G 72 Patrick J 72
EPPLE, Henry 91 94
ERB, Thomas 30 William R 30
EUEH, John 52
EVANS, Britton D 96 James 53
EVERETT, Anna 92 R L 92 Robert L 92 Thomas 94
EVERITT, Martin W 93
EWALD, 52 Frank B 88
FARBER, Caleb 87 89 96 Nicholas 87
FARLEY, D H 65
FARRELL, Frank 96 Mrs John 95
FAULL, William A 48
FEAKES, Edward C 11
FEENY, John 52
FELLOWS, A F 10
FENWICK, Lily L 18
FICHTER, J S 68

FIELDS, John 88 Mrs John R 96
FISHER, B 72 Effie 33 George B 76
FITCH, Charles W 9 Grant 8 54
FITHIAN, Dr 26
FITZGERALD, J N 6
FLAGGE, Frederick W 96
FLANIGAN, Henry 43
FLUKE, Charles 94
FLYNN, Martin M 49 Patrick 36
FOGELSON, N 72
FOLK, H W 77 Henry 77
FORCE, Abram B 91
FORD, David 54
FORSHEE, Willard 86
FOSTER, 52 C K 48 49 David Lunn 8 Robert E 3 5 8 10 Sarah 8
FOUNTAIN, J W 88 Jesse W 87
FOWLER, Samuel 14 34 35
FRACE, George W 48 Ralph 95
FRANKLIN, William 46
FREDENBURG, Charles 92
FREEMAN, 26 Elihu M 25 V B 25 26 Virgil B 26
FRENCH, E 90
FRIEDMAN, Philip 94
FRITTS, Benjamin 87 Lee R 88
FULLER, Lester J 88
GARFIELD, 10
GARIS, Fletcher S 87
GARRIS, 29 Charles M 93 Peter E 87 Wesley 89
GEORGE, Iii King Of England 46
GESSLER, Theodore A 88 Theodore A K 88
GIBBS, M T 91 Morris T 90 Mr 7 Whitfield 7 9 10
GIBSON, John S 9
GILBERTSON, H W 23 92
GILLAM, John W 9
GIVEANS, Charles L 92 Emma P 92 Mrs C L 92
GLYNN, John 38
GOBLE, David 76 Samuel W 49
GOODMAN, Aaron C 3 Edward 7 Mr 7 Paymaster 7 R F 49 95 Richard F 3 6 8 10 49 92 94 95
GOODRICH, Elias 25
GORDON, B C 75 Benjamin C 88 R F 94
GORMAN, John T 49
GOTTLEIB, 52
GOULD, Charles 93 Chas 96 William 93
GRAEY, Chas 65 Francis 51
GRAHAM, E R 89
GRANT, 6 Milton E 47 95
GRAY, Whitfield 89
GREEN, Ephraim 52 Ephraim 16 54 Ephraim Jr 54 Gov 60 Samuel 13 William 93
GREER, 36
GREESPON, I 38
GRIGGS, George V 14
GRIMM, Amelia 93 J 94 Jacob 48 88 94
GROVER, Albert 48 93 Florence 93
GRUVER, Charles M 88
GUNN, J K 41 Jennie 94

GUSTIN, 29 Annie J 50 John 54
HAGERMAN, J W 90
HAGGERTY, Bonnell M 52 D S 83 J D 83 James 29 Thomas 94 Uzal C 29
HAINES, Alanson A 14
HAIRLOCKER, Henry 13 25 45
HAIT, Walter J 88
HALL, Edward 88 Eleanor 95 J C 89 James E 7 John H 3-5 8 47 50 52 53 Judge 3-5 Mary 95 Mr 3 56
HALLOCK, Agnes 50 Harvey L 24 I L 23 48 49 Israel L 48 53
HALSEY, Charles 77
HALSTED, Job S 52 54
HAMILTON, Carrie V 50 Edgar A 14 Howell 87 88 James 89 Morris R 9 Robert 16 45 60
HAMM, Roy 93
HAMMELL, John S 96
HAMMOND, Peter V 87
HAMPTON, Jonathan 13 46 49
HANCOCK, 10
HANEY, Charles P 87 89
HANOVITZ, H 79
HARDEN, Harry 93 Ora 82 Reeve 39 94 W W 91 William 95
HARDIN, Clinton R 88 George 49 Reeve 95
HARRIS, George N 21 49 94 Henry S 10 John 52 W N 88 96 William N 94 96
HARRISON, H W 37 Wm H 4
HART, 67 A C 18 Archibald C 18 Geo P 87 George P 88 Lily L 18 Lydia 92 N H 66 95 96 Nathan H 23 53 55 95
HARTRIM, Alfred 88
HAVENS, H N 83 Henry N 88 James C 16
HAWKEY, Richard 94 Richard W 93
HAWKINS, Minnie 24
HAYES, 6
HAYS, Thomas 16 Thomas M 19
HAZELTON, W Frank 94 William F 92
HELLER, Anna 96
HELM, James I 50
HELMECRI, Alex 91
HEMINGWAY, John R 48
HENDERSHOT, 74 Andrew J 88 Charles J 88 George M 87 Harry H 94 J B 10 S B 63
HENDERSHOTT, J B 87 97 J C 97
HENDERSON, George M 88 Philip W 87
HENRY, John 29
HERMAN, Jacob 92 95
HERMANN, J 63
HERRICK, Benjamin F 95
HERZENBERG, J A 87 Joseph 33 Joseph A 88
HETZEL, D B 49 Frances L 91
HEWITT, Mr 15
HIBLER, Samuel 90
HIGGINS, Alex M 90
HILL, Amanda J 16 B T 92 Edward M 84 F Blanche 95 Joanna 52 Jonathan 47 Luther 21 26 55 Miss 90 Mrs T 92 Sarah 47
HILLIARD, S W 6
HILLS, J A 90
HILLYER, Asa 90

HINDS, C J 94 95 Henry 26 Henry S 87
HISSAM, Alvah 93
HOCKENBERRY, Merritt L 90 Peter 91
HOFFMAN, E E 90 H D 91 John 49
HOLBERT, Frank 83 88
HOLLEY, William Welles 46
HOLLY, R M 92 Richard M 92
HOLMAN, Edwin C 90
HOLMES, John 52
HONIG, Joseph 33
HOOD, Bruno 49 58
HOOEY, William 93
HOOKER, George 88
HOPKINS, 23 30 Alice R 20 B K 20 Fred O 50 Harvey S 20 21 87 89 92 N H 29 Noah H 29 S H 48
HOPPAUGH, Halsey 87 Mr 50
HOPPER, Russell 94 William 90
HORNBECK, Isaiah 87 93 96 Jacob E 10
HORNER, Mae 96
HORNICK, Benjamin 94
HORTON, 13 45 Mrs Loton 96
HORVATH, Joseph 38
HOTALEN, John M 49
HOUGH, 30 A D 89 Edgar 93 94 F M 68 Frank M 16 Martin E 53 Peter 48 W B 92
HOUGHTALING, Monroe 88
HOUSE, Charles 49 Jason C 88 89 N D 86
HOWE, James 90
HOWELL, Amzi 10 Jennie 93 John C 16 48 49 Mary 94 Mrs D C 92 Susan 22 W F 65 William F 21 48 87 William J 91 Willis M 93
HUDSON, Hendrick 12
HUFF, A W 92 Eugene 88 93 George 49 Joseph E 88 Schooley J 93 William S 87
HUFFMAN, William 88
HUGHES, Hugh 14 Martin 95 Wm 18
HULL, A 87 Charles 94 David R 16 54 98 David R Jr 49 R T 95 Roland T 95 Rolland T 55 Roy 94 Sidney 88
HULMES, Amy 93
HUMMER, Elizabeth 93 Peter 93
HUMPHREYS, John R 48 92 95
HUNT, Dr 52 Etta 81 Halloway 46 Henry C 8 81 Louis N 92 Marshall 81 87 Samuel H 16 Sarah A 81 Theodore 89 Theodore Jr 88 William T 90
HUNTER, W F 90
HURD, Pierson 53
HURSH, Geo E 92 George E 92
HUSTON, 3 42 Henry W 89 95 Mrs Henry 96
HUTT, William 89
HUTTON, Margaret 94
HYDE, James C 94 Michael J 88
HYNARD, Mary 60
IKE, Lewis 93 Rosa 93
ILIFF, 26 66 67 Anna 19 23 Floy 95 J H 89 James 23 47 90 John 63 89 L S 49 95 97 Lewis S 23 87 95 Lucy 23 Mrs John 94 William 19 87 88 92 93 William M 25 26 90 Wm M 25
INDIAN, Shawuskukhking 12

INGERSOLL, Elizabeth 93 G N 30 George N 96 Mae 93 95 S E 87 Samuel 47 Samuel E 23 W H 89
INSCHO, Daniel 88 R M 79 Robert M 88
INSLEE, 48 Thos E 96
JACKSON, 67 George T 90 Mrs John 95
JAEAC, Tmre 91
JAMES, Fred 95 W C 91
JARVIE, J N 27 James N 28
JENSEN, Edward I 69
JOHNSON, D M 88 Edgar D 96 George V 29 James 95 John 22 Judge 52 Robert T 22 26 74 87 Samuel 45 49 64 Whitfield H 53 William 26 William H 3
JOHNSTON, John 46 Minnie 94 O P 42
JONES, 48 Charles 49 J E 90 Nathaniel 88 William H 94
JULIER, Amelia E 68
KALLBERG, John 63
KAMMER, A M 36 91
KANOUSE, Edward 58 Peter 90
KARPPI, 13
KATZENSTEIN, John S 92
KAYS, Henry 24 Henry T 19 87 88 95 Martin R 96 Mary 24 Thomas 9 81 Thomas M 95 William B 93
KEECH, George T 11
KEEN, Alvah S 95
KEEPERS, George M 93
KELLAM, 67
KELLEGER, Frank N 88
KELLEY, E W 91
KELLY, Chris 79 John W 79 Peter J 79
KELPINGER, W L 95
KELSEY, Henry C 9 45 55
KENT, C L 39
KEPLINGER, Mrs W L 95 William L 95
KERN, Irving J 48
KERNICK, H M 82
KERR, Edna 93 94 Polly 52 Robert 49 88
KICE, H V 96
KILPATRICK, 14 Gen 36 Judson 10 36
KIMBALL, R W 93 Richard M 93
KIMBER, John B 10
KIMBLE, R J 44
KINCAID, James R 83
KINDRED, Louise 95
KING, A A 79 David W 87 88 Of England 13 Orren W 90 Silas E 90
KINNEY, 26 A P 25 26 Amos 48 C A 96 Clark M 87 Clark N 88 David F 87 J D 93 John D 93 L F 88
KINNICUTT, Isaac 93
KINTNER, John S 49
KISHPAUGH, Ada 93 Lewis J 67 93 Martin 89 Maude L 67
KISTLER, Jennie 96
KISZ, F P 80
KITCHEN, J C 39
KITHCART, Joseph H 94
KLEPACKY, M 67
KNAPP, Sarah 8
KNIGHT, Peter M 93 Thomas J 93

KNOX, Geo E 93 George E 87 88 W A 91 William 94
KOHN, S 33
KOLLOCK, 4
KONKLE, Andrew H 50 Mrs Andrew 95
KRALL, Marguerite 33
KRAMER, John C 49
KUSER, A R 9
KYMER, George O 88 James L 93 Luna 68
LA'HOMMEDIEU, Elias 53
LABAR, Fred R 88 I L 85 87 95 William H 85
LAFORGE, John 94 Julia 94
LAMBERT, E E 88 95 Edward E 94 Wilbert 96
LANCE, Alice 93 Josephine 93 Pearl 93 Roy 94
LANE, Samuel 52
LANTZ, Flora A 93 Flora M 93 Thomas R 41
LASIER, Irene 33
LAVENE, Wm 94
LAWRENCE, 26 J L 24 S H 82 Seymour H 93 Thomas 39 53
LAYTON, Edward 89 Lester 92 Mrs Edgar 95 Mrs Lester 95 Ophelia 92 Stewart 92
LEE, 56 Fitzhugh 18 John R 36
LEHMAN, 73
LEIGHTON, Nathan 90
LEONARD, 6
LEPORT, George R 48 Kate 50 Katy 50
LERIEW, F J 96
LEWIS, E S 96 George W 87 J M 15 Robert 94
LEZETTE, Max 93
LINCOLN, 6
LINDEN, Sadie 93
LINDSEY, Ben B 16
LINN, C H 39 Miss 50
LIPSKY, Jacob 75
LITTELL, Lyman A 43 Watson 38 87
LITTLE, Frank H 96 W S 39 Wm S 39
LOCKBURNER, Conrad F 93 Frank H 30
LOGES, Fred Jr 48 49 Fred Sr 48
LONGACRE, Seth W 89
LONGCOR, Anna D 63 D H 87 H 88
LONGDON, C W 96
LOOMIS, John 10
LORD, Frank W 93
LOSEE, A 48 Henry S 24
LOSEY, Alice V 19 Charlotte 64 George 26 Jacob 90 John C 64 94 96 William 64
LOWE, I B 83
LUDLOW, Gov 60
LUNGER, 97 G H 93 97
LYONS, Albert T 21 87
LYTLE, J G 90
MABIE, Martin 90
MACKERLEY, A V B 87 88 Ackerson J 51 88 C E 89 Charles E 87
MADDEN, J P 75 94
MAINED, Draper C 49
MAINES, Draper C 49 Edward C 19 21 87 George B 77 Ida 93 Jacob 89 Mr 20 William C 93

MAJOR, Frank 41
MALLAY, Maggie 93
MANLEY, David A 88
MANN, 4 Leo 63
MANNING, 82
MARGARUM, F W 83 Ford 95 Ford W 16 94 Theodore F 16
MARSHALL, D K 96
MARTENIS, R L 39
MARTIN, Eleanor 17 Frances M 17 George S 17 30 James J 17 Joseph 89 96 L H S 92 L R 89 L R Jr 86 Lebeus 92 Lebus 92 Lewis J 10 16-18 21 Mrs E K 92 Sarah 92 Sayre 17 Sayre S 21 87 96 Scott 17 W Scott 83 William 91 Winfield S 88
MARVIN, T W 84
MASAKER, Aaron 87
MASEKER, J W 76
MASKER, John 48
MASTERS, Harry 93
MATTHEWS, Geo P 95
MAXIM, Hudson 88
MAY, James 90 Lucy 33
MCCARRICK, John A 24 88 93 95 96 Mary E 93
MCCARTE, George 87
MCCARTER, 48 52 Agnes 50 64 Daniel S 53 George H 52 53 George R 9 John 45 52 Robert H 53 Thomas N 6 Uzal H 58
MCCARTHY, D W 38 87 David W 23 38
MCCARTY, Jacob 89
MCCLINTOCK, James 89
MCCLOUGHAN, H J 3
MCCOLLUM, Charles 48
MCCONNELL, 26 William 90
MCCORMICK, Edward 51
MCCOSKER, Edward 51 Rev 36
MCCOY, Eleanor 17 Etta 81 John L 96 Parker S 88 Samuel 81
MCCRACKEN, C E 68
MCDANIELS, Alex 26
MCDANOLD, H J 43
MCDANOLDS, Cora 93 James S 14 T J 93
MCDAVIT, Frank 90
MCDAVITT, 26
MCELROY, H G 93
MCENTEE, William 94 Wm 94
MCGUINNESS, M F 36
MCINTIRE, Thomas 47
MCKAIN, 26 Alexander 25 John 25
MCKEEBY, Frank 87
MCKIM, Leon C 20
MCKINLEY, Lorenzo 93 Pres 7
MCKINNEY, 26 Lewis 25 Lorenzo 88
MCMAHON, Father 36 51
MCMICKLE, Augustus 87 George 88 L B 90
MCNALLY, James J 9
MCNEILIE, Cynthia 93
MCNEILLIE, Irene 93
MCPEEK, Ivan 94 O A 87 Roswell 88 Wm 94 Wm H 93
MCQUAID, B J 51
MCQUEEN, Glenroie 90
MEDDAUGH, C C 91 Frank A 88

MEEKER, Dr 26
MELLOR, Bertram J 71 W H 95 William H 71
MENSCH, Audrey 81 Harry R 81 96 Maud G 81 Sarah 81
    Stephen A 81
MERRIAM, 74 E W 57 Edwin W 58 H F 57 H W 7 22 56 84
MERRILL, 30 Thomas 89
MERSHON, Robert 93
MEYER, Charles 27 Charles A 26 87 Charles Anthony 27
MIDDLETON, John 89
MILHAM, Ed S 49
MILLARD, W W 90
MILLER, John 25 26 Joseph Y 52 Levi D 25 Rhoda 26 William
    A 93
MILLIKEN, 67 John P 67
MILNE, Charles 90
MINER, Asher 4
MINGLE, F A 43 89 Mr 43
MINNIKIN, Leonard 93
MINTURN, James F 87
MOFFAT, John 94
MOFFET, William H 46
MONTROSS, Abbie 19
MOONEY, John R 91
MOORE, D W 90 Edward C 52 George H 92 Ira C 49 J R 83 Mr
    50 Nelson P 3 Thomas M 7
MORAN, Francis 47
MOREHOUSE, J 39 John 39
MORFORD, L M 49 55 Lewis M 16 48 55 95 Mae 95 May M
    95 Samuel D 16 54 Theodore 16 45 54 Virginia 95
MORGAN, B J 90
MORRIS, Abraham S 22 Dennis 88 Laura B 22 Levi H 16 22 58
    64 87 92 95 96 Mrs William 95 Richard R 53 Susan 22 W J
    96 W R 88 William R 94
MORRISON, E 95 96 Ephraim 16 John 36 Joseph H 82 W F 82
MORROW, Jeanette 52
MORTON, James 90
MOTT, F A 86 89 G S 6 George S 46 Virginia 95 W 31
MOWERY, William H 93
MUIR, Cyrus 94 E A 47
MULLER, Charles F 88 John P 88
MUNSON, Amos 36 Asa 34 S C 39 Samuel T 19 32 87
MURRAY, Thomas E 67 95
MYERS, Wallace 49
NELDEN, George H 45 H H 79 John H 29 96
NELSON, Alva 88 Warren C 90
NESTOR, Wm C 88
NEWMAN, 52
NICHOLLS, W Earl 68 W H 95 William H 49 64 95
NICHOLS, Frank 49 J V 45
NICKELS, Frank 95 Frank H 94 Fred 94 Margaret 94
NILSSON, Fritz H 88
NIPER, Edward 96 Mrs William 93 William 88 93 94
NOBLE, William H 9
NORRIS, Stephen 48
NORTHRUP, 26 James L 90 Joseph 25 26 Joseph Jr 53 Mary 24
    R V 86 Richard V 24 Theodore F 83
NORTON, Oliver W 90

NOYES, Stephen D 90
NYCE, Carrie 19
O'CONNOR, John J 51
O'DONNELL, A F 49
O'MALEY, Myles 36
O'MALLEY, John 94 Thomas 94
OAKES, Charles M 68 93
ODENHEIMER, Bishop 46
OETTING, Philip W 88
OGDEN, 34 Elias 34 Uzal Jr 46
OLNEY, Eugene 46
OSBORNE, Frances A 6 Joseph A 6 Margaret 6 William 88
OWEN, Edwin 9
PADDOCK, B F 89
PALMER, W H 56 William G 89
PARCEL, Simeon M 87
PARCELL, S M 89
PARCELLE, Bertha 93
PARKER, William D 87
PARLIMAN, Millard E 88
PEATFIELD, George 71 87
PELLET, Fred M 89 Obadiah 53
PELLETT, L W 92
PEMBERTON, Charles 26 Col 52 Sarah 52
PENNEY, Bruce A 87
PENNY, Bruce A 89
PEREZ, William C 93
PERLEE, George 39
PERRY, Elinor 92 Frank 95 Harry 94
PETERSON, H C 94
PETTIT, John 52 Jonathan 13 Nathaniel 13 46 52
PFLUG, Anthony 93
PHILLIPS, 52 A G 48 Harold H 96 Henry S 90 W S 95 96
PHLEGAR, G E 41
PIERSON, A A 49 Austin A 49 Foster 94 Samuel 94
PITMAN, W M 90
PLOTTS, W E 89
POLHEMUS, William 95
POOLE, J W 94
POOLEY, Thomas R Jr 95
PORTER, Joseph W 90 Wilson R 94
POTTER, C A 93 94 Dr 26 E B 47 H S 89 96 L 94 Mrs E B 47
POWELL, S W 95
POWERS, James 93
PRICE, 29 45 J C 88 Jacob C 29 Saml 29 Z H 92 Zachariah H 53
PRICKETT, George M 87
PRIEST, J Addison 46
PUDER, Albert 92 Wesley C 49
PULLIS, Seymour 96 Seymour R 87 William 49
QUACKENBUSH, John 68
QUICK, Edwin M 95 J Linn 92
QUINCE, J Frank 87 S Frank 22 94 W H 87
QUINN, E J 71 94 95 Joseph P 37 88 95
RAHALEY, Daniel 36
RANDALL, J W 95 Wesley J 88
RANDOLPH, 4 Reuben F 53
RANKIN, William 49

RAYMOUTH, F C 91
REBERZER, William 91
REDHEAD, R J 49
REED, E N 90 Jacob 96 Mahlon J 96
REINBERG, Gustave 87 88
REINHARDT, C 92 Fred 87 Rose 92
RENOUF, Thos P 89
REULE, Philip 96
RIBBLE, Sarah 50
RICKER, C R 88 Clayton R 95
RICKHORN, Rudolph 39
RIDDELL, Elizabeth Fair 93
RIDELL, H E 93
RIKER, Wm 96
ROBBINS, A 44 Robert 96 V M 44 Victor M 87
ROBERTS, Abigail 90
ROBESON, Minnie 93
RODIMER, Florence 93 Howard 93
ROE, Charles 64 Charles J 16 Charles L 94 Elias 92 Elias H 92
    Elmer T 84 Ernest 29 95 Frances 95 Frank 29 George W 87
    93 Hannah 93 Huldah 92 Jesse G 96 Jessie G 64 John 95
    Leonard 95 Minerva 77 Mrs Ernest 95 Mrs Frank 95 Mrs
    Frank Arthur 96 Mrs Thomas C 92 Theodore M 94 Thomas
    C 88 W W 49 95 96 William W 55
ROGERS, 86
ROHN, W L 89
ROLESON, Jesse L 88
ROOF, Charles W 87 James 66 94-96
ROOSEVELT, Pres 7
RORBACH, Charles P 53 John 52 Samuel 52
ROSE, Clark 49 Joseph R 25
ROSENBERG, Dr 26
ROSENKRANS, 3 Amanda 93 B F 93 Benjamin F 87 Eugene 88
    J B 41 J Victor 92 Lillian 50 Martin 10 48 53 Sarah E 21
ROSS, Wm E 23
ROUSE, Clarence W 46
ROWE, Samuel 90
ROY, Condit B 94 J Hampton 88 Lu Ella 21 Mrs Brice 92 W W
    92 William A 83
RUBAN, L C 43
RUDE, Abram B 87 Horace E 16 J W 42
RUNDLE, I S 92 Isaac M 94
RUNION, Fannie 92 William F 90
RUNYON, J H 91 Theodore 6
RUSBY, S O 90 Samuel O 91
RUTAN, C L 94 Joseph F 88
RUTGERS, Anthony 34
RYDER, J W 91
RYERSON, 52 69 David 16 54 George M 45 H O 49 96 Henry
    Ogden 14 Martin 45 N P 88 89 Thomas 45 48 Thomas C 52
SALMON, Herbert K 88
SANBORN, John B 5 Mrs John B 5
SAUNDERS, George E 94 Harold 94 Hector 93
SAVACOOL, George H 70 John 52 Margaret 93
SAYER, Stephen H 9
SCHEELS, John 92

SCHILLING, Gerhard J 91
SCHNEIDER, Henry 89 Henry J 88
SCHOOLEY, G V 39
SCHOONOVER, R H 89
SCHWANHAUSSER, Frederick 88
SCOTT, James 34
SELMES, George 94
SESSION, 90
SHACKLETON, James H 58
SHAFER, Jonathan F 45 Joseph Linn 46 Robert F 53
SHARP, Anthony 34 Joseph 34
SHAW, A P 86 92 Frances M 17 G L 87 George C 17
SHAY, Allen R 16 22 87 Amanda J 16 Catherine 16 Cora 16 E
    A 94-96 Ernest Arthur 8 Evi 94 James 8 James M 92 Mrs
    Allen R 94 Seth 41 Susan 8 Timothy E 16
SHEE, Walter L 53
SHEPARD, F N 87
SHERMAN, 4
SHERRED, Andrew 92 Mrs Wm 94 W H 89 W H? 65 Wm H 95
SHIMER, Cora 16 H E 94 Howard E 50 92 95 96 Joseph 89
SHINER, Charles 48
SHIPMAN, Sarah A 81
SHORTER, Irvin D 10
SHOTWELL, Lulu A 68 Robert 93
SHUMAN, Henry J 87 J H 76 Jacob H 76 W L 76
SHUMO, Dr 26
SHUSTER, E D 87 88
SICKLES, William 93
SIGLER, John A 87
SILVERS, Sarah 93
SIMMONS, Benjamin D 53 J D 48 82 Peter 89
SIMONSON, Mary Hynard 60 Theodore 16 22 48 49 54 55 60
    82 88 94-96 Thomas T 60
SIMPSON, Harold M 82 Jonas 91 Magdaline 82 Ora C 20 82 92
    95 Oscar 25 R D 43 87 Smith 89
SIMS, C N 91
SIPLE, M C 49 Morris C 94
SKINNER, Asenath 96 Cortland 46 Mary 93
SLAGHT, Amelia 94 John H 88
SLATE, Elmer 91
SLATER, J Britt 25 Mary 92 R Lee 87 Sylvester 92 Wm S 26
SLAUGHTER, Eugene 92 Joseph 90
SLOAT, William H 89
SLOCKBOWER, 26 A Watson 83
SMALE, Thomas 67
SMALLEY, Andrew A 53 D D 91 James 20
SMITH, 83 A A 96 Albert O 20 Ambrose C 90 C B 96 D L B 94
    Daniel 89 Dr 24 26 E M 88 Edward M 93 Eugene 77 94
    Frank 53 91 Franklin 45 53 92 Fred C 48 Geo C 92 George
    C 92 96 George W 87 Irwin 9 J K 39 Jehiel T 26 John 91
    Lester T 41 53 Lewis 90 Morford 51 88 Mrs George A 95
    Nathan 53 Peter 90 91 Peter D 90 R D 90 R M 80 R T 26
    Raymond E 94 Robert 96 Robert T 23 25 26 87 94 Robert
    Thompson 23 Russell 94 S R 90 91 Samuel T 90 91 Stephen
    90 Sylvanus 40 T H 90 Thomas E 48 W H 95 Warren H 49
    88 89 92 William 88

SNOOK, A 94 A C 88 Alfred C 87 Alfred D 75 Asher E 96 Frank T 87 Fred 89 Frederick 90 H C C 96 Harvey 21 51 87 88 Hiram 21 Lu Ella 21 R H 95 William E 94
SNOVER, Andrew 94
SNYDER, Fred R 48 88 89 92 Laura B 22 Martin R 48 Mrs Harry 94 Raymond 22 92 Robert 93
SOUTHWICK, Mr 56
SPRAGUE, Samuel D 96
SPRANGER, Frank W 87 88
STACKHOUSE, Frank 93 Harry 26 Harry A 87 N A 26 95 Nathan A 26 95 Samuel W 90
STANTON, Brice 90 Brice B 92 96 Chris N 96 Ella O'Gorman 96 James E 36 John J 7 9 10 36
STEEL, Charles L 46
STEELE, C S 49 Charles S 48 49 55 88 94 95 Chas S 49 Florence 95 W D 48 49 Whitman D 49
STEFFEN, Henry 96
STEIBIG, Louis 93
STEPHENS, James C 88 William 88 93
STEVENS, Alonzo 93
STEWART, Daniel 16 John T 53
STICKNEY, Amelia 21 Chas E 11 21 95 Erastus 11 John E 88
STIDWORTHY, 79 Reuben 88
STILES, William A 10
STOKES, Gov 60
STOLL, 8 Arthur 93 Frank 92 Ira 88 92 James 54 James M 41 53 Joseph 29 Oscar 90 William 93
STONE, Gabriel 93 Hiram 87 88 94 T S 94
STOREY, W A 63
STORMS, T B 86 89
STRADER, Emma C 67 John 53 M P 48 Moses 94
STRALEY, Dr 26 I F 88 Mrs S V 64
STRAULINA, Joseph 94
STRAWAY, Charles 88 94
STROH, Maud G 81
STRUBLE, 26 A C 93 Emmet B 88 H J S 93 Hugh D 26 Joe 26 Martha 93 Mrs Alfred 93 William P 88
STUART, Daniel 54
SUNDERLAND, A J 89
SUTTON, Daniel E 54 George W 88 J H 43 90 James 88 John 96 John H 53 Mary 43
SWAIN, George R 75
SWANBERG, Svante 92
SWARTS, P P 91
SWARTWOOD, M 44
SWAYZE, Jacob L 7 9 10 16 John L 16 20 Justice 96 Mr 10
SWEENEY, John 75 88
SYMMES, John Cleves 14
SZOTO, Mike 91
TALMADGE, John 90 R N 49 Reuben N 95
TALMAGE, R N 49
TAYLOR, 34 Kathryn 95 Walter R 93
TEETS, Ernest 94
THOMPSON, C D 49 C E 39 Charles D 81 David 16 52 54 Henry C 91 J S 90 J W 26 John 88 John W 26 87
TICE, Harry 93 Levi 93
TIDABACK, Michael 88 90
TILLMAN, Nicholas 29
TIMBRELL, Charles H 93 H A 80 88 93 Heman A 53
TIMES, George 91
TITMAN, Geo B 88 George B 87
TITSWORTH, Kate 92 W W 89
TOOMATH, James A 95
TOWNSEND, Fannie 60 William 74 88
TOZER, John 56 57
TRAUGER, H L 96
TRELOAR, Lillian 33 Thomas J 90
TRIBUS, Lewis C 50
TRIMBLE, James M 21
TRUEX, D C 27 David C 53 94
TRUMBULL, A R 43
TRUSDELL, John 52 Kittie 50 Wesley 48
TULLY, A C 83 88 Andrew 90 M P 21 71
TUTHILL, E C 95 Ernest C 46 92 95
TUTTLE, 4 C E 94 R 89 Rutherford 50 51 62 88 S Leroy 28 92
UNDERWOOD, Oscar W 18
UPTEGROVE, Edward P 87
UTTER, E M 96
VAIL, Harry 88 Theodore 86
VALE, Harry 93
VALENTINE, 26 George C 87 88 William H 90
VANARSDALE, A S 88
VANATTA, John A 88
VANAUKEN, A C 94 Barret A 90 Bowdine 48 George B 93 Jacob N 87 Nathaniel 87
VANBLARCOM, 3 49 A J 53 Andrew J 50 53 55 92 95 Joseph 90 L 52 69 Lewis 6 14 87 94 95
VANCAMPEN, 65 Mrs S J 52 Sherwood D 92
VANCE, Alanson A 47
VANDINE, John 52 N 94
VANDRUFF, Evi 92 F B 83 Samuel S 83 88
VANETTEN, Daniel E 88 Fritz 48 L F 48
VANFREDENBURG, H A 10 Henry A 10
VANGELDER, George 48 49
VANGILDER, Isaac 90
VANHORN, Charles 88 George W 88 Lester 96 O 87 92 Obadiah 53 93 Philetus R 92
VANHORNE, Thomas 13
VANNATTA, Wm 25
VANNESS, George 96 John 52 Peter 25 29 90
VANORDEN, Fred 39 Nelson 93
VANREED, Mabel 33
VANSANT, I N 89 Isaac 90
VANSICKLE, 15 A P 73 92 94 Abbie 19 Abram P 92 Alice V 19 John J 14 19 87 W H 88 W N 96 W P 96 Warren H 87
VANSTONE, Charles 93 Mrs Samuel B 96
VANSYCKLE, 26 F N 26 95 Frank N 26 87 J V 90 Reuben 90
VAUGHAN, Judson V 96 Richard 96
VOORHEES, Mrs H L 95 Mrs Shepard 94 Shepard 96
VOUGHT, W J 89 William S 87 89
WAKELEE, Edmund W 18
WALKER, Chancellor 81 Charles A 93 97 James 14 Lillian 96
WALLACE, F Ernest 94 95 George D 9 Nellie 94 R D 86 Richard D 53

WALLIN, Caroline 82
WALLING, Joseph 39
WALTERS, John 96
WALTON, Isaak 14
WARBASSE, Citizen 52 J E 57 Samuel 95
WARD, Henry M 49 John 90 Martin Jr 63 Rev Mr 90
WARNER, C 94 Edson P 87
WASHER, Mabel 94 Nelson 88 Park 96
WASHINGTON, 89
WATERMAN, 52
WATT, Alex A 92
WEIDNER, David P 91
WEILAND, Gottfried S 44
WEISS, Fabian 95
WELLS, 83 Harry E 87 94
WERNER, Joseph 93
WERTS, Gov 60
WESTBROOK, Charles 88 Mr 3 Richard B 3 4 William N 87
WESTERVELT, William G 90
WESTFALL, G W 27 Willis 27
WHITAKER, John A 16 Jonathan 16 O M 96 Ole M 93 96
WHITE, George W D 90 S R 26
WHITEHEAD, Mortimer 92
WHITNEY, J E 63 95 John E 88
WHITTAKER, Jonathan 53
WHITTE, W H 89
WHITTEMORE, Walter F 55
WHYMS, Frank D 49 92
WILBUR, F P 87 Fred P 95 Frederick P 32
WILD, W D 96

WILGUS, S G 93
WILLEY, F G 91 93
WILLIAMS, 23 C M 96 E F 96 George 93 George A 67 Isaac 87 S E 96 Samuel A 86 William J 49
WILLIS, Margaret 96
WILLS, John 55 80 88 94 S S 27
WILLSON, 26 Charles E 87 L H 68 94 Lewis O 88 S J 26 William D 87 William E 26 87
WILSHIRE, Mrs George 95
WILSON, 4 Abiah 92 Alice R 20 Charles G 83 E 94 Frank 82 88 Gov 16 20 22 23 27 42 Harry G 87 James A 87 John P 92 L H 95 Levatus 91 Mrs William 95 Philip S 94 95 Pres 18 20 Sarah 92 Simon 39 William D 24 88 96
WINNER, Isaac 89
WINTERMUTE, D S 84 George A 48 M B 84 M F 63
WISE, Jacob S 96
WOLF, George 94
WOLFE, 42 A E 83
WOLVERTON, Helen 93 Thomas 13
WOOD, Arthur G 96 J H 92 John H 92 Josephine 92
WOODRUFF, Augustus 88 C M 48 N A 88 Stephen 48
WOODS, John L 89 Jonas S 87 96
WOODWARD, H J 96 Henry J 96 W W 8 96 William W Jr 95
WOOLSEY, Elijah 89
WRIGHT, John 43 W D 64 W S 82
WYKER, Daniel 92 L D 29 Lynch 89 Sarah 92
YETTER, Willard A 87
YOUNG, 26 Alexander H 46 Dr 26 G O 95 George O 26 87 William I 96

www.ingramcontent.com/pod-product-compliance
Lightning Source LLC
Chambersburg PA
CBHW080406170426
43193CB00016B/2828